D0371787

BATTLE SCARS

305.409
C617b

BATTLE SCARS

Gender and Sexuality in the American Civil War

Edited by Catherine Clinton and Nina Silber

WITHDRAWN

LIBRARY ST. MARY'S COLLEGE

OXFORD
UNIVERSITY PRESS

2006

OXFORD
UNIVERSITY PRESS

Oxford University Press, Inc., publishes works that further
Oxford University's objective of excellence
in research, scholarship, and education.

Oxford   New York
Auckland   Cape Town   Dar es Salaam   Hong Kong   Karachi
Kuala Lumpur   Madrid   Melbourne   Mexico City   Nairobi
New Delhi   Shanghai   Taipei   Toronto

With offices in
Argentina   Austria   Brazil   Chile   Czech Republic   France   Greece
Guatemala   Hungary   Italy   Japan   Poland   Portugal   Singapore
South Korea   Switzerland   Thailand   Turkey   Ukraine   Vietnam

Copyright © 2006 by Oxford University Press, Inc.

Published by Oxford University Press, Inc.
198 Madison Avenue, New York, New York 10016

www.oup.com

Oxford is a registered trademark of Oxford University Press

All rights reserved. No part of this publication may be reproduced,
stored in a retrieval system, or transmitted, in any form or by any means,
electronic, mechanical, photocopying, recording, or otherwise,
without the prior permission of Oxford University Press.

Library of Congress Cataloging-in-Publication Data
Battle scars : gender and sexuality in teh American Civil War /
edited by Catherine Clinton and Nina Silber.
p. cm.
Includes bibliographical references and index.
ISBN-13 978-0-19-617445-8 ; 978-0-19-517444-1 (pbk.)
ISBN 0-19-517445-3 ; 0-19-517444-5 (pbk.)
1. Sex role—United States—History—19th century. 2. Women—
United States—History—19th century. 3. United States—History—
Civil War, 1861–1865—social aspects. 4. United States—Social
conditions—To 1865. 5. United States—Social conditions—
1865–1918. I. Clinton, Catherine, 1952– II. Silber, Nina.
HQ1075.5.U6B38 2006
305.3'0973'09034   2005048796

9 8 7 6 5 4 3 2 1

Printed in the United States of America
on acid-free paper

for Susan Ferber

CONTENTS

CONTRIBUTORS

Thomas J. Brown is Associate Professor of History and Associate Director of the Institute for Southern Studies at the University of South Carolina. He is the author of *Dorothea Dix, New England Reformer* (1998), the editor of *The Public Art of Civil War Commemoration: A Brief History with Documents* (2004), and coeditor, with Martin H. Blatt and Donald Yacovone, of *Hope and Glory: Essays on the Legacy of the Fifty-fourth Massachusetts Regiment* (2001).

Lisa Cardyn received her Ph.D. and J.D. degrees from Yale University, where she is now a Research Affiliate at the Gilder Lehrman Center for the Study of Slavery, Resistance, and Abolition. She is currently revising the manuscript of her first book, a study of sexual terror and the Reconstruction klans. Her next project, tentatively titled *The Trials of Evelyn Nesbit*, takes up the contested meanings of sexualized violence in the context of one of the most notorious "crimes of passion" of the last century—Harry Thaw's murder of the architect Stanford White. It is the subject of her most recent article, "Spectacles of Sex and Violence in Old New York: The Nesbit-Thaw-White Affair," published in 2004.

Catherine Clinton is the author and editor of over twenty books, most recently *Harriet Tubman: The Road to Freedom* and *Hold the Flag High* (an illustrated book for young readers). She is currently working on a biography of Mary Todd Lincoln.

Jim Downs earned his undergraduate degree from the University of Pennsylvania; and his M.A. and Ph.D. from Columbia University. He is revising his dissertation, "Diagnosing Reconstruction: The History of the Medical Division of the Freedmen's Bureau," for publication. Downs is the co-editor of *Taking Back the Academy: History of Activism, History as Activism* (2004), and the editor of *Why We Write* (2005). He has published articles in *The Southern Historian* and *Women and Performance: A Journal of Feminist Theory*. He is currently teaching in the Department of History at Princeton University.

Virginia Meacham Gould is an Adjunct Faculty Member at Tulane University. She is the author of *Chained to the Rock of Adversity: To Be Free, Black, and Female in the Old South* (1998) and co-editor of *No Cross, No Crown: Black Nuns in Nineteenth Nineteenth-Century New Orleans*. She has published numerous essays in books and journals, including "Piety, Social Activism, and the Dynamics of Race: The Foundation of the Sisters of the Holy Family," in *Free Women of Color in the Americas*, edited by David Barry Gaspar and Darlene Clark Hine. She co-authored, "The Feminine Face of Afro-Catholicism," published in the *William and Mary Quarterly* and winner of the A. Elizabeth Taylor Prize from the Southern Association for Women Historians. She is presently writing a biography of Henriette Delille, the founder of the Sisters of the Holy Family in New Orleans.

Stephen Kantrowitz received his Ph.D. from Princeton University in 1995 and since then has taught U.S. history at the University of Wisconsin–Madison. He is the author of *Ben Tillman and the Reconstruction of White Supremacy* (2000), which won the Ellis W. Hawley Prize from the Organization of American Historians. This essay draws on the research for his new project, "Radical Reconstruction in the Deep North."

Elizabeth D. Leonard is the John J. and Cornelia V. Gibson Associate Professor (and Chair) of History, and the Interim Director of Women's, Gender, and Sexuality Studies, at Colby College in Waterville, Maine. She is the author of three books: *Yankee Women: Gender Battles in the Civil War* (1994); *All the Daring of the Soldier: Women of the Civil War Armies* (1999); and *Lincoln's Avengers: Justice, Revenge, and Reunion after the Civil War* (2004).

Anne Sarah Rubin is an Associate Professor of History at the University of Maryland, Baltimore County. She is the author of *A Shattered Nation: The Rise and Fall of the Confederacy, 1861–1868*, a study of Confederate nationalism and identity. She is also a co-author (with Edward L. Ayers and William G. Thomas III), of *The Valley of the Shadow Project*, a multimedia history of the Civil War in two communities, which won the 2001 E-Lincoln prize. She is currently working on a study of Sherman's March in history and memory.

Nina Silber is Associate Professor of History at Boston University, where she specializes in classes on the Civil War, women's history, and the U.S. South. In addition to the original volume of essays on gender and the Civil War, *Divided Houses: Gender and the Civil War* (co-edited with Catherine Clinton and published in 1992), her publications include *The Romance of Reunion: Northerners and the South, 1865–1900* (1993); *Yankee Correspondence: Civil War Letters between New England Soldiers and the Homefront* (co-edited with Mary Beth Sievens and published in 1996); and *Daughters of the Union: Northern Women Fight the Civil War* (2005).

John Stauffer is Professor of English, History of American Civilization, and African and African American Studies at Harvard University. He received his Ph.D. in American Studies at Yale University in 1999, where he received the Ralph Henry Gabriel Prize for the best dissertation from the American Studies Association. His first book, *The Black Hearts of Men: Radical Abolitionists and the Transformation of Race* (2002), won the 2002 Frederick Douglass Book Prize from the Gilder Lehrman Institute; won the Avery Craven Book Prize from the Organization of American Historians; and was the Lincoln Prize runner-up. He is the editor of Frederick Douglass's *My Bondage and My Freedom*, for the Modern Library; the co-editor (with Zoe Trodd) of *Meteor of War: The John Brown Story*; and (with Tim McCarthy) of *Democratic Vistas: New Essays on American Abolitionism*. He is at work on a new book, *Dreaming of Democracy: American Interracial Friendships in History and Myth*.

BATTLE SCARS

1

INTRODUCTION

Colliding and Collaborating:
Gender and Civil War Scholarship

Nina Silber

In the past fifteen years, since the initial appearance of *Divided Houses*, our original volume of essays on gender and the Civil War, scholarship on the sectional conflict has, in its own way, been nudged in new directions. Of course, a quick tour through the bookstore, or a glance at most television documentaries, will reveal that the dominant picture of the Civil War still revolves largely around leading generals, great battles, and famous political leaders. But, even if only occasionally, subtle hints emerge documenting a different kind of Civil War experience: news articles on women who cross-dressed as men and fought like soldiers; an occasional book exploring the exploits of a Civil War heroine; even a Hollywood film that devotes considerable screen time to the trials of women trying to survive on the homefront. And while Hollywood directors may not have always been the most assiduous readers of the latest historical writing, their future artistic creations might be enhanced by turning to the work of a growing number of scholars who have begun to complicate the traditional story-line of the U.S. Civil War by reminding us that significant numbers of Civil War–era Americans were not men. We can now read more carefully about the problems and contributions of a diverse corps of female nurses, the work done by women spies and soldiers in advancing the war's agenda, and the way that women writers crafted their own critical interpretations of wartime events. The study of emancipation, a pivotal development of the Civil War years, has also moved forward by leaps and bounds, again with far greater attention paid to the ways the abolition of slavery uniquely affected the status of women, both black and white, in the Civil War era.[1]

As our original volume made clear, and as this new collection continues to emphasize, the recent scholarly trend has looked not just at the experiences of women but also at the larger issue of gender. This perspective places the focus on the cultural and ideological systems that have shaped the behavior and activities of both men and women, and the interaction between the Civil War and that larger cultural framework about sex roles. Certainly these essays, as well as the new literature more generally, are interested in documenting men's and women's distinct experiences; but those experiences are put in the context of the ideas and expectations about sex roles and how those roles were sanctioned in American society. In other words, we look at how gender has been a cultural construction in American history and how that construction influenced the social, political, and even military landscape during the Civil War years. With this new volume of essays, we hope to explore ways in which considerations of gender have opened up new directions in how historians understand the era of sectional conflict and slave emancipation, exploring such topics as black and white abolitionists' conceptions of masculinity, the roles played by Catholic nuns in the Civil War South, and sexual violence during Reconstruction. In this introductory essay, we also aim to take stock of how this specific field of study has unfolded in the last few decades and what insights it has (and perhaps has not) brought to the study of the Civil War era.

To a great extent, the study of gender and the Civil War represented a kind of collision between three different subdisciplines in the historical profession: traditional Civil War scholarship, the development of women's history, and a new emphasis on social and cultural history that dominated the historical profession toward the end of the twentieth century. Traditional Civil War scholarship, from the time the war ended and extending into the present day, has continued to be largely focused on military activity, political leadership, and, to a lesser extent, the interaction between battlefield developments and wartime politics. Certainly through the 1950s, virtually no Civil War study gave much attention to women, let alone to issues of gender. Indeed, as James McPherson noted in his foreword to *Divided Houses*, the biases of the traditional historians could be detected in the population more generally, perhaps most notably in the insistence on the part of Civil War Round Tables (gatherings where mostly amateur historians discussed the war), as late as 1976, on excluding women from membership. As one member of the Chicago Round Table explained, admitting "the ladies" would "inevitably lead to an erosion of the purpose of this organization." Traditional Civil War historians, in short, believed there was little overlap between their own battle-driven focus and "women's" concerns.[2]

But away from the Civil War limelight, beginning in the middle years of the twentieth century, a few pioneers began to study the question of women's place in the American past. These early historians, many working on the periphery of the historical profession, produced studies examining women's roles in industrialization and economic life, while also giving attention to the more prominent political declarations and activities of American women, especially those pursuing female suffrage. One of the few encounters between Civil War scholarship and the early women's history appeared in 1966 in the form of Mary Massey's pathbreaking volume *Bonnet Brigades: American Women and the Civil War*. Massey, like other women's historians of her generation, was largely interested in women's activities in the public sphere and in understanding how the war pushed women into spaces previously considered exclusively masculine preserves. Perhaps most of all, Massey was interested in the increased economic opportunities made possible by the military conflict. Along these lines, she documented women's inroads into professions such as teaching, nursing, and government service, as well as industry. "The economic emancipation of women," Massey concluded, "was the most important single factor in her [sic] social, intellectual, and political advancement, and the war did more in four years to change her economic status than had been accomplished in any preceding generation." To a great extent, Massey initiated (or perhaps confirmed) a view that would inform popular perceptions about women and the Civil War for many years to come: that the Civil War represented a liberating turning point for the women of the United States, north as well as south. In subsequent years, scholars would draw on Massey's abundant research and expand on many of her findings. Inevitably, too, they had to confront, and sometimes reassess, her emancipationist paradigm.[3]

In the 1970s and 1980s, historians brought a whole new range of questions and methodological tools to the study of the American past, including the Civil War, by drawing on new approaches in social and cultural history. Inspired in part by the social movements of the 1960s and 1970s, scholars developed a new appreciation for the historical experiences of "ordinary" people, those who had not commanded armies or held political office or dominated American business but had spent their lives toiling in factories, laboring in their homes, working the land, and supporting (but seldom leading) various types of political movements. Lacking the highly verbal documents traditionally used to examine the lives of elites, social historians often used quantitative methods to consider how groups of non-elites, including women, may have affected historical outcomes. Still, much of the early social history scholarship tended to overlook the Civil War altogether, reflecting the determination of these scholars to see American history from a new vantage point. Less focused on the crucial moments of the traditional political story of the American past, the new social history offered a different narrative, one driven more by changes in the industrial process or by experiences in local communities than by national upheaval and federal elections. In light of this tendency, one scholar, at the end of the 1980s, wondered if social historians had "lost the Civil War" altogether. Were American social historians, queried Maris Vinovskis, now going to the extreme of completely overlooking this pivotal event in their study of the past?[4]

This temporary blind spot notwithstanding, not all historians had "lost" the war. Some now began to bring a social history focus to the study of the conflict, quantifying recruitment activities in local communities or closely observing relief efforts at the community level. And, in the meantime, the new generation of women's historians was, on its own terms, finding its way back to the Civil War. The field of women's history had been rejuvenated with the new turn to social history, with numerous studies undertaken to document the ways that masses of women, as well as more notable females, had contributed to various social movements and historical developments. But the new women's history also began to strike out in new directions, going beyond the framework laid out by an earlier generation of women's historians and by the social historians of the 1970s and 1980s. More specifically, the new women's history began revisiting the central components of the traditional political narrative, using the profoundly different experiences of women to come to new assessments of critical watersheds and well-established turning points. Some, for example, reexamined the revolutionary era, documenting numerous instances of women's contributions during the American Revolution. In doing this work, they offered new ways to read the political culture of this period, calling attention to the conservative bent in republican thinking, especially with respect to female citizenship, by observing how a new type of ideology emerged that illuminated women's highly circumscribed civic status. By reading women's experience, and ideas about womanhood, back into the revolutionary period, women's historians suggested new ways to think about the broader accomplishments, and limitations, of the American Revolution.[5]

And so, it seemed only logical that if scholars might revisit such a fixture on the historical landscape as the American Revolution, they might do the same for the U.S. Civil War. By the 1980s, a number of scholars had begun to do just that, an impulse that was captured, in part, by the essays that appeared in the original *Divided Houses*, and by subsequent work that was spawned by that volume. Some of that work has continued to pursue the methods of social historians by looking at specific groups of women (and men) and considering how their experiences intersected with the disruptions of wartime. Other scholars, including many whose work appears in this volume, have pushed their work into the realm of cultural history, raising questions about how notions of gender—as a cultural ideal—have been redefined in the course of the sectional conflict.[6]

Among the most enduring questions, for both social and cultural historians, is the one that was central to Mary Massey's interpretation of women in the Civil War era: how should we evaluate the experience of women in this period? Did the war encourage advancements in women's status, or did it have little effect on the standing of American womanhood and on established gender roles more broadly? Of course, as many recent scholars have acknowledged, any type of answer to these questions would require a more detailed investigation into the numerous other factors that shaped women's lives—especially variables such as race, class, and region. Region, in particular, has been a crucial determinant in studies of Civil War women. Most historians have assumed that notions and practices associated with gender have differed considerably in the Southern states, where slavery was a dominant factor in daily life, and the Northern states, where it was not. Most see evidence of a more deeply rooted patriarchal system in which white male plantation owners stood at the pinnacle of a clearly gendered chain of command. And as most students of history realize, Southern women obviously experienced the war itself in very different ways from Northern women. Closer to the chaos of the battlefield, frequently subjected to the constraints of Union occupation, and often shaped by the trauma of defeat, Southern women felt the repercussions of war far more directly than Northern ones. In fact, perhaps the drama and trauma of Southern women's wartime experience has also been one reason why more studies have focused on women of the South than on their Yankee sisters. The South, after all, produced (even if only in its imagination) a Scarlett O'Hara, while the North has yet to create her Yankee counterpart.

As a result, Southern women have, especially in recent years, received considerable scrutiny in the historical literature. But even among women of the South, their wartime experience varied considerably, as well as their standing both during and after the war, depending on whether they were free or slave, white or black, Union or Confederate supporters. While women's historians may have once used the experience and voices of privileged women as a way to understand and represent the world of "women" more generally, most scholars today recognize how much class and race, in particular, have significantly shaped the lives of their historical subjects. Indeed, even while scholarship still tends to focus more on women of means, historians today are more conscious of understanding the privileged status of their subjects. To some extent, in fact, the turn away from "women's history" and toward "gender history" has allowed scholars to give greater attention to crucial variables of class and race. By studying the power and influence of gender ideology, historians recognize how different groups of women and men, depending on their social and racial status, often experience that gender ideology in very different ways.

Not surprisingly, recent scholarship has often delivered very different pronouncements about the wartime experience of white slave-owning women than about the experience of Southern women who were black and enslaved. White plantation women, many have found, frequently showed a keen awareness of the privileges they had to lose and were sometimes reluctant to make the kinds of sacrifices that might jeopardize their prewar gender status, that is, as "ladies." Some historians, in fact, have even suggested that Southern plantation women eventually felt betrayed by the Confederate enterprise for the way it compromised their positions of privilege. Yet, the desire to protect privileges was, in many cases, offset by a growing sense of autonomy that even wealthy women gained during the war, some of which they put to use in the post-bellum era in creating new types of organizations and various forms of political expression. Perhaps most notable among these postwar activities—as many scholars have observed—were the efforts of elite Southern white women to construct and preserve the memories of the South's Civil War experience.[7]

Enslaved men and women, by contrast, experienced the war through the prism of emancipation, a revolutionary event that dramatically transformed their status both politically and domestically. As several recent studies have suggested, black female slaves actively participated in advancing liberation for both themselves and their children and in establishing themselves in new social and household positions. Former slaves could, for example, make new claims as legally recognized husbands and wives in the postemancipation South and could use those claims to make their own assertions about broader questions of power and control, whether in negotiating with white landowners for greater economic autonomy or casting ballots—in the case of African American men—for candidates who would be more responsive to the needs of the black community. Focusing on these postwar power dynamics, the new scholarship on gender and the Civil War has inevitably pushed into the Reconstruction period, and even beyond, in order to understand how tensions over gender roles continued to simmer in postwar America. Thus, as scholars have suggested, Confederate defeat and the aftermath of emancipation propelled the postwar South into a multifaceted "gender crisis," with ex-slaves working, often without success, to hold onto wartime gains, defeated white men working to reassert their positions of prominence in their societies, and white women working to both restore features of the status quo and advance some of their own ideas about independence.[8]

As should be clear, these "gender crises" were not simply about women's experiences and positions. Rather, the study of men, and the way both white and black men have, like women, been shaped by a range of social and cultural understandings of gender, has also been integral to some of the newest Civil War scholarship. Enlisting, going into battle, facing conscription, and remembering wartime experiences have, as scholars have recently pointed out, played crucial roles in shaping male identities. Moreover, the South's highly patriarchal plantation system—and its wartime disintegration—also had unique effects on black and white men in terms of how they thought about themselves—as husbands, as fathers, and as participants in their larger communities. This complex shaping of male identities in the Civil War era could, historians have noted, have significant political and military effects, influencing men's performance as soldiers, as abolitionist activists, or as upholders of a system of white supremacy.[9]

Speaking to this wide variety of issues and considering the experiences of both men and women, black as well as white, several essays in this new collection respond to questions regarding the wartime and postwar crises of gender in the Civil War South. In his essay on slave women and sickness during the war, James Downs complicates the picture of enslaved women's emancipation experience. By studying issues of health and physical well-being, he reminds us how much black women in this period had to endure in terms of illness and death, and how that might make black women's path to freedom different from that of black men. The fact that black women often suffered the most in terms of food and clothing and exposure to disease clearly had profound consequences for enslaved women's wartime experience. Other essayists present new complications to the traditional picture of Southern white womanhood. Looking at a much-overlooked group of white women in Southern society—Catholic sisters—Virginia Gould suggests how such women formed affinities with the plantation system and for the broader Confederate enterprise. Even more, she finds ways the war allowed nuns, in places like Natchez, Mississippi, and New Orleans, to step outside traditional Catholic constrictions regarding women's behavior. Thus, for at least one group of Southern white women, the turmoil of war may have offered a route to greater freedoms and opportunities.

Essays by Anne Rubin, Tom Brown, and Lisa Cardyn draw our attention to the political and social turmoil of the postwar South and how those tensions often assumed a gendered component. Rubin and Brown, in particular, point us toward the shift to cultural history as a new terrain for understanding ways gender was being redefined. Rubin, who writes here about two seemingly female news columnists (the identity of only one of her writers can be documented as female), argues that literary offerings provided a vehicle for white Southerners to understand and address the postwar gender crisis. More specifically, these columnists challenged the politics of radical Reconstruction, but offered their critique in a feminine voice that could appeal to a white Southern audience extending beyond those who read the latest political news. Even more, Rubin's columnists advised Southern white women to rein in the kind of aggressive and politicized behavior that may have been acceptable during wartime but, they maintained, was no longer proper in the postwar South.

A similar reining-in process is documented in Tom Brown's essay, although the restrictive message is conveyed here through a memorial statue, not a newspaper column. Brown projects the postwar gender crisis further into the future by considering a topic that has greatly intrigued scholars in recent years: the reconstruction of Civil War memories in the post-bellum years. As Brown shows in his discussion of the two Civil War memorials constructed in Columbia, South Carolina (one erected by the women for the men, and a later one erected by the men for the women), a significant shift in gender politics occurred. According to Brown, the first tribute offered, from the women to the Confederate soldiers, reflected a sentimentalized ideal of manhood, placing emphasis on the power of female emotions to ennoble men's cause in war. Yet, while this tribute suggested some public recognition of women's wartime and postwar influence, the second memorial, sponsored by men in recognition of Confederate women, offered a far more traditional reading of male and female roles. Returning to an antebellum ideal, the new statue depicted Southern women as demure, pure, and, ultimately subservient to men. In short, the white men and women of South Carolina used their monuments to speak to and resolve, at least in part, the postwar gender crisis.

Finally, Lisa Cardyn looks at the postwar gender crisis from a very different perspective: the sexualized violence of the Ku Klux Klan (KKK). Although, as Cardyn notes, the Klan has been widely studied, few have considered the sexual dimension of its terrorist assault against the freedmen and freedwomen. But, as Cardyn suggests, rape and sexual assault were critical weapons in the KKK arsenal, serving to revive the image (and, in many cases, the practice) of white slave-owners' sexual domination of black men and black women. As she notes, this ugly and vicious crusade could have chilling consequences on black men's and women's continuing struggle for freedom.

Clearly, even with the work already done and the new contributions before us, questions remain about gender and the Civil War South. Given that most Confederate soldiers came from the less privileged class of non-slave-owning whites, the question of how the men and women of this class were affected by the secession crisis clearly deserves more scrutiny. How did the war transform the thinking, and the experience, of poorer white women, those less concerned with the loss of privileges and slaves? What role might these women's wartime experiences have played in establishing the new post-bellum climate of gender relations? And how might religion and ethnicity have affected the status of less privileged Southern women? More, too, must be learned about the experience of enslaved women in the transition from slavery to freedom. How were slave women affected by the transformed domestic and political relationships of wartime? How should we understand the emancipation experience in light of the very different circumstances—like the health problems observed by James Downs and the violent sexual attacks investigated by Lisa Cardyn—in which the men and women of the slave class found themselves? Finally, we must learn more about regional permutations within the South, especially in light of the not insubstantial political divisions that many see at work in different parts of Dixie. How, for example, did the war affect the men and women of the slaveholding Border States?

How did that region's very different experience of emancipation affect gender roles for both enslaved and slave-owning men and women?

Although less of the new gender history has focused on the Civil War North, similar questions and problems have shaped the scholarship in this field. Thus, historians studying the women of the North, like their counterparts studying the South, also confront the question of how the war affected women's status, of just how much the war served to liberate women from prewar restrictions. Even more, with an eye toward Northern women's growing determination to fight for female suffrage, some see evidence of Yankee women's emerging political activism in the Civil War era. Female nurses, for example, who found themselves doing grueling labor in wartime hospitals, on hospital transport boats, and sometimes on the fields of battle, learned important lessons in self-assertion and professionalism. Quite a few, in fact, learned to challenge male surgeons and army bureaucrats as they advanced the interests of their "boys" and their own right to work in a public capacity. Northern women who remained on the homefront likewise gained new experience in organizing and fund raising, especially through the extensive relief apparatus of the United States Sanitary Commission. Many of these women learned new lessons in advancing their opinions and positions, even defying well-positioned male leaders. And quite a few gained a new public voice through literature. Although Southern women also wielded fiery pens during this period, the wartime era seemed to be an especially critical launching point for Northern female authors (consider such prominent scribes as Harriet Beecher Stowe and Louisa May Alcott), as many took advantage of the more extensive publishing field that existed in the North. With the wartime crisis allowing greater opportunities for women to write, female authors used this occasion to weigh in on matters of national import.[10]

Again, though, as in the South, the problem of gender in the Civil War North also requires further refinement and consideration based on questions of class and race. While the prevalent stereotype of Civil War nurses has generally presented these women as privileged and middle-class, recent scholarship has suggested that many nurses were black and working-class women who were often poorly paid and badly treated in Civil War hospitals. Such studies certainly call into question the notion that women might have achieved a sort of liberation from prewar constraints. Instead, it seems, quite a few female nurses experienced new forms of oppression and exploitation. More, too, must be learned about the experiences of poor white women in the North, who, even more so than Southern women, were divided by religion and ethnicity. Many of these less privileged women increasingly came to voice objections to wartime policy, and especially wartime conscription. For these women, too, the wartime realities of widowhood, economic dependency, and low-paying employment also meant their experiences were, in many ways, far from liberating.[11]

Although the "crisis of gender" that affected the Civil War North has received less attention than that in the South, authors in this present collection do point to significant tensions in the Yankee states with respect to gender during the prewar and wartime years. Elizabeth Leonard, for example, observes how some women—nurses and relief workers, in particular—managed to bend the prevailing gender system to make inroads for women in employment and public health. Yet, as she argues, if that antebellum gender system might bend to accommodate women who still upheld essential gender differences, the system showed little flexibility when it came to women who more openly defied the notion of gender difference. Thus, in this way, she explains the obstacles encountered by Mary Walker, a radical, pants-wearing physician who was constantly shunned by Union officials. The inflexibility of the gender system was also manifest, or so she suggests, in the considerable consternation expressed in the aftermath of Mary Surratt's execution, when Northerners voiced second thoughts about holding a woman accountable, in such an extreme fashion, for her political, even allegedly treasonous, actions.

Significantly, too, essayists in this volume have addressed the question of masculinity in the Civil War North. Stephen Kantrowitz discusses the competing notions of manhood evident in the rhetoric and work of black and white male abolitionists in Massachusetts. While black men in antebellum New England felt a strong compulsion to assert their manhood within the framework of "respectability," white men were more inclined, he suggests, to prove themselves as "insurrectionaries," secretly working and training to physically defy the capture of fugitive slaves. These differing perspectives, Kantrowitz maintains, had a significant effect on the route that black and white men ultimately took to military service during the war itself. And, as John Stauffer observes, many New England authors, both male and female, were also greatly affected by shifting notions of manhood in this period of intense military activity and influential female writing. Indeed, as Stauffer notes, several male authors wrote with a new appreciation for masculine vigor and martial values, and even the young female writer Louisa May Alcott appreciated the need for her female protagonists to assume masculine characteristics in the face of wartime crises. In contrast, Stauffer finds that an older generation of women writers, like Lydia Maria Child and Harriet Beecher Stowe, tried to defend, albeit ineffectively, the old sentimental ideals of femininity. The North's wartime crisis of gender, or so Stauffer suggests, was resolved, at least in literature, in favor of a new and vigorous masculine ethos, perhaps not unlike the manly resolution that Tom Brown sees in Confederate memorials. It would not be hard to imagine how such a climate of intense virility might have stifling consequences for women's writing in postwar America.

Perhaps one of the most interesting ways in which the study of gender has begun to transform our understanding of the Civil War era has been through new studies of wartime and postwar political culture. A number of scholars have thus concerned themselves with the ways in which ideas of gender have informed the political rhetoric and cultural politics of the time, even if women themselves have not had formal and direct access to the political machinery. Antebellum and wartime women could, for example, influence party leaders and party policies and even carry out important political work, such as gathering and presenting petitions and even making speeches on behalf of party candidates. In turn, political parties of the prewar and wartime era demonstrated, in varying degrees, a certain responsiveness to women's issues. Even Southern white women, long considered to be more backward than their Northern sisters with respect to political activity, have surfaced in a number of historical accounts as active political participants, lending their voices to those urging prewar moderation and reconciliation and to those encouraging force and secession. In their political work, both Northern and Southern women were encouraged to express themselves in order to help cement an image of wartime nationalism and cross-class (as well as interethnic) unity within each of the sections.[12]

Yet, if there was some room for women to negotiate in the political spectrum, Catherine Clinton's essay reminds us of the very complicated path that women who emerged in any kind of public spotlight during the Civil War had to pursue. Indeed, as she notes, with so much worry and publicity during the wartime years about prostitution, women who stepped into any kind of public role—defying Union soldiers in the streets of New Orleans, protesting the price of bread in Richmond, Virginia, or enduring the wrath of General Sherman—could frequently find themselves cast as despised and morally suspect "public women." Even more, as Clinton observes, both Confederate and Union authorities were adept at casting such aspersions on women. Thus, if the Civil War did offer an opportunity for women to take up some forms of public expression, the image of being a "public woman" during the wartime years could also have a chilling effect on female voices.

Ultimately, the vast array of work that has been, and continues to be, done on gender and the Civil War has helped us gain a clearer picture of the social and political fabric of American life in the middle years of the nineteenth century. We can see more clearly where women—white and black, Northern and Southern—have made strides and where they have faced looming obstacles. We can see more clearly, too, how men in both sections have grappled with the unique challenges of wartime and shaped their own sense of identity in the process. And we have a better sense, too, of how much the politics of this period—whether that politics took the form of speech-making, newspaper reporting, novel-writing, monument-building, or Klan violence—has been shaped by the shifting terrain of gender. Ultimately, this work may help us confront one of the thorniest problems to beset scholars who study gender and the Civil War: how might our insights into women's and gender history change our traditional picture of the military and political narrative of the war? In other words, having learned about some of the ways the war did and did not change the status of Southern white women, or about the tremendous work undertaken by women on the Northern homefront, or about the participation of black men and black women in bringing on their own emancipation, can we offer a new assessment about how factors related to gender may have contributed to the failure of the Confederates or the ultimate success of the Union? Some historians have already begun to offer tantalizing suggestions, pointing us in the direction of Southern white women who began to sour on the Confederate cause and urged their menfolk to come home, or the enslaved men and women who played active roles in weakening the slave foundation of Confederate society. In addition, we now have a growing body of evidence that speaks to different notions of manhood that influenced black and white men, in both regions, and that may have affected their determination to continue, or cease, their struggles for military victory and emancipation. Still, barriers separating scholarship on gender and military pursuits remain, in large part, to be crossed. Scholars undertaking new investigations may find it useful to consider ways a growing state apparatus—clearly a hallmark of the wartime era—responded to the Civil War's gender crisis. Much, for example, might be learned by looking at how the Confederate government responded to the poor and increasingly desperate female kin of the soldiers, or at how the Union army pursued its objectives of occupying the Confederacy by compelling Southern white women to swear oaths of loyalty? In both cases government authorities found it necessary to weigh in on matters of gender, and these "official" pronouncements could significantly shape the political and military contexts of the war. No doubt, as historians continue to pursue these and other questions related to this pivotal moment in the American experience, we will find new book titles, new kinds of studies, perhaps even new types of motion pictures that will give us an even more vivid picture of life during the Civil War.

NOTES

1. Among the most recent literature considering gender and the Civil War is Jane Schultz, *Women at the Front: Hospital Workers in Civil War America* (Chapel Hill: University of North Carolina Press, 2004); Elizabeth Varon, *Southern Lady, Yankee Spy: The True Story of Elizabeth Van Lew, A Union Agent in the Heart of the Confederacy* (New York: Oxford University Press, 2003); DeeAnne Blanton and Lauren M. Cook, *They Fought Like Demons: Women Soldiers in the American Civil War* (Baton Rouge: Louisiana State University Press, 2002); and Catherine Clinton, *Harriet Tubman: The Road to Freedom* (New York: Little, Brown, 2004).

2. James M. McPherson, foreword to Catherine Clinton and Nina Silber, eds., *Divided Houses: Gender and the Civil War* (New York: Oxford University Press, 1993), xv.

3. Mary Massey, *Bonnet Brigades: American Women and the Civil War* (New York: Knopf, 1966), 340. Other mid-twentieth-century works reflecting an interest in women's history include Eleanor Flexner, *Century of Struggle: The Woman's Rights Movement in the United States* (Cambridge, Mass.: Harvard University Press, 1959), and Mary Beard, *Woman as Force in History: A Study in Tradition and Realities* (New York: Macmillan, 1946).

4. Maris Vinovskis, "Have Social Historians Lost the Civil War? Some Preliminary Demographic Speculations," *Journal of American History* 76 (June 1989), 34–58.

5. Early social history studies of the Civil War can be found in *Toward a Social History of the American Civil War*, edited by Maris Vinovskis (Cambridge, Eng.: Cambridge University Press, 1990). On women in revolutionary America, see Mary Beth Norton, *Liberty's Daughters: The Revolutionary Experience of American Women, 1750–1800* (Boston: Little Brown, 1980), and Linda

Kerber, *Women of the Republic: Intellect and Ideology in Revolutionary America* (Chapel Hill: University of North Carolina Press, 1980).

6. Catherine Clinton and Nina Silber, *Divided Houses: Gender and the Civil War* (New York: Oxford University Press, 1992).

7. Among the works examining Southern white women are Drew Faust, *Mothers of Invention: Women of the Slaveholding South in the American Civil War* (Chapel Hill: University of North Carolina Press, 1996); George Rable, *Civil Wars: Women and the Crisis of Southern Nationalism* (Urbana: University of Illinois Press, 1989); Catherine Clinton, *Tara Revisited: Women, War, and the Plantation Legend* (New York: Abbeville Press, 1995); Marli Weiner, *Mistresses and Slaves: Plantation Women in South Carolina, 1830–1880* (Urbana: University of Illinois Press, 1997); and Laura Edwards, *Scarlett Doesn't Live Here Anymore: Southern Women in the Civil War Era* (Urbana: University of Illinois Press, 2000).

8. Among the works examining slave women are Edwards, *Scarlett Doesn't Live Here,* and Edwards, *Gendered Strife and Confusion: The Political Culture of Reconstruction* (Urbana: University of Illinois Press, 1997); Leslie Schwalm, *A Hard Fight for We: Women's Transition from Slavery to Freedom in South Carolina* (Urbana: University of Illinois Press, 1997); Tera Hunter, *To 'Joy My Freedom: Southern Black Women's Lives and Labors after the Civil War* (Cambridge, Mass.: Harvard University Press, 1997); and Thavolia Glymph, "'This Species of Property': Female Slave Contrabands in the Civil War," in *A Woman's War: Southern Women, Civil War, and the Confederate Legacy,* edited by Edwards D. C. Campbell, Jr., and Kym S. Rice (Charlottesville: University Press of Virginia, 1996), 55–71. LeeAnn Whites, among others, has studied the postwar tensions over gender in the South, and has identified the conflict as a "crisis of gender." See LeeAnn Whites, *The Civil War as a Crisis in Gender: Augusta, Georgia, 1860–1890* (Athens: University of Georgia Press, 1995).

9. Works looking at Southern men's Civil War experiences and identities include Stephen Berry, *All That Makes a Man: Love and Ambition in the Civil War South* (New York: Oxford University Press, 2003); Jim Cullen, "'I's a Man Now': Gender and African American Men," in Clinton and Silber, *Divided Houses,* 76–91.

10. Works considering Northern women's Civil War experience include Elizabeth Leonard, *Yankee Women: Gender Battles and the Civil War* (New York: Norton, 1994); Lyde Cullen Sizer, *The Political Work of Northern Women Writers and the Civil War, 1850–1872* (Chapel Hill: University of North Carolina Press, 2000); Jeanie Attie, *Patriotic Toil: Northern Women and the American Civil War* (Ithaca, N.Y.: Cornell University Press,1998); Judith Ann Giesberg, *Civil War Sisterhood: The U.S. Sanitary Commission and Women's Politics in Transition* (Boston: Northeastern University Press, 2000); and Nina Silber, *Daughters*

of the Union: Northern Women Fight the Civil War (Cambridge, Mass.: Harvard University Press, 2005).

11. For more on black and working-class women as nurses see Jane Schultz, "Seldom Thanked, Never Praised, and Scarcely Recognized: Gender and Racism in Civil War Hospitals," *Civil War History* 48, 3 (2002): 220–236.

12. Scholarly works considering gender and wartime political culture include Elizabeth Varon, *We Mean to be Counted: White Women and Politics in Antebellum Virginia* (Chapel Hill: University of North Carolina Press, 1998); Stephanie McCurry, *Masters of Small Worlds: Yeoman Households, Gender Relations, and the Political Culture of the Antebellum South* (New York: Oxford University Press, 1995); Nina Silber, *The Romance of Reunion: Northerners and the South, 1865–1900* (Chapel Hill: University of North Carolina Press, 1993); Kathleen Diffley, *Where My Heart Is Turning Ever: Civil War Stories and Constitution Reform, 1861–1876* (Athens, Ga.: University of Georgia Press, 1992); and Melanie Lawson, *Patriot Fires: Forging a New American Nationalism in the Civil War North* (Lawrence: University Press of Kansas, 2002).

2

FIGHTING LIKE MEN

Civil War Dilemmas of Abolitionist Manhood

Stephen Kantrowitz

In the decade before the Civil War, many of Massachusetts's black and white abolitionist men mobilized themselves into unofficial armies against the slave power. They did much else, of course, some of it in collaboration with one another as well as with black and white women: speaking and petitioning against slavery, producing and distributing abolitionist literature, and providing aid to fugitives. But when it came to conceiving of themselves as soldiers in the war against slavery, black and white abolitionist men in the Bay State took dramatically different routes. Black men formed militia units and sought acceptance by the state, while white men assembled in secret societies and drilled for confrontation with slaveholders and their henchmen.

Yet these two sets of activities were not as distinct as this simple description would suggest. In both mobilizations, men struggled to balance rebelliousness and respectability, forging understandings of martial manhood out of this unstable amalgam. By the time the war arrived, both black and white abolitionist men had come to see collective, armed struggle both as a form of virile rebelliousness and as proof of disciplined respectability. The relationship between the two virtues remained complex; so did the relationships between the two groups, as the divergent histories of black and white manhood presented these allies with markedly different challenges.

Those challenges came to the fore during the Civil War. Once the Lincoln administration called for troops, abolitionist men's prewar struggles, fantasies, and symbolic activities shaped their response to the federal military mobilization. As they debated whether to serve and how to respond to the unequal treatment of black troops, abolitionist men confronted both the power and the limits of the competing martial histories they had forged before Sumter fell. They forced one another to consider what it meant to fight like men.[1]

By the time John Brown's body lay a-moldering in the grave, abolitionists understood their struggle against the Slave Power as paramilitary, revolutionary, and heroic. Abolitionists, black and white, celebrated acts of rebellion, and most had moved away from a principled opposition to liberation through violence.[2] Their convictions led them to violate the law and to celebrate such violations—breaking fugitives out of courtrooms and jails, providing them with shelter, food, and transportation, and funding conspirators who sought to weaken the Slave Power's grip or (in the case of John Brown) deal it a devastating blow. They did act in the realms of electoral or constitutional politics, but a striking feature of both black and white men's activities during the years just before the Civil War was their celebration of collective physical struggle against the agents of the Slave Power.

Black and white Massachusetts men mobilized collectively and forcefully against slavery. In 1851, shortly after the passage of the Fugitive Slave Law, the clothing dealer and former slave Lewis Hayden led a largely black group that rescued the fugitive Shadrach Minkins from a Boston courtroom and ferried him to safety in Canada. To protect the fugitive William Craft from his pursuers, armed African Americans kept watch over Hayden's house; Hayden threatened to blow up the dwelling—himself, Craft, slave-catchers and all—rather than see the fugitive reenslaved. In 1854, Hayden and Harvard-trained minister Thomas Wentworth Higginson were among a small group of abolitionists who battered down the door of the Boston courthouse in an effort to free another fugitive, Anthony Burns. Their raid failed but left a constable dead—probably from a shot fired by Hayden as he sought to protect Higginson—and impelled President Pierce to send federal troops to the city to ensure Burns's return to slavery. Hayden and Higginson were likewise among the many state abolitionist leaders involved in John Brown's 1859 interracial military assault on the federal arsenal at Harpers Ferry, Virginia. These clashes all became national events, forcing the federal government to act and polarizing regional opinion. Brown's failed raid—the terror it sent through slaveholding society, and the wave of Northern sympathy for Brown after his execution by Virginia authorities—accelerated the nation on its course toward civil war.[3]

Abolitionists celebrated slave rebellions as military campaigns for black liberation. John S. Rock, a black orator trained in dentistry, medicine, and law, declared to a Boston audience, "I believe in insurrections."[4] When a prominent white abolitionist suggested that black men would not rise to the defense of a woman in peril in the same way that white men would, Rock "urged Negroes to undertake some daring or desperate enterprise in order to demonstrate their courage."[5] Higginson published scholarly accounts of Caribbean maroon colonies and American slave revolts, but as his activities demonstrated, even before the war he was never simply a scholar of rebellion. "I can only make life worth living for, by becoming a revolutionist," Higginson had told a Boston audience shortly after the storming of the courthouse in 1854.[6] Black historian and *Liberator* veteran William Cooper Nell published *The Colored Patriots of the American Revolution*, a compendium of historical accounts that not only sought to establish the role of black Americans in the country's founding military struggle but linked that activity to later acts of liberatory violence, culminating with an account of fugitive slaves violently resisting recapture at Christiana, Pennsylvania, in 1851.[7] On this celebration, at least, black and white men could agree.

One implication of the emphasis on armed struggle was the masculinization of radical antislavery.[8] Not all rebels were men: indeed, both black and white women were essential to abolitionist organizing and fugitive defense, and black women had participated in at least one fugitive rescue in Boston during the 1830s.[9] But during the 1840s and 1850s, shifts toward military and electoral antislavery strategies made it harder for men to see women as central players, despite their absolutely crucial roles in the abolition movement. The revolutionary soldier became a central figure, and at least in abolitionists' letters and speeches, the rebel army against slavery was an army of men. Though some women did take on martial roles, they could be presented as exceptions that proved the rule; female rebels could even be transformed into men. John Brown called Harriet Tubman, the fugitive slave who returned south to lead wave after wave of escapees, "General Tubman," referring to this powerful woman as "he" and describing Tubman as "the most of a man, naturally; that I ever met with."[10] Brown's idiosyncratic approach reflected a deeper sense that was shared among his sympathizers and colleagues, black and white: forceful, aggressive leadership in the service of revolutionary ends was something performed exclusively by men.[11]

Yet the call to rebellion did not by itself constitute either the sum of manhood or the measure of wisdom. For some, this may have been a response to the catastrophic history of slave insurrections in the United States. At an 1858 convention of black Massachusetts men, freeborn black Northerner Charles Lenox Remond proposed inciting a slave revolt in South Carolina, arguing that death was preferable to life in slavery. His proposition was voted down: many members of the convention, particularly those born in the slave South, did not believe that such a plan could succeed; slaves lacked weapons and means of coordination for the struggle and would be hanged en masse if they rose. "When I fight," explained the former slave Josiah Henson, "I want to whip somebody."[12] The delegates' skepticism about uncoordinated action had local roots as well, for the record of Boston's would-be revolutionaries was, put charitably, a spotty one. Even successful rescues of fugitives lay just moments away from utter disaster. Lewis Hayden was said to have kept the fugitive William Craft's would-be kidnappers at bay by literally holding a match over a powder keg. The celebrated Minkins rescue in 1851 had nearly come to grief as a jubilant crowd of supporters repeatedly brought the carriage containing the escaping fugitive to a standstill. For the 1854 raid to free Anthony Burns from the Boston courthouse, Higginson and others had envisioned a tightly planned raid led by a cohesive abolitionist leadership, but miscommunications and perhaps faltering courage threw this plan into chaos. This was no way to run a railroad.[13]

But more was at stake than practicality. Although these men advocated and celebrated violent insurrection, they also insisted on presenting themselves as gentlemen—as men whose character and comportment even those who disagreed with them would be bound to respect.[14] Not for them the chaos of mob action—instead, both black and white abolitionist men organized themselves into bodies that were simultaneously militant and gentlemanly, rebellious and orderly. Yet these complementary virtues of rebelliousness and respectability did not mean quite the same thing for black and white men. "Respectability" was something that white men had to lose, but it was something black men could rarely gain. Proper dress, bearing, and verbal and written expression—even if the particulars were subject to debate—might allow rising black men and women to present themselves as worthy additions to a (nonracial) democratic society.[15] Or they might not. The 1850s taught black Northerners hard lessons about their place in national life. The Fugitive Slave Law of 1850 required Northern citizens and authorities to aid in the recapture of men and women who had escaped from slavery; it put all black Northerners, especially but not only fugitives, at risk of enslavement or reenslavement. The efforts made by abolitionists in Boston and elsewhere to rescue fugitives—particularly the failed 1854 effort to rescue Anthony Burns—provoked an overwhelming military response by the federal government, which sent soldiers and deputized the state militia to march Burns through the streets of Boston and back into slavery. The Supreme Court's 1857 Dred Scott decision voided African Americans' historical and contemporary claim to American citizenship, making inequality a constitutional as well as practical reality. Even in comparatively egalitarian Massachusetts, no law prohibited the exclusion of black men and women from public hotels, restaurants, transport, and places of entertainment, and Afro-Bostonians could not know when they would be rudely treated, expelled, or set upon. They did know that polish in dress and manners guaranteed them nothing. In the 1850s, that is, there could be nothing conventional about the notion "respectable colored persons."[16]

Boston's black leaders felt their social inferiority most keenly with regard to the state's militia law. The state militia was organized under the terms of the federal law of 1792, which restricted membership to adult white men. Beginning in the early 1850s, members of Boston's black abolitionist leadership waged a campaign of petition, protest, and self-organization against this exclusion. In wave after wave of petitions, they asked the legislature to remove the word "white" from the state's militia law. They formed their own informal militia companies—the Massasoit Guards, and later the Liberty Guards—and then sought state arms and sanction.[17]

Militia membership offered a way to reconcile black militancy with full belonging. If black men could find a legitimate place in the American martial tradition, they would not stand as perpetual outsiders, the slave rebels against whom white solidarity was forged, and with whom foreign enemies sought alliance. And successful militia service would demonstrate that black men could be both as fierce as white men, and as disciplined. One of the leaders in this venture, William J. Watkins, made his case in language that emphasized the amalgam of rebelliousness and respectability at the heart of this project. His remarks, later published as a pamphlet entitled "Our Rights as Men,"[18] described the petitioners "as men, proud of, and conscious of the inherent dignity of manhood; as men, who, knowing our rights, dare, at all hazards, to maintain them." Here were the two critical components of arms-bearing manhood: propriety, respectability, "dignity" on the one hand; an uncompromising insistence on rights on the other. The petitioners, he continued, were "law-abiding, tax-paying, liberty-loving, NATIVE-BORN, AMERICAN CITIZENS," the appeal to emerging nativist sympathies coming only after his insistence on a less partisan set of class and patriotic appeals. Christian forbearance was all well and good—Watkins prefaced his pamphlet with a bow to the principles of Christian justice, mercy, and humility—but the moment called for something else. Writing as *Uncle Tom's Cabin* was emerging as the bestselling novel of the century, Watkins derided Uncle Tom's "Christian meekness and becoming resignation" as wholly inadequate to the challenge that racial caste presented to the ideal of American liberty.

Yet the critical companion to the demonstration of respectability and probity was the willingness, as Watkins put it, to "dare, at all hazards." The head of the militia movement was Robert Morris, a pioneering black lawyer whose practice included a long list of Irish clients. In his remarks to a legislative committee, Morris did not echo Watkins's nativist emphasis on black men's status as native-born Americans; instead, he told the legislative committee that he admired the pluck of Irish immigrants who had formed a militia company despite native-born Protestants' opposition.[19] Action mattered, and acted they had. Rather than wait for the hesitant state to allow them the same privileges, black men did the same: Morris and his fellows created an unofficial company they dubbed the "Massasoit Guards." Pressing for its inclusion in the state militia, they corresponded with like-minded men in other Northern states and sought interviews with the governor.[20]

But over and over, the state turned them down. Finding neither dignity nor daring in being repeatedly rejected, the Massasoit Guards disbanded in frustration. Another unsanctioned company, the Liberty Guards, captained by laborer and coachman Lewis Gaul, arose and became a fixture in black activist politics. When Boston's black delegation arrived in New Bedford, Massachusetts, on West Indian Emancipation Day, 1858, for the Convention of the Colored Citizens of Massachusetts, Gaul's Liberty Guards performed a military display alongside their colleagues in the New Bedford Blues before formally escorting their fellow Bostonians to the convention hall. But Robert Morris, inside the hall, disavowed any connection with the armed and uniformed men outside: "It did not represent the colored young men of Boston," he claimed. "This company was dressed up in uniform, but it was training against the law. The colored men of Boston would not recognize any such military organization until they had it by right." He wanted to be a soldier only if he would be accepted as such.[21]

In 1859, after six years of persistent petitioning and self-organization, the campaign for black militia service came within sight of victory: the state legislature finally voted to remove the word "white" from the state's militia law.[22] But this triumph on Beacon Hill came to grief in the mountains of Virginia. While the militia reform bill moved toward passage, John Brown was a name known only to those on the frontline of the struggle over slavery; by the time the bill reached the Massachusetts governor's office, Brown was imprisoned and awaiting trial for the raid on Harpers Ferry, and the Southern countryside was alight with the fires of the worst insurrection panic in a generation. Massachusetts men, including Higginson and Hayden, had been hip-deep in the conspiracy, and the governor may have reflected that to take that particular moment to distribute arms to the state's black citizens could bring him a different sort of national fame than he sought. He vetoed the bill. In 1860, when faced with another such bill, he did the same. Undaunted, a protest meeting of black citizens "pledged a renewal of persistent agitation."[23]

But even as Boston's leading black men sought to integrate themselves into the nation's revolutionary and military traditions, they—and many of their white allies—wondered if that integration was in fact possible. David Walker's 1829 *Appeal to the Colored Citizens* had famously framed the issue in conditional terms: "What a happy country this will be, if the whites will listen." That "if" resonated throughout Watkins's testimony to the legislative committee, and, by the 1850s, through abolitionism as a whole. Boston's abolitionists, white as well as black, expressed great skepticism about the potential of the United States for realizing their dreams of universal freedom and citizenship. Many white radicals were disunionists, seeking the secession of the free states, both in order to avoid compromising with slaveholders and to bring the border of freedom that much closer to Southern slaves. Some black radicals were emigrationists, who had more or less given up on the United States as a site of black freedom and instead sought it in Haiti, Liberia, or Canada. James Redpath, the white Boston abolitionist who ran the Haitian government's emigration program for black Americans, did not see America as the model for black regeneration in Haiti; rather, he imagined Haiti as "the black England of the future."[24]

And even those who espoused neither disunion nor emigration doubted whether America would ever acknowledge black men as legitimate heirs to its revolution. It was not hard for an abolitionist to feel that America in the 1850s represented a betrayal of whatever of value might be found in the revolutionary legacy. Some still sought to rehabilitate the nation, but all recognized the seriousness of the challenge. Black men's efforts to argue and act themselves into the American revolutionary tradition could be as full-throated as William Nell's pamphlets and books, but they could also express deep ambivalence. Watkins mocked a hypocritical "American Republicanism" and "American Christianity (?)" that seemed "determined if there is any manhood in us, to crush it out of us."[25] Like Nell, though, Watkins did argue that Revolutionary War service proved black men's fealty to the ideals of the nation, and that acknowledgment of that fealty required the recognition of black men's full rights as citizens. Others expressed a deeper skepticism. At the 1860 celebration of Crispus Attucks's martyrdom at the Boston Massacre—an event William Nell had labored to add to the abolitionist calendar as a way of asserting black Americans' inextricability from the revolutionary heritage—John S. Rock's speech reflected the depth of ambivalence many felt. "I am not yet ready to idolize the actions of Crispus Attucks," he demurred, for the government Attucks's sacrifice had helped create "has used every means in its power to outrage and degrade his race and posterity."[26]

While Boston's leading black men drilled without authority and petitioned the legislature for recognition, white men who suffered under no such disabilities ordered themselves in different sorts of ranks. Many white abolitionists imagined themselves not as rejected heirs seeking recognition but as insurrectionaries who would form an entirely new political order. They did not need to demonstrate their respectability: though some of their conservative detractors no doubt disagreed, leading white abolitionists did not seem to have had much doubt that they would be treated as full citizens. They could have formed a militia company had they wished, but until sectional conflict appeared imminent, few white radicals seemed interested in public military service. During the 1850s, while their black compatriots were protesting, petitioning, and drilling for inclusion in the state militia, white abolitionist men instead formed a secret paramilitary society whose aim was collective, physical defiance of the federal Fugitive Slave Law. In a sense, while black abolitionist men sought recognition as equal citizens doing their civic duty, white abolitionist men were imagining themselves as outsiders, criminals, and members of a vast conspiracy against an unjust republic.

The League of Massachusetts Freemen and its dozens of local auxiliaries—most notably the Boston Anti-Man-Hunting League—grew up in the wake of the Anthony Burns crisis of 1854. Its stated goal was to prevent any future fugitives from being returned from Massachusetts to slavery. The League's leaders imagined—and to an impressive degree created—a clandestine and oath-bound statewide network of clubs whose members were prepared to obstruct, and if necessary to kidnap, would-be slave-catchers.[27] The League built on and collaborated in the work of fugitive defense that the Boston Vigilance Committee had undertaken since the 1840s, including purchasing a yacht for use by Bearse—a member of the Boston Anti-Man-Hunting League—on his raids.[28] But the League envisioned something more. Its leaders developed a constitution, a cipher, and a system for checking the credentials of new members. In a bow to the deep involvement of abolitionist women in the movement's activities, they provided for the wives of members to be let in on its secrets by taking an oath. The membership itself, though, remained entirely male.

This exclusion reflected the League's military character: like the men of the Massasoit and Liberty Guards, the men of the League prepared for combat. Members were divided into squads based on their willingness or unwillingness to use force in the defense of fugitives. (Less than a fifth of the Boston League's members demurred.) They prepared for confrontations with slave-catchers by drawing up diagrams and conducting secret drills according to them. A dozen men would stealthily surround the "slave-catcher," while one would approach him and seek to persuade him to desist. If he refused, he would be seized and carried off, and his intended victim freed. "This drill," a leading member wrote,

> was always carried out amid great merriment especially when a stalwart farmer from the country came from one of the leagues. He was told to use any means of defense (fists, feet &c) but with perfect ease, in less than half a minute, he was laid prostrate & borne around the room as we intended to kidnap the Slave Hunter *in case we had a chance.*[29]

They imagined repeating—but perfecting—the kind of rescue black men had effected in 1851 and that black and white men together had botched in 1854.

The gentlemen in question were almost exclusively white. This was not simply a matter of social class: the "stalwart farmer" whom the Anti-Man-Hunters carried merrily about the room was not the only white man of modest means involved in the League. Worcester's Martin Stowell was one of several white working-class radicals who took part. But only one African American, the well-known caterer Joshua B. Smith, was invited to join. No proscription was written into the League's constitution, and the surviving records do not demonstrate any overt resistance to an integrated membership (though racial exclusion and white supremacist expression among white abolitionists was hardly rare). Indeed, it is possible that the resistance ran another way: perhaps black abolitionists expressed little interest in such an elaborately formal approach to physical resistance to slave-catchers—an activity for which they needed no oath to bind them, individually or collectively. The League's members may well have enjoyed the sense of belonging to a secret brotherhood, an experience otherwise denied them by virtue of the apolitical or conservative character of the existing white fraternal societies. Of the prominent white male abolitionists in Boston, only one seems to have been active in the white fraternal orders. Black abolitionist men, by contrast, already had oaths and fraternity aplenty in Prince Hall Freemasonry, an African American order to which virtually every leading black male abolitionist in Boston belonged.[30]

If Watkins and his compatriots feared that black militiamen would be seen as rebels playing gentlemen, the League's founders seemed to have worried about the reverse: that they would appear to have been gentlemen playing at revolution. The League's archivist seemed sensitive to this possibility in the 1880s when he annotated the body's records before depositing them at the Massachusetts Historical Society: of the great chart, four feet square, that represented how a squad of numbered League members would surround a slave-catcher like numerals on a clock face, he wrote: "Of course the committee would not so *formally* surround the man, but each committee man would know exactly what part he was to seize and at the proper moment would do his part of the work."[31] Higginson, who belonged to the Boston chapter, noted that the League "was an excellent thing, though perhaps it had a few unnecessary formalities."[32] He spoke generously, for all the ciphers and regulations and drills in the end amounted to nothing: the League, as such, rescued not a single fugitive.

And yet this was more than play, and the League's members remained eager to put their plans into action. In early 1860, many men believed to have conspired with Brown were subpoenaed to appear before a Senate investigating committee, and it was widely feared that those who submitted would be extradited to Virginia, where they would be tried and executed. James Redpath, as a well-known associate of Brown's, fully expected to be arrested by U.S. authorities. In April 1860, hoping to further Brown's work by provoking a direct confrontation with the federal government, Redpath's associates—including his publisher, William Thayer, and Higginson—plotted to bring armed men to a future hearing. "If his case is tried in Boston," they said, they proposed "to have in the court room during the trial 25 men *well armed* under a competent leader. If the judge decrees that [Redpath] must go to Wash[ington] . . . we will encircle and defend him against the Sergeant or U.S. Marshall." Thayer regretted that the League (the "L___ of F___," as he carefully put it in a letter to Higginson) was not "under thorough organization."[33] But it was not too late—and the League appears to have reorganized and conducted drills as late as early 1861, after South Carolina's secession.[34] Perhaps members of the League were among those who protected Wendell Phillips from antiabolitionist mobs during the secession winter.[35]

When the war finally came, it played out differently from the way either the black men of the Massasoit Guards or the white men of the Anti-Man-Hunting and associated leagues had imagined. And though by its end black and white abolitionist men had found common cause in the ranks of the Union military and the Lincoln government's policy of emancipation, the path to that consensus was anything but straight. Indeed, the war turned some of these men's worlds upside down: aspiring patriots settled into campaigns of defiance, while would-be rebels donned the uniform of the national army and urged others to compromise and accommodate.

After secession, black and white men continued to predict slave revolts on a scale never before seen. The slave rebel was alive and well, and Boston's abolitionists insisted that his moment had come. Once the Civil War began, John S. Rock claimed, "fifty negroes would take the State of Virginia without the loss of a man. . . . One thousand negroes would sweep the slave States from the Potomac to the Rio Grande."[36] Higginson, too, had the image of the slave rebel on the brain. As the war began, he continued his paramilitary scheming, "trying to get means for equipping a picked company for John Brown, Jr. [the abolitionist martyr's son and coconspirator]—to be used on the Pennsylvania border." Whatever else occurred, "I want at least to get the *name* of John Brown rumored on the border & then the whole party may come back & go to bed—they will frighten Virginia into fits all the same."[37]

James Redpath went further. Like Rock and Higginson, he delighted in suggesting that the war would bring slave revolts on a scale never before seen. His emigrationist sheet, the *Pine and Palm*, printed the report of a traveler (no doubt Redpath himself) who had stumbled upon a South-wide secret "freemasonry" of slave rebels. "The blacks," he reported, "only *bide their time*."[38] But more tangibly and verifiably, Redpath reported that an associate of his, the fugitive slave Abraham Galloway, had returned from Haiti in order to go "South to incite insurrections." Galloway, who had spent time in the black communities of Boston, Canada, and Haiti, would soon become a spymaster reporting directly to Union commanders in Virginia and North Carolina; by 1863, he would be playing a crucial role in the recruitment of North Carolina freedmen for the Union military. Slave rebels did exist; they had in fact been biding their time; and now their allies were finally in a position to offer them meaningful help.[39]

The firing on Fort Sumter recast old arguments. Most abolitionists, historian James McPherson has concluded, moved to support war against the Confederacy,[40] and the Lincoln administration's halting moves toward enlisting black troops brought white abolitionists ever deeper into the military struggle. By the end of 1862, Higginson had taken command of the First South Carolina Volunteers, one of the very first black regiments, recruited from among the freedmen in the Union-occupied southeast. Many young men of abolitionist leanings followed suit, including William Lloyd Garrison's son George and his wealthier neighbor Robert Gould Shaw.[41] The prominence of Massachusetts men followed in large part from the critical role played by the state's governor, John Albion Andrew, an abolitionist lawyer who had defended fugitives and participated in vigilance committee activities for over a decade. It was to Andrew that Lincoln turned when the Union moved toward the enlistment of black Northerners in 1863.

But by the time Andrew mobilized his allies to recruit black Northern men, the frustration felt by Massachusetts' black abolitionists had reached dangerous heights. Black abolitionists traveled a far more difficult path than their white peers in translating their martial commitments and antislavery impulses into Civil War service. Some of the contours of that story have become familiar, particularly the struggle of black Northerners over equal pay. Yet the struggle over black military service took place at an even more fundamental level than that oft-told story suggests.

Within days of Lincoln's call for volunteers, a mass meeting of Boston's black citizens had resolved to fight for the nation and to prepare for service by organizing into drilling companies. Their services were not accepted. Over the next two years, repeated efforts to remove the word "white" from the state's militia law went nowhere. So did efforts to create a black "Home Guard." Unlike their white male allies, who could choose whether or not to enlist, Boston's black men had been shut out.[42]

The result was a new kind of rebellion. It began early, drawing on the brimming well of bitterness on the subject of military service. At a public meeting in Boston just days after the first Massachusetts regiments had left for Washington, a reporter for the *Weekly Anglo-African*, the nation's preeminent black newspaper, found "that the division of sentiment was large on the subject of volunteering." Robert Morris, the leader of the militia movement, offered a set of resolutions that on the surface appeared to occupy the nonconfrontational ground suggested by Republicans and other nonabolitionists. "Very modestly written," and avoiding the word "slavery," Morris's resolutions "expressed the patriotic feelings of the colored men towards the States and the Union declaring themselves ready to defend the flag of the common country against the common foe." But to this commitment Morris appended a critical qualification: "when the removal of disabilities allowed them to do so on terms of equality." And that meant the removal of the word "white" from the state's militia law. The resolutions were popular, but not universally so—and at least some of the challenge appears to have come from those who took an even more militant position than Morris. William Wells Brown, for example, "thought that self respect demanded that the people should not beg for the removal of disabilities." Black men should not have to ask for what the nation should already have given.[43]

These men's feelings of wounded pride and disregarded patriotism seethed as the war progressed. In the radically altered political world of early 1863, Massachusetts governor John Andrew worked his longstanding connections among black and white abolitionists on behalf of the Lincoln administration, trying to get recruiting under way for what would become the Fifty-fourth and Fifty-fifth Massachusetts infantry regiments and the Fifth Massachusetts Cavalry. William Wells Brown wanted to cooperate, but he still objected to service on terms of less than perfect equality. He told an antislavery audience that he would not help until the hated word "white" had been removed from the statute books. "While the State of Massachusetts refuses the black man as an equal in every sense of the word, it would be an insult to ask them to fight." "Equality first," he insisted, "guns afterwards."[44] Robert Morris, though a longtime associate of Andrew, not only concurred but went further: "He thought it the colored man's duty to 'go right.'" Not only should the word "white" be struck, but: "Let black regiments be officered by men of their own color and a great blow would be struck. He for one would go when he could go as he should."[45]

This was not idle talk. During the first year of recruitment of black Northerners, Morris's objections seem to have gained traction. Recruitment among Boston's militarily eligible black population lagged behind expectations, and the words of men like Morris and Brown appeared to be responsible—or at least William Nell thought so. In June, 1863, he lamented publicly that, "owing to a combination wholly unexpected and never to be too much regretted, numbers of young men were induced to refrain from enlisting in the 54th, and thus lost the golden privilege of having their names enrolled in the first colored regiment from the North." He noted a countercampaign, in which "the young ladies of Boston organized themselves" to persuade their reluctant peers.[46] Clearly, Nell implied, it was somehow not self-evident to the black men of Boston that this had become their fight, and it had fallen to the city's black women to remind them of their responsibilities.

The challenge to recruiting by black abolitionist men should not be overstated. Morris's friend and colleague Lewis Hayden served as a recruiter for the black regiments, as did many other black abolitionists, eventually including even the doubting William Wells Brown. Like many others, John S. Rock offered a mixture of rage, pragmatism, celebration, and protest. In a speech to the New England Anti-Slavery Convention that spring, he urged all who could "conscientiously" enlist to do so, but thought it was not surprising that "after pressing their claims for two years . . . many should have become discouraged and disheartened." Given the wording of the state's militia law and the absence of black commissioned officers, "you ought not to be surprised why we have hesitated, and not rushed pell-mell into the service, and urged others to follow us." Yet he also lauded the "proficiency of drill and manly bearing" of the Fifty-fourth Massachusetts on its march through Boston, and foresaw great fruits from this undertaking.[47] But Morris continued to play the rebel, refusing to follow along in a practical policy that did not match his sense of the right. Twenty years later, a eulogy by his protégé Edwin G. Walker celebrated Morris's stand—one that Walker thought had brought Morris to the verge of being locked up as a foe of conscription—as part and parcel of the career of defending fugitives that had made Morris famous.[48]

Even after men became recruiters, they could be subject to moments of grave doubt and second thoughts. William Wells Brown had urged black men to go to war, he told an August 1863 meeting, "to convince this God-forsaken nation that black men are as valiant as other men. But our people have been so cheated, robbed, deceived, and outraged everywhere, that I cannot urge them to go." John S. Rock, though a friend of Governor Andrew, agreed.

> If we are not to be treated as men now when in this hour of peril we have come forward and forgiven two centuries of outrage and oppression what reason have we to expect anything, how do we know that it may not be wrested from us? Is this nation any better at heart now than it was four years ago?

And Robert Morris continued to argue that the unequal treatment of black troops was reason enough to doubt any promises, however honestly intended.

> We told you this is the way they would treat us. No, I want you to understand I am not going to the war; God forbid, that I should ask any man to go. . . . But if any one chooses to make a fool of himself he can do so. We have rights as well as the white people, and it looks to me as though they intend to use us and do not mean to do anything for us. If we are not careful they will give us what they gave our fathers in the Revolution.

And contra William Nell's assertions, at least one black female activist agreed: Mrs. Carteaux Bannister urged support for the soldiers who were already in the field, "but she did not want any more to go to aid a government that had treated them so cruelly. She would rather beg from door to door than that her husband should go to war."[49] And this was a month *after* the Fifty-fourth Massachusetts had made its famous assault on Fort Wagner.

While black abolitionists wrestled earnestly and often angrily over the question of equality before the law, their white allies wavered. In the radically new circumstances of the war, rebelliousness struck some habitual mavericks as a bit self-indulgent. James Redpath reflected in 1862 that "of course we abolitionists delight in embarrassing administrations, but national safety sometimes demands that we should forego the pleasure of performing *such* duties."[50] Even the famously obstinate Wendell Phillips, who had argued for the dissolution of the United States as late as 1861, believed the time had come to support the government. In a public meeting in Boston in February 1863, he openly disagreed with Robert Morris and encouraged Boston's black men to enlist. "True, all that could be desired was not yet granted," he admitted, "but nevertheless the time was near at hand when colored men would enjoy their full rights."[51] He alluded directly to one of Morris's main objections: "I hear there is some reluctance because you are not to have officers of your own color. This may be wrong. . . . But if you cannot have a whole loaf, will you not take a slice?"[52] Phillips's appeals may not have been fully persuasive, for he himself had often been unwilling to make the kind of compromise with principle that he now urged upon his black allies. John S. Rock, certainly, resented being urged to defer indefinitely in the hope that all would be "right in the end." "This living entirely for posterity sounds well from the rostrum," he argued a few months after Phillips's speech, "but a loaf of bread to-day is worth a barrel of flour next year."[53]

White abolitionists more skilled at political cajolery made more nuanced appeals. In an open letter, antislavery editor and vigilance-committee member Elizur Wright urged his black allies to take up the government's invitation to serve—not as an end in itself, but as a means to greater things. "I grant," he admitted, "with a twinge of shame, that the invitation does not come in man-fashion. There is a higgling about the *color* of the officers and other conditions." Nonetheless, he urged them to see Union military service, even under unequal conditions, as a moment of white indecision that they might transform into an opportunity for self-liberation. He had been in the courtroom twelve years before during the rescue of Robert Morris's client Shadrach Minkins, and in language that was doubtless aimed squarely at Morris, he made a case for once more seizing the day. Just as in 1851, he argued, black men might use their armed bodies to pry open a door that had been opened a crack. During the Minkins riot, Wright explained, "I noticed that the brave and patriotic colored men who vindicated their manhood and the constitution on that occasion, did not wait until the court room door was pried open, but squeezed in as soon as ever they could." Their decisive action in a moment of crisis could become a potent metaphor for present possibilities: "There will be no excluding you from the full and just share in the however-bounded republic which is due to your mind and manhood, forever and forever more, the moment you begin to pour into its armies with fixed bayonets."[54] The Lincoln administration had opened the door a crack; the rest was up to them.

Legislative changes at the state and federal level finally addressed black activists' demands. In September 1863, under a reorganization of the state militia, Lewis Gaul's petition to form a black company of infantry was accepted, and on September 21, he was formally named captain of the new unit.[55] In February 1864, the Massachusetts legislature formally struck the word "white" from the state's militia laws.[56] The door Wright had invoked was finally open, and by early 1864, Gaul was formally reporting his men's names on the roster of the Fourteenth Unattached Company of Militia. Gaul's company, known as the "Shaw Guards," in honor of the fallen white colonel of the Fifty-fourth Massachusetts, quickly became regular participants in Boston's civic affairs.[57] That summer the federal government finally followed suit, granting the black regiments equal pay and back pay.[58] The war with the Union had ended, less than a year before the war with the Confederacy.

This seemed to clarify the relationship between black militancy and the American state. And at the National Convention of Colored Men in Syracuse, New York, in October, John S. Rock took a step past the profound ambivalence that so often characterized black abolitionist views of the United States. He began in familiar terms: "Many of our grandfathers fought in the Revolution, and they thought they were fighting for liberty; but they made a sad mistake, and we are now obliged to fight those battles over again, and I hope, this time, to a better purpose." But he also celebrated the new laws and concluded that "there are but two parties in the country today. The one headed by Lincoln is for Freedom and the Republic; and the other, by McClellan, is for Despotism and Slavery. . . . The friends and the enemies of the country are defined."[59]

In the end, the rebellion led by Robert Morris proved less powerful than the recruitment efforts of Rock, Brown, Hayden, and others. Nearly two hundred thousand black men served in the Union army and navy, forging a military claim to American citizenship that overwhelmed and reversed the trend of the 1850s. By 1864, Lincoln would suggest that military service might entitle black men to voting rights; this was not a bold new insight, but a strategy black communities had already adopted and would successfully pursue in earnest during the crucial years immediately following the war. It had been a remarkably successful strategy, driving Lincoln and the Union government toward an ever more unambiguous acknowledgment of black men's capacity for and right to full citizenship.

Yet the moment of victory between 1865 and the ratification of the Fifteenth Amendment in 1870 disguises a more complex history of race, gender, martial struggle, and citizenship. The moment marked not the final triumph of the ideal of equality, but a high-water mark in the struggle for nonracial citizenship that would not be reached again until another century had passed. In between would come the overthrow of Reconstruction, the collapse of interracial political movements, and the long winter of Jim Crow. The partisans of equality during these years did not lack commitment, but they did lack the Civil War, the catalyst that had allowed their forebears to press the case for universal citizenship on so many fronts.

On one of those fronts, their struggle was not helped, and may even have been hindered, by the preoccupation with martial manhood. Abolitionists had always been among the strongest supporters of women's rights, including the rights of political citizenship. Yet one effect of abolitionist men's emphasis on military struggle as the essence of citizenship seems to have been to constrict their political imaginations. Although men and women who had been prominent in the abolition movement persistently advocated woman suffrage during the late 1860s and 1870s, the political and military campaigns of the 1850s and 1860s helped make citizenship's virtues into more explicitly martial ones. Abolitionist men did not in any sense create this dynamic, but they were drawn into it, sometimes nearly as fully as those who supported woman suffrage less ardently or not at all. In the late 1850s, an eccentric like John Brown might regender Harriet Tubman in order to make sense of her as a political and military leader; by the late 1870s, even longtime suffrage advocate Lewis Hayden, articulating the case for woman suffrage to a friendly audience of black activist women that included his wife and colleague Harriet Hayden, could stake women's claim in the weakest possible realm: that of military activity. As proof that black women had earned the right to vote, Hayden offered the example of an eighteenth-century black woman who disguised herself as a man and served in the patriot army during the Revolution.[60] If this was the best a committed women's-rights man could do, the outlook was bleak indeed. Martial manhood, once a critical but missing component of the African American struggle for full civil equality, had become the sine qua non of political citizenship, and the full enfranchisement of men left women—even "General" Tubman—behind. It remained for men and women who were committed to women's rights to think and struggle their way out of the dead end that their victory had inadvertently helped create. But that is another story.

ACKNOWLEDGMENTS   Thanks to John Stauffer, Tim Tyson, Susan Ferber, Catherine Clinton, Nina Silber, David Blight, and an anonymous reader for helpful readings of this essay.

NOTES

1. James Oliver Horton and Lois E. Horton show black men in the antebellum era negotiating competing ideals of masculinity while discussing violence and nonviolence in "Violence, Protest, and Identity: Black Manhood in Antebellum America," in James Oliver Horton, *Free People of Color: Inside the African American Community* (Washington, D.C.: Smithsonian Institution Press, 1993), 80–97. On savagery and civilization in the abolitionist imagination, see John Stauffer, *The Black Hearts of Men: Radical Abolitionists and the Transformation of Race* (Cambridge, Mass.: Harvard University Press, 2001), 182–207.

2. "By the end of 1859 almost no nonresistant voice remained to be raised against force and violence." Lewis Perry, *Radical Abolitionism: Anarchy and the Government of God in Antislavery Thought*, rev. ed. (Knoxville: University of Tennessee Press, 1995) (originally published 1973), 260.

3. Gary Collison, *Shadrach Minkins: From Fugitive Slave to Citizen* (Cambridge, Mass.: Harvard University Press, 1997); Albert J. Von Frank, *The Trials of Anthony Burns: Freedom and Slavery in Emerson's Boston* (Cambridge: Harvard University Press, 1998); Benjamin Quarles, *Allies for Freedom: Blacks and John Brown* (New York: Oxford University Press, 1974).

4. Rock's speech in C. Peter Ripley, ed.; Jeffreys, Rossbach, associate ed., et al., *The Black Abolitionist Papers*, vol. 5, *The United States, 1859–1865* (Chapel Hill: University of North Carolina Press), 58–66.

5. Quotation from Benjamin Quarles, *Black Abolitionists* (New York: Oxford University Press, 1969), 228.

6. Quoted in Tilden G. Edelstein, *Strange Enthusiasm: A Life of Thomas Wentworth Higginson* (New Haven: Yale University Press, 1968), 162.

7. William Cooper Nell, *The Colored Patriots of the American Revolution* (1855; reprint, Salem, N.H.: Ayer, 1986).

8. See, for comparison, Kristin Hoganson, "Garrisonian Abolitionists and the Rhetoric of Gender, 1850–1860," *American Quarterly* 45, 4 (December 1993): 558–595.

9. Leonard Levy, "The 'Abolition Riot': Boston's First Slave Rescue," *New England Quarterly* 25 (March 1952): 85–92.

10. Catherine Clinton, *Harriet Tubman: The Road to Freedom* (New York : Little, Brown, 2004), 129.

11. For one intriguing introduction to this theme, see Maggie Montesinos Sale, *The Slumbering Volcano: American Slave Ship Revolts and the Production of Rebellious Masculinity* (Durham, N.C.: Duke University Press, 1997).

12. "Convention of the Colored Citizens of Massachusetts," reprinted in *Proceedings of the Black State Conventions, 1840–1865*, vol. 2 (Philadelphia: Temple University Press, 1980), edited by Philip S. Foner and George E. Walker, 96–107.

13. Austin Bearse, *Reminiscences of Fugitive-Slave Law Days in Boston* (Boston: Warren Richardson, 1880); the (possibly overdramatized) account of Hayden's actions is in Nina Moore Tiffany, "Stories of the Fugitive Slaves I: The Escape of William and Ellen Craft," *New England Magazine* 7, 5 (January 1890): 524–531; Collison, *Shadrach Minkins*; Von Frank, *Trials of Anthony Burns*; Quarles, *Allies for Freedom*.

14. As Kristin Hoganson suggests, abolitionist men, no less than other Northern men, had come to value "responsibility, regularity, [and] self-control" as essential qualities. Hoganson, "Garrisonian Abolitionists," 583.

15. On "respectability," see Patrick Rael, *Black Identity and Black Protest in the Antebellum North* (Chapel Hill: University of North Carolina Press, 2002), 130–135.

16. For portraits of this community, see James Oliver Horton and Lois E. Horton, *Black Bostonians: Family Life and Community Struggle in the Antebellum North*, rev. ed. (New York: Holmes and Meier, 1999) (originally published 1979), and George A. Levesque, *Black Boston: African American Life and Culture in Urban America, 1750–1860* (New York: Garland, 1994).

17. On the Massasoit Guards: Robert Morris Papers, "Massasoit Guards" folder, Boston Athenaeum; on the Shaw Guards: *Weekly Anglo-African*, November 26, 1864, p. 1, c. 6. The background of the local movement to 1855 is analyzed in Hal Goldman, "Black Citizenship and Military Self-Presentation in Antebellum Massachusetts," *Historical Journal of Massachusetts* 25 (winter 1997): 19–45. For a brief overview of black militia activity in national context, see Quarles, *Black Abolitionists*, 229–230.

18. William J. Watkins, "Our Rights as Men," reprinted in *Negro Protest Pamphlets: A Compendium* (New York: Arno Press, 1969), edited by Dorothy Porter, quotations pp. 4, 8.

19. On Morris's clients, see *In Memoriam Robert Morris* (Boston, [1883]), pamphlet, Printed Materials Collection, Massachusetts Historical Society (MHS), Boston; "Speech of Robert Morris, Esq. Before the Committee on the Militia, March 3, 1853," clipping, "Massasoit Guards" folder, Morris Papers.

20. Ferguson, Cincinnati, to DeGrasse, Boston, August 29, 1855, Morris Papers, "1880s" folder; also see Quarles, *Black Abolitionists*, 229–230.

21. *Liberator*, August 13, 1858, p. 4, cs. 2–6; see also "Massasoit Guards" folder, Morris Papers.

22. Commonwealth of Massachusetts, *Journal of the Senate*, 1859, esp. October, 19, 26, 31, Commonwealth of Massachusetts Archives (hereafter CMA).

23. "Meeting of Colored Citizens," *Liberator*, June 15, 1860, p. 1.

24. *Pine and Palm*, September 4, 1862, extra leaf.

25. Watkins, "Our Rights as Men," 8.

26. Rock's speech in Ripley, op. cit., *Black Abolitionist Papers*, 5:58.

27. On the Boston Anti-Man-Hunting League and the League of Massachusetts Freemen, see Bowditch Family Papers, and Boston Anti-Man-Hunting League Records (hereafter BAMHL), both at MHS. Also see Records of the Vigilence [sic] Committee, Special Collections, Boston Public Library.

28. Bearse, *Reminiscences*. For evidence of collaboration, see Record Book 2, January 17, 1855, BAMHL Records.

29. Untitled Document, p. 118, folder 1, BAMHL Records.

30. Book 1: Constitution; Book 4: Applicants for Admission; and Book 5: Names of Members, BAMHL Records. For an excellent starting point on

Prince Hall freemasonry, see Peter P. Hinks, *To Awaken My Afflicted Brethren: David Walker and the Problem of Antebellum Slave Resistance* (University Park: Pennsylvania State University Press, 1997), esp. 70–73. The white abolitionist-Mason was editor and politician Charles Slack. The only prominent black abolitionist man in Boston who stood clearly outside the Prince Hall lodge was William Cooper Nell.

31. Untitled Document, p. 118a, folder 1, BAMHL Records.

32. Higginson, Worcester, to Dear Sir, December 30, 1860, Book 10, BAMHL, Bowditch Family Papers.

33. James C. Malin, "Plotting after Harpers Ferry: The 'William Handy' Letters," *Journal of Southern History* 8, 1 (February 1942): 81–87, quotation on 85–86.

34. Untitled Document, p. 118, folder 1, BAMHL Records.

35. For a brief sketch of these events, see McPherson, *Struggle for Equality* (Princeton, N.J.: Princeton University Press, 1964), 42–44.

36. Ripley, op. cit. *Black Abolitionist Papers*, 5:65.

37. Higginson, Worcester, to Mother, April 23, 1861, Higginson Papers, Houghton Library, Harvard University.

38. *Pine and Palm*, January 2, 1862, "Away Down South in Dixie," p. 3, cs. 1–2.

39. *Pine and Palm*, July 20, 1861, "Two Slanders on Hayti Refuted," p. 4, cs.1–2; David S. Cecelski, "Abraham Galloway: Wilmington's Lost Prophet and the Rise of Black Radicalism in the American South," in *Democracy Betrayed: The Wilmington Race Riot of 1898 and its Legacy* (Chapel Hill: University of North Carolina Press, 1998), edited by David S. Cecelski and Timothy B. Tyson.

40. James McPherson, *Struggle for Equality*, 47–51.

41. Joseph T. Glatthaar, *Forged in Battle: The Civil War Alliance of Black Soldiers and White Officers* (New York: Meridian, 1991).

42. Benjamin Quarles, *Negro in the Civil War* (Boston: Little, Brown, 1953), 26–27; "Equal Militia Rights," *Liberator*, June 14, 1861, pp. 3–4; Commonwealth of Massachusetts, *Journal of the House,* May 15–23, 1861, January 23, 1863, CMA; see also petitions of Robert Morris and J. Sella Martin, in House Unpassed Legislation, 1861, CMA.

43. *Weekly Anglo-African*, May 4, 1861, p. 3, c.1

44. Ibid., February 14, 1863, p. 1, cs. 4–5.

45. Ibid., February 28, 1863, p. 2, c. 6.

46. Ibid., June 13, 1863, p. 2, cs. 3–5.

47. *Liberator*, June12, 1863, p. 4, cs. 3–6.

48. *In Memoriam. Robert Morris, Sr.* (n.p., n.d. [1883]), pamphlet, Printed Materials Collection, MHS, 39.

49. *Weekly Anglo-African*, August 13, 1863, p. 2, c. 6–p. 3, c. 1.

50. Redpath to Watkins, March 4, 1862, James Redpath Correspondence, 1861–1862, Schomburg Center, New York Public Library.

51. *Weekly Anglo-African*, February 28, 1863, p. 2, c. 6.

52. Luis F. Emilio, *A Brave Black Regiment: History of the Fifty-Fourth Regiment of Massachusetts Volunteer Infantry, 1863–1865* (1894; reprint, New York: Arno Press, 1969), 13.

53. *Liberator,* June 12, 1863, p. 4, cs. 3–6.

54. Broadside, "To the Men of Color," Boston, February 15, 1863, in Executive Letters, Series 567x, vol. 21b, CMA.

55. Massachusetts *Acts and Resolves* 1863, chap. 243; petition of Lewis Gaul and 124 others, n.d., and Enlistment Roll, September 2, 1863, Commonwealth of Massachusetts, Adjutant General's Office, Enlistment Rolls of the Mass. Volunteer Militia, series 486x, CMA; *Boston Evening Transcript,* September 22, 1863, p. 2, c. 4; *Weekly Anglo-African*, October 10, 1863, p. 3, cs. 3–4.

56. Commonwealth of Massachusetts, *Journal of the House,* January 27–February 5, 1864, CMA.

57. See, e.g., *Weekly Anglo-African*, November 26, 1864, p. 1, c. 6.

58. *Weekly Anglo-African*, July 16, 1864, p. 1, cs. 5–6.

59. Rock's speech at Syracuse, October 6, 1864, in Ripley, op. cit., *Black Abolitionist Papers,* 5:304–306.

60. Hayden speech in *An Account of the Labors of the Ladies' Charitable Association of Boston, In Recognition of, an Homage to, the Declaration of Independence* (Boston, 1876), 11. It should come as no surprise that Hayden was citing Nell, *Colored Patriots of the American Revolution.*

3

"OH, I PASS EVERYWHERE"

Catholic Nuns in the Gulf South during the Civil War

Virginia Gould

On April 8, 1863, Marie Hyacinth LeConnait, the mother superior of the Daughters of the Cross in Avoyelles Parish, Louisiana, wrote to her mother and father in Plounez, France. Penning her letter in her native French, LeConnait did not offer reassurance to her elderly parents as the Civil War closed in on her and her convent.[1] Instead, she filled her pages with news of the deprivations suffered by her congregation and alerted her parents to the dangers they faced. She reported that she had lost contact with the Daughters of the Cross in Isle Breville and Shreveport the preceding fall when New Orleans was captured by Union forces. By early May the situation had worsened. The "Federals (Yankees they are called here), our enemy," she wrote, "have a camp five miles from us." On May 2, she wrote again, warning her mother and father: "No one knows when this terrible war will be over, but do not worry about us." Until now, she added, they have "respected the religious communities."[2] Although the threat had thus far been negligible and manageable, she had heard that thirty thousand Union troops were advancing on the parish. With no other recourse, Mother Hyacinth ordered her religious sisters to sew a French flag and hoist it over the convent. Then she prayed that their declaration of French citizenship, and thus their neutrality, would save them.[3]

The French flag flying over the convent did not spare the Daughters of the Cross. On June 12, 1864, LeConnait wrote her parents again, telling them that a month earlier, on Pentecost Sunday, her convent and its

41

gardens had been a battleground. From dawn until midafternoon, Union soldiers gathered on one side of the convent, while Confederate soldiers gathered on the other.[4] Before the battle was struck, Mother Hyacinth sent all but four of her religious sisters and their students into the woods to hide. The four sisters left in the convent were forced to take cover in the oven for three hours while the battle raged. When it ended, their convent and its chapel were severely damaged; their livestock killed. After surviving the battle, the sisters watched as angered Union soldiers ransacked their convent. According to Mother Hyacinth, the defeated "Federals" had taken revenge on the countryside, and even the convent was not spared.[5]

Marie Hyacinth LeConnait, like other religious sisters in the region, refused to desert her convent or her apostolate. Instead, after the battle she ordered her sisters to clear out the rubble and resume their duties, educating and providing succor to the pupils who remained under their tutelage. The determination, resiliency, and self-sufficiency demonstrated by LeConnait and her religious sisters were typical attributes of women religious who defined social action, or good works, as a part of their spirituality. The tradition they followed, of communities of religious sisters serving the poor, the uninstructed, and the uneducated, was an old one. It first took form in seventeenth-century France as a consequence of the evolution of a complex of social services. According to Elizabeth Rapley, seventeenth-century French women imbued with religious energy sought and found ways to channel their energy into meaningful action. As these women formed themselves into socially active groups, they needed protection and maintenance, which is what the Catholic Church could and did provide. The effect of this movement of Catholic women into socially active communities changed the face of modern France, since no alternatives developed to the systems of female-run schools and hospitals.[6]

Convents of women dedicated to spiritually directed social activism, following their seventeenth-century foremothers,[7] peppered the Gulf South by the time Union forces advanced into the region in 1862, serving as a testament to the vibrancy of Catholicism in the region. French missionary priests first transported Catholicism to colonial Louisiana in the eighteenth century. Their goals were twofold. The first was to ensure the salvation of the inhabitants, whether French, Indian, or African, and to impose social order, with female piety as one of its principle conventions. In 1727, French colonial administrators sent twelve Ursuline nuns to New Orleans. By the following spring, the Ursulines had established a school with boarding and day divisions.[8] Though alone in reinforcing feminine piety, the Ursulines spread their fervor throughout the region as they educated the daughters of planters, merchants, and skilled and unskilled tradesmen and women.[9] Most of their students were white, though Indian girls and free girls of African descent were also educated by the nuns. Most of the students were from New Orleans; yet, girls from Mobile and Natchez, Natchidoches and New Iberia boarded with the women. The Ursulines attracted female students from all classes and races. Their ministry to instruct enslaved women and girls in the fundamental principles of Catholicism was particularly successful.[10] By the end of the eighteenth century, the Catholic worshippers at the St. Louis the King of France Cathedral in New Orleans were overwhelmingly black and female.[11] By the nineteenth century, the majority of inhabitants in the Gulf South were Catholics, even if just nominally so.[12]

The foundation of Catholicism laid in the eighteenth century did not go unchallenged in the nineteenth century. When the region was ceded to the United States in 1803, the majority of priests and nuns withdrew.[13] In 1812, when Guilliaume Louis DuBourg was appointed apostolic administrator of the diocese of Louisiana, which then included Mississippi and Alabama, and eventually Florida, only a handful of Ursulines and priests were ministering to thousands of Catholics living in every corner of the immense wilderness. In response to the "barren field" he found in Louisiana, DuBourg traveled to France seeking financial and missionary aid for his flock.[14] DuBourg's success can be gauged by the growth of a variety of French feminine missions, based in convents, in his diocese.[15]

The Catholic sisters who transplanted their apostolates to the region did not pose a challenge to the traditions of Southern womanhood, since their roles were not altogether inconsistent with those of secular nineteenth-century Southern women. Their inferior status was most visible in their ban from ministering the sacraments. Their mannerisms and dress symbolized their submission and their subjugation to Church fathers who acted as spiritual and administrative advisors. Their charitable good works—the care they extended to the needy, the sick, and the orphaned—did not challenge the ideals of Southern womanhood. The schools for girls they founded within their convent walls, schools meant to educate girls to be good Catholic wives and mothers, and the programs they instituted to instruct the enslaved in the religious principles of the Catholic Church perhaps stretched the bounds of womanhood but were nonetheless acceptable and welcome within the Deep South.

Yet the complex of social services the women founded, managed, and manned were something of an anomaly. Southern women were limited to roles defined by family, children, and individual forms of charity and devotion, while religious women addressed their social action to the public. And while Southern women were considered intellectually inferior to men, influenced too much by emotion to be capable of leadership or decision making, the educational academies founded and run by women religious were applauded for their excellence.[16]

The women who disguised their abilities with habits and veils also administered hospitals and provided quality medical care to the sick and injured. They were self-supporting; they owned and maintained their own property; they held administrative positions; they were free from the dominance of fathers and husbands; they were released from the duties of motherhood; and oftentimes they were viewed as spiritually superior to the male clergy who were more comfortable behind their pulpits. Religious sisters might have rejected the ideal of Southern womanhood for themselves, though they disguised their actions by avoiding extremes, hiding their femininity, and conveying the spirit of humility and sensible piety. Indeed, their competence in the most trying of circumstances during the war smoothed the way for the advancement of their status and their ministry in the years that followed the war.[17]

If the roles religious sisters assumed posed a challenge to Southerners, their attitudes about slavery did not. To have challenged slavery in the Deep South would have been unpopular and even dangerous. In 1840, a French missionary priest and vicar general of New Orleans, Etienne Rousselon, summed up the dilemma nuns and priests faced in a letter he wrote to the editor of the *Annals of the Propagation of the Faith.* Rousselon begged the editor to resist discussing the topic of slavery in the *Annals.* The Church in his region, he pointed out, could not judge the question of slavery the same as it was judged in France. To do so he concluded would be "a matter of life and death. From the moment when one suspected the clergy to be abolitionists, one would have to expect in our slave states certain deplorable excesses."[18]

The abolitionists were, overwhelmingly, Northerners and Protestants. Slavery had either been abolished or gradual emancipation had been enacted in the Northern states by 1800. The 1820s and 1830s saw a rise in the prohibition of slavery in new territories, though the issue of continuing slavery in the South remained. In 1817, a group dominated by Quakers formed the first American Colonization Society, which proposed to emancipate slaves and send them to Africa. Free blacks rejected that plan and instead during the 1820s and 1830s called for immediate emancipation. During the 1830s, William Lloyd Garrison mounted a sweeping antislavery crusade that radicalized Northern antislavery Protestant groups. The Protestant reform movements of the 1820s and 1830s were the foundation of the growing antislavery movement of the 1840s and 1850s. By the 1850s, the reformist, individualist Protestant antislavery movement had also turned anti-Catholic. Northern Whigs, who stood together as antislavery advocates, disdained immigrants, who were mostly poor, mostly Catholic, and mostly antitemperance. Many believed that the hierarchical nature of Catholicism was inimical to the ideals upon which the American Revolution had been fought. Catholics did not respect the notion of the separation of church and state, they insisted.[19] Whigs were also suspicious of the Catholic leaders who opposed European revolutions. For their part, Catholics, North and South, shared the belief that abolitionists were linked to the revolutionaries and radicals who voiced anticlerical, liberal, and secular ideologies.[20]

In the minds of Southern Catholics, abolitionism was so directly associated with Protestantism that it was believed to be a "Protestant Crusade." Sarah Grimké, who, along with her sister Angelina, was the first women to give voice to abolitionism, linked Catholics and slavery when she argued that slavery was even worse than "Catholic superstition" with its "wicked system of bigotry and despotism."[21] In response to anti-Catholic attacks, Catholic leaders went out of their way to prove themselves to be good Americans and avoided involvements in the political struggles of the day, including the controversy that raged around slavery. Their failure to take a stand against slavery reinforced the belief that they were proslavery, sectional loyalists.

In fact, there is little evidence to suggest that either priests or nuns in the Gulf South held antislavery views.[22] Catholic missionaries who spread their fervor around the world traditionally fashioned their institutions to fit local norms. Had Catholic leaders, whether male or female, opposed slavery, they would have antagonized lay men and women who were slaveholders, thus interfering with their mission. In the South, nuns fashioned their institutions and their curriculum to fit the needs of the populace. They educated young women who were the daughters of slaveholders, and they educated them to become the wives and mothers of slaveholders. What is more, many of the priests and nuns who sought to spread their fervor were slaveholders themselves.

Soon after they arrived in New Orleans in 1727, the Ursulines incorporated slavery into their way of life. They first incorporated domestic slaves into their daily routines. Soon afterward, they began to reap the benefits from plantation slavery. Perhaps the Ursulines set the standard for the nuns who arrived in the nineteenth century. At first, most groups were uncomfortable with slaveholding, though they were soon justifying the institution by arguing that enslaved laborers were the only laborers available. The experience of Mother Hyacinth of the Daughters of the Cross is typical. On November 17, 1855, she wrote to her brother, Yves-Marie LeConnait, a missionary priest in Natchitoches, explaining that her community had twenty-four acres of land that they could not cultivate. The population, she explained, was "composed of white and black people, or negroes." The white people did not work, she told him, because they have "Negroes to do the work on farms or plantations, that produce cotton, sugar, rice, and corn." She added: "These poor negroes are *really* slaves. They are absolutely sold and bought like the beasts or animals in Europe." She then explained to Yves-Marie that the first time she had seen a human being exposed for sale was in New Orleans, where she was "seized with horror." She confessed that when the bishop proposed she purchase a slave she could not help but show her "repugnance, and he did not insist." She concluded the letter by pointing out that slaves were "treated like beasts with little pity. And yet, they are children of God!"[23]

Marie Hyacinth LeConnait's opinion about slavery changed quickly. In a letter to Bishop Martin two months later, in January 1856, she complained that her community could not find labor; they could not even "hire any good Negroes." Then she asked him if she could purchase a man who was good and industrious. The following March she told her brother that she had purchased a slave. "I forgot to tell you I have never witnessed such a strong repugnance as I did in seeing the buying of human flesh!" Then: "The day I signed the bill of sale for our slave I wanted to cry all day."[24]

The Ursulines, the Daughters of Charity, the Sisters of the Sacred Heart, and the Sisters of Mount Carmel, who were either French immigrants or affiliated with French communities, were slaveholders. The Dominican Sisters, the School Sisters of Notre Dame, and Mercy Sisters, who were Irish and German immigrants, were not slaveholders. The latter group found laborers to hire. The former found ways to justify their willingness to hold humans in bondage. Nuns who were slaveholders had reason to fear "the Federals, our enemy." They knew they would be stripped of their slaves, who constituted a considerable portion of their capital. But whether they owned slaves or not, all Catholic sisters of the South saw the advancing "Federals" as an invading, disruptive force. They feared for their safety and for the safety of their charges, and they feared their property—their convents, schools, asylums, and hospitals—would be destroyed or confiscated. Their property belonged to them, not the Church. It was where they lived, where they worshipped, where they advanced their ministries.

In 1863, after their grounds were used as a battlefield, the Avoylles Parish Daughters of the Cross were able to repair their convent and school and revive their apostolate. But not all the convents survived the war. The Mercy Sisters in Natchez remained in their convent until it became a target of Union gunboats. A few teaching congregations were forced to close their schools when their convents were destroyed or claimed by federal forces. The Daughters of Charity were forced to close their convent and school at Donaldsonville; the Daughters of the Holy Cross could not sustain their convent and school at Isle Breville; the Marianites of the Holy Cross abandoned their convent and school at Plaquemines; the Sisters of Mercy at Natchez did the same.[25]

Though some of the communities suffered less than others, none were spared the disruption and deprivation of the war. After New Orleans fell to Union gunboats in late April 1862, news of the capture frightened the residents in Vicksburg, who knew there was nothing between them and New Orleans to "hold back the gunboats."[26] Many of Vicksburg's inhabitants frantically fled the city. The Sisters of Mercy stayed, continuing their classes for the few children who stayed in town with their parents. As federal gunboats drew closer to Vicksburg in early May, the sisters closed their school, but refused to leave their convent until their spiritual advisor, Father Leray, insisted they take refuge at a plantation outside the city.[27]

Despite the losses, the majority of women managed to keep their convents safe and their schools open. Women from France, Ireland, and Bavaria held the status of foreign nationals and were thus, in principle, protected from the ebb and flow of either Union or Confederate forces. Officially viewed as neutrals, they were not forced to take an oath of allegiance, and their property was supposed to be exempt from destruction and confiscation. When the Daughters of the Cross in Avoyelles Parish hoisted the French flag and flew it over their convent, they were proclaiming the neutrality they believed was available to them. The Sisters of St. Joseph of Bourg at Bay St. Louis, also hinged their safety upon their status as foreign nationals. Soon after Ship Island, in the Mississippi Sound, was occupied by federal forces they raised the French flag over their convent, declaring their neutrality. French religious sisters whose convents were within traveling distance to New Orleans, women like the Sisters of St. Joseph, at Bay St. Louis, Mississippi, had received French flags from the French consul in New Orleans at the outbreak of the war.[28]

When the Daughters of the Cross returned to their badly damaged convent, they resumed their duties. The Sisters of St. Joseph of Bourg managed to keep their girls' academy in Bay St. Louis, open throughout the war, but only because their superior, Mother Esperance, traveled to New Orleans for supplies. According to the report Mother Esperance sent her superior in France, she spent four to five days on each trip passing back and forth through the blockade as she made her way through the Gulf in an small open schooner named *Hard Times*. The boat, manned by Father Leduc and his choirboy, Pierre Prudeaux, ran supplies between New Orleans and Bay St. Louis until it was captured by federal gunboats. The nun was not aboard when the crew was arrested and subsequently jailed, though she admitted that she had to force herself to get used to that kind of travel "so as not to let the Community die of starvation." For a long time, she reported, "famine has made itself cruelly felt" on the Confederate side of the blockade. Under the circumstances, Mother Esperance thought it nothing short of a miracle that "in spite of the misery of the times . . . we have thirteen boarders."[29]

What Mother Esperance endured was not that unusual. In 1864, Anna Shannon, the Mother Superior of the Academy of the Sacred Heart in St. Michaels's, Louisiana, crossed enemy lines to travel to New York. She had been summoned by her sisters, who told her that the General Chapter in Paris had appointed her vicar of all the convents and schools in Louisiana, which included a school at St. Michael's, one at Grand Coteau, and another at Natchitoches.[30] As superior to the three convents, Mother Shannon was in an unusual and unfortunate situation. When federal forces captured New Orleans in the spring of 1862, the river parishes, where St. Michael's was located, had fallen into federal hands, while Grand Coteau and Natchitoches were located in parishes that remained in Confederate control. Shannon, who was located at St. Michael's, could correspond with her sisters in Paris and New York but was separated from her sisters at Grand Coteau and Natchitoches. Furthermore, because she had access to New Orleans, which was reasonably supplied by the federal forces, she had access to the necessities of life.

When New Orleans fell under Union control in 1862, Louisiana became a divided state. Union troops tried to extend their victories from New Orleans through the lower river parishes and into the rest of the state. Shannon's Sisters of the Sacred Heart suffered the consequences of the battles that raged across the interior of Louisiana. The scarcity at Grand Coteau began in early 1863, when federal troops stripped the inhabitants of the Attakapas region of their crops, supplies, and livestock. Once

Shannon had amassed clothing, wine for mass, and various staple foods from New Orleans, she had to strategize a way to get past the stockades and deliver the items to the rebel-controlled parishes. She first considered using a smuggling operation run by federal officers, but she feared that if it was intercepted, she and all the rest of her convents would come under fire from federal authorities. Instead, she decided to transport the supplies herself. She approached Archbishop Jean-Marie Odin in New Orleans to apprise him of her plan to take a companion and several other people, including several priests, to shepherd supplies across the border safely. The group that would travel under her protection needed passports. Odin gave her a letter written to the commander of the Artillery Corps of the Federal Army of Louisiana, General Michael Kelly Lawlor, who, as Odin described him, was a good Catholic. Shannon then paid a visit to Mr. George Byrnes, a Confederate sympathizer she knew from St. Michael's who was an agent in New Orleans for the planters in the region. She wanted him to receive General Lawlor and his wife for dinner, where she might be introduced to them. Despite his intense dislike of the "enemy," Byrnes agreed to extend the invitation, and General Lawlor accepted. At dinner, Lawlor listened as Shannon made her case for resupplying her convents. His response: "Madame, you may count upon me. You should reach your destination if I have to take you there myself on one of my caissons."

General Lawlor paved the way for Mother Shannon to meet the Union general Nathaniel P. Banks, whose daughters were being educated by the Sisters of the Sacred Heart at their academy in Manhattanville, New York. The convent and school in New York were under the direction of Mother Superior Aloysia Hardy and mistress general Susannah Boudreau. The two women had been associates of Mother Shannon in Louisiana before they were assigned to the convent in Manhattanville. General Banks responded in the only way he could. He addressed Shannon as Mother and promised his support to her.

With General Lawlor's permission, Mother Shannon and her party assembled supplies for the stranded convents. She also packed supplies for the Jesuits at Grand Coteau, who had been sharing their scarce supplies with the nuns and their pupils.[31] She knew she would have to hide the Jesuits' supplies from federal authorities, who would refuse her any request to aid them. Under her protection, the group crossed the blockades and reached Grand Coteau, where food was so scarce the sisters and their pupils were living off cornbread and blackberry preserves (the convent was surrounded by blackberry brambles and located in the middle of the sugar parishes). After resupplying the convent at Grand Coteau, Shannon traveled to Natchitoches to resupply the convent there.[32]

The following year, in 1864, Shannon returned to Grand Coteau and Natchitoches on a similar mission, though this time her work did not proceed as smoothly. Just before she arrived at the Grand Coteau, Confederate authorities seized her supply wagon.[33] Shannon's reaction was swift and thorough. She first took her case to Confederate authorities at Opelousas. When she was not successful there she went to Washington, another small settlement. After several days of negotiations, days laced with novenas, holy hours, and mortification, Shannon convinced the authorities to allow her to place her supplies in a locked storeroom inside the Grand Coteau convent. After placing the keys to the storeroom in the chapel in the hands of the statue of St. Joseph, she traveled to Marshall, Texas, to plead her cause to the governor of Louisiana and the commander of the regional Confederate forces, General Richard Taylor, son of Zachary Taylor. When she arrived at the headquarters of General Taylor, her path was blocked by two sentinels, who raised their bayonets and shouted, "You can't pass." Shannon smiled and gently parted the bayonets, as she responded, "Oh, I pass everywhere." Taken by surprise, the soldiers relented. General Taylor's response was not dissimilar. After meeting the determined woman, he quickly agreed to the release of the supplies.

Even then, Mother Shannon's mission was not complete. Before she left Marshall, Texas, she was confronted by another challenge. Church fathers appealed to Shannon to secure the release of a priest who had been incarcerated by Confederate officials in a small Texas town not far from Marshall. Shannon secured the priest's release and then returned to Grand Coteau, where she found that most of the supplies she had secured had spoiled. That it fell on Shannon to free a priest challenged the gendered traditions of a Church that assigned clergymen to protect clergywomen. No doubt Shannon and the priest understood that necessities created by war could trump gender conventions, whether they were Church-sanctioned or not. Even before the war, religious women in the frontier Gulf South were often unable to follow strict rules first devised in medieval Europe, and the scarcity of priests and bishops had long fostered autonomy. During the Civil War, clergymen often found themselves in a position of dependence upon the Catholic sisterhood. Whether it was smuggling supplies to the Jesuits in Grand Coteau or providing cover for a priest who needed to pass through the blockade, a habit went further than a robe and collar.[34]

With the help of Mother Shannon, the Sisters of the Sacred Heart continued to board and educate girls in their convents throughout the war. They provided for girls whose parents believed they were safer living in a convent than staying at home, and at the same time they offered a curriculum laced with anti-Union rhetoric. In 1862, when the Union general Benjamin Butler, known to angry New Orleanians as "the Beast," organized a public school system, he failed to win the hearts and minds of most of the inhabitants of the port. A year later, only 12,500 of the eligible 38,000 pupils attended public schools. Some simply were not interested in attending school. Others attended the 141 private and mostly Catholic schools in the city. The reason: it was not a secret that most of the residents nurtured antipathy for the occupying Union forces.

Teaching nuns struggled to avoid disruption in their lives and in the lives of their students. The daily routines of convent life were closely regulated. Religious sisters rose before dawn, dressed quickly and modestly, attended morning prayers, ate breakfast, attended to their assigned duties, attended prayer again, ate lunch, returned to their duties, attended prayer, ate dinner, and went to bed. These strict routines, punctuated by long periods of silence, defined lives dedicated to a prayerful, productive life. Disruption was antithetical to their purpose. Yet with war came disruption, for some more than others. After being forced out of their convent and school by the 1862 siege of Vicksburg, the Sisters of Mercy transformed themselves from teaching nuns into nursing nuns.[35] When the Mercy Sisters came to the United States, they had a tradition of visiting the sick and were thus trained to provide simple nursing care. They were taught the basics of cleanliness and nourishment, and they knew how to administer medication. Their duties in the kitchen, the laundry, and on the sick ward taught them the importance of schedules, supervision, and organization.[36]

The Mercy Sisters in Vicksburg were not the only sisters to turn their attention from teaching to nursing. Over the objections of her spiritual director, the mother superior of the Ursulines in Galveston transformed her convent and school into a hospital. The Marianites and the Sisters of Mount Carmel in New Orleans followed suit. Their ministry to the troops was so effective that they often replaced the societies of lay women in the region who had joined together to furnish food and clothing and blankets for the troops and nurses for the ill and wounded. The patriotism and good will of volunteer lay women could not hide their lack of skill or the social unease they caused when they were seen caring for strange men.[37] Eventually, the majority of the organizations disbanded, as few of the women possessed either the organizational or medical skills to effectively respond to the growing crisis. Faced with limited options, both Confederate and Union authorities called upon the Sisters of Mercy, the Daughters of Charity, the Marianites of the Holy Cross, the Sisters of Mount Carmel, and the Ursulines to minister to the needs of the sick and wounded.

The Daughters of Charity bore the heaviest burden of nursing during the war. Headquartered in Emmetsburg, Pennsylvania, they ran a network of hospitals, orphanages, and nursing schools. At the beginning of the war, they operated nearly a dozen schools in the Gulf South. In New Orleans, they cared for 170 female orphans at the New Orleans Female Orphan Asylum and 700 patients at Charity Hospital. They ran St. Vincent's House in Donaldsonville, Louisiana, where they housed forty orphans and several sick people. In Mobile alone, they welcomed 400 poor students into their school, tended to 105 in their orphan asylum, and nursed 200 patients housed in their hospital. They excelled as administrators and nurses in all their institutions.

The Daughters of Charity were uniquely prepared to provide care for sick and wounded soldiers. They, above all other sisters, followed a centuries-old apostolate of nursing. Novices were trained by experienced senior nuns. They were taught to ventilate sick wards without permitting air to chill their patients and to clean the sick to avoid sores. They also learned that they must provide adequate and pleasingly nutritious food to their sick and wounded patients. They were even told that overheated broth became too salty for the patients' good. As time went on, the sisters refused to work with "Lady volunteers," or lay women. They reported that they found them more of a hindrance than an aid. They insisted on being in charge of their own hospitals and ambulances and demanded that they be reimbursed for their expenses in treating soldiers.

The Daughters of Charity dictated the terms of care they provided and then wrapped them within the mantle of spirituality, which advanced their vows to seek religious perfection through good works. The first rule of the Daughters of Charity was that sisters sent to hospitals or the Hotel-Dieu were there "to honor Our Lord Jesus Christ, the Father of the sick poor . . . corporally and spiritually." They were to instruct the sick in what was necessary for their salvation and to advise them to confess their sins so that those who died could depart "in a state of grace." Those who recovered would be resolved to never more "offend him."

When she was attending to soldiers felled by fever at Warrington, Florida, Sister Mary Agnes Kelly, a Daughter of Charity, found men who had little or no religion, despite the ministers who "kept a vigilant eye upon us for fear we might elude from their grasp one of those poor souls and bring him into the true fold."[38] Sister Mary Agnes was clearly distressed that so many of the men brought in with fever were delirious, which meant that she could "do absolutely nothing for their poor souls." [39]

Religious sisters who directed their attention to nursing were viewed as neutrals and were equally attentive to the needs of both Confederate and Union soldiers. In September 1862, Union general Benjamin Butler wrote a letter to Sister Maria Clara, the superior of the Daughters of Charity in Donaldsonville, Louisiana, apologizing for the destruction of their buildings after a bombing campaign. No one, he wrote, could more fully appreciate the self-sacrificing labors of the sisters than himself. His soldiers, he continued, were daily indebted to the sisters, who knew "no nation, no kindred, neither war nor peace." He continued by saying that their "all-pervading charity" was like the "boundless love of Him who died for all." Butler then promised to do for them what he did for their sisters in New Orleans: to fill their orders for provisions and medicines.

Civil War nursing sisters treated soldiers suffering devastating diseases and injuries that were further exacerbated by crude medical care or no medical care at all. At one point, the hospital at Warrington, Florida, had more than eight hundred sick men on its wards. Sister Mary Agnes Kelly was appalled at the conditions there. The men, she reported, were obliged "to lie on the floor with their knapsack[s] under their poor heads and one blanket for evening and it fairly alive with vermin and fleas."[40] The patients, she reported, had serious bedsores, some of which had become "fetid with gangrene." She found two patients whose bed clothing had grown into their backs. Upon investigation she found that some of the men had been lying in the same position for seven weeks without being moved, changed, or cleaned. The men, repelled by their own smell, would not help the women cleanse their sores. The secular lay nurses, Sister Mary Agnes thought, did "what suited their fancy."[41]

Nursing sisters, lured into the thick of battle, unflinchingly continued to provide for the sick and wounded. The Daughters of Charity at Warrington were roused in the middle of the night and told to pack and be ready to leave at dawn. The rebels had launched an attack against the Union forces at Fort Pickens, which was across the bay and clearly in sight of Fort Barrancas. The sisters remained in suspense, concerned primarily with the seriously sick in their care, with enemy guns "pointed directly at the hospital." By the time the "Federals" launched their counterattack, three of the sisters had moved the most seriously injured and ill into a temporary shelter in the woods. The other three sisters, at the request of the commanding general, stayed at the hospital in order to provide cover for those who were retreating. Sister Mary Agnes Kelly reported that from time to time during the day, "the sisters would pass and repass in front of the enemy's fort to let them see the place had not been evacuated."[42]

When nursing sisters arrived at field hospitals, they usually found soldiers who openly feared them. Sister Mary Agnes Kelly reported that on one occasion she and her religious sisters entered a ward where a large group of sick soldiers had just been brought. When the women entered, Sister Mary Agnes wrote, the men "covered their heads with blankets" and nothing could convince them to come out for "three or four days." The men, she noted, were "frightened" at the sisters' appearance or, in their words, "skerte." Some soldiers, she said, were "anxious to know to what regiment we belonged to or if we had been engaged in any battles for if ever we were the 'Yankees' would be more afraid of us than any gun the boys could show them."[43] Another wounded soldier, frightened by the Sister of Mercy bending over him, shrieked "Great Heavens, are you a man or a woman? But your hand is a woman's hand; its touch is soft, and your voice is gentle."[44] The astonishment expressed by the soldiers who were not familiar with the habits and veils worn by nuns was not unusual, and, in fact, the sisters were mostly amused by it.

What they were not amused by, nor tolerant of, was frank prejudice. When Sister Valentine Lautouradais, a Daughter of Charity, arrived with several of her sisters at a hospital in Montgomery, Alabama, in February 1863, she found that the surgeon in charge "hated Catholics." "He told me plainly that he did not want us in his hospital." He explained that he had his own servants, under the direction of a matron, and that he did not need their services. The sisters sought out the surgeon of the post and explained to him that they would not work under this man. The surgeon of the post retorted that any prejudice against them would disappear as soon as the dissenting surgeon saw their devotedness. The sisters insisted, maintaining that the offending doctor had gone too far when he said he knew the sisters in New Orleans and "wanted nothing to do with them."[45]

By 1863, both Confederate and Union wounded were being cared for by the Daughters of Charity in the City Hospital in Mobile. Sister Gabriella Larkin, one of the Daughters of Charity, urged her sisters to treat all the patients with prudence and impartiality, "looking upon them all as the wounded members of Jesus."[46] The neutrality demonstrated by the sisters proved to be rewarding in other ways. A novice of the Daughters of Charity explained how she benefited from the policy of impartiality. Late in the war, a small group of sisters, all Daughters of Charity, traveled from their convent in Mobile to the one in New Orleans. The mission of the young novice among them was to petition the archbishop to allow her to take her vows. While en route, the young novice later wrote, she sat on the train by a lady who tried to make her admit she was on the side of the Confederacy. The sister refused, explaining that she and her sisters cared for Confederates and federals alike. Later, when the sister reached the federal line, she was told she must take an oath of allegiance. She wrote: "I said we never take the oath, for while we are nursing the sick and wounded Confederates here, our Sisters in the North are nursing the Federals." The Union guard asked her what she would do if they would not let her pass without taking the oath, to which she reportedly smiled and said, "We will only have to go back." The little band of sisters were allowed to pass, and then when they reached the boundary on their return journey "the Federal Officers sent for the Confederate Officers and asked them to see us safely home, which they did."[47]

Religious sisters, living and working within their institutions, wrapping their social activism within the language and behavior of piety and fervor, possessed the tools to react effectively to the chaos of war that threatened to engulf them and their ministries. Their ability to safeguard their convents and schools allowed them to continue to educate and to protect their pupils. When their convents were destroyed or confiscated, they regrouped, joining other convents or moving into battle zones to care for the wounded. Their dedication to the sick and dying of both armies allowed them to travel back and forth through blockades, transporting supplies and people. Nursing sisters won the respect of both Union and Confederate troops and leaders, which helped reduce openly intolerant anti-Catholic feelings. The skills, organization, and dedication that the nursing sisters demonstrated during the war set a new standard for the professionalization of nurses, though nursing sisters were not alone in extending their ministries. Those religious sisters who dedicated their lives to teaching privileged and poor white girls before and during the war extended their reach to include freed slaves after the war. The Sisters of the Holy Family in New Orleans included freed girls in their classrooms at war's end. Finally, in spite of the hardships or war, or perhaps because of them, religious sisterhoods increased their numbers and their ministries at war's end.

NOTES

1. Hyacinth LeConnait was the mother superior of the Daughters of the Cross in the United States. As mother superior, she was responsible for the well-being of all the sisters and their work in the convents of the Daughters of the Cross in the United States. The Daughters of the Cross were Belgian female immigrant missionaries who brought their particular charism to their foreign missions. The Daughters of the Cross were educators of girls. Their schools included provisions for both boarders and day schools. The letters she wrote were dated April 8 and May 2. Sister Dorothea Olga McCants, *They Came to Louisiana: Letters of a Catholic, 1854–1882* (Baton Rouge: Louisiana State University Press, 1970).

2. McCants, *They Came to Louisiana*, 163–164.

3. Ibid.

4. The sisters feared the small Confederate force camped near the convent. They knew if they did not leave, the Union forces would attack. On May 16, 1865, forty thousand Union soldiers, retreating from the battle of Mansfield, engaged the Confederates on the convent grounds. After the battle, Confederate troops withdrew in order to reorganize their unit for the last engagement of the Red River campaign, which was fought on Yellow Bayou near Simmesport, Louisiana. McCants, *They Came to Louisiana*, 168.

5. Ibid.

6. Elizabeth Rapley, *The Dévotes: Women and Church in Seventeenth-Century France* (Montreal: McGill-Queens University Press, 1990), 77. At the end of the seventeenth century, after women were returned to cloister in their convents, one group of women, the Dames de la Charité, continued to defy the edict of the Council of Trent that forbade religious women to mix with the world. This group, led by Vincent de Paul, adopted a rule, dressed simply but distinctly, took vows and continued their charitable work. These *filles seculiares* lived a modified religious life.

7. The priests assigned to New Orleans were Capuchin friars. They were few in number and did not pursue a program of catechesis among the enslaved of the city and its environs. There is some evidence that the Capuchins hoped to convert Indians, but such plans were not carried to fruition. Jesuits, known for a more proactive ministry to enslaved populations, were prohibited from evangelizing in the area. Archives Coloniale, Section C 13A, 10: 43–46v; 11:217–19, and Charles Edwards O'Neill, *Church and State in French Colonial Louisiana: Policy and Politics* (New Haven: Yale University Press,1966), 55, 70–77, 130, 162–173.

8. The Ursulines were the first order of teaching nuns established in the Catholic Church. Before their foundation in northern Italy in 1535, all nuns

were cloistered contemplatives who conducted no ministries to the public. The Ursulines broke with that tradition, but remained an obscure congregation until they spread to France at the end of the sixteenth century. In France, they grew rapidly and by 1700 counted some ten thousand nuns in over three hundred convents throughout France. Their apostolate was a radical departure from past practice in several ways. It advocated the propagation of Catholicism through the catechesis and education of women, recognizing the essential role that mothers played in inculcating faith in their children and enforcing a regimen of pious observation within their families. It also provided a rationale for female education and insisted that in order for the program to succeed, it must not be limited to the elite but extend to all women, regardless of social standing. The Ursuline plan was to catechize all women, training them to become catechizers themselves, creating an army of lay women, each shouldering responsibility for ensuring the future of Catholicism through her own pious acts.

9. Marie-Madeleine Hachard, *The Letters of Marie Madeleine Hachard, 1727–28*, translated by Myldred Masson Costa (New Orleans: LaBord, 1974), 59.

10. It's true enough that some enslaved Africans, particularly living on far-flung plantations, did not receive instruction and baptism. The majority of those in the colony, however, did. And surely many understood only the rudiments of Catholicism. Even so, Catholicism was one of the basic tenets of the social system, and thus the inhabitants understood themselves to be Catholic, whether they received the sacraments on a regular basis or not.

11. Emily Clark and Virginia Meacham Gould, "The Feminine Face of Afro-Catholicism, 1727–1852," *William and Mary Quarterly*, 3rd ser., 59, 2 (April 2002): 409–448.

12. For a full discussion of the Ursulines and their apostolate, see Emily Clark, "'By All the Conduct of Their Lives': A Laywomen's Confraternity in New Orleans, 1730–1744," *William and Mary Quarterly*, 3rd ser., 54, 4 (October 1997): 769–794; and "A New World Community: The New Orleans Ursulines and Colonial Society, 1727–1803" (Ph.D. diss., Tulane University, 1998), 74–79.

13. France ceded Louisiana to the United States in 1803; Mobile and the region around it was ceded in 1811; the area around Pensacola was ceded in 1821.

14. Roger Baudier, *The Catholic Church in Louisiana* (New Orleans: Roger Baudier, 1939). Annabelle M. Melville, *Louis William Dubourg: Bishop of Louisiana and the Floridas, Bishop of Montauban, and Archbishop of Besançon, 1766–1833*, vols. 1 and 2 (Chicago: Loyola University Press, 1986). Also see the Diary of Father Tessier in the Archives of the Sulpiciens of Baltimore,

which are incorporated into the Archives of the Archdiocese of Baltimore, St. Mary's Seminary, Baltimore.

15. In 1817, nine women missionaries left France to join the Ursulines in New Orleans. The Sisters of the Sacred Heart founded two convents and schools a few years later. The Visitation Sisters opened a boarding school in Mobile in 1831. The Sisters of St. Joseph of Medaille opened two schools at Bay St. Louis, Mississippi, in 1855. In 1857 and 1858 they added orphanages, an asylum for the aged poor, and a school in New Orleans. The Daughters of the Cross opened schools in Avoyelles Parish, Isle Breville, and Shreveport, Louisiana. In 1861, the Sisters of St. Joseph (of Bourg) were educating girls in Bay St. Louis, Mississippi. Irish and German sisters joined them. The Irish St. Mary Dominican Sisters opened a school in New Orleans in 1860. Another Irish group, the Sisters of Mercy, opened a school in Vicksburg, Mississippi, in that same year. A Bavarian group, the School Sisters of Notre Dame, opened a school in New Orleans in 1856. In the 1830s, the Daughters of Charity sent American nursing sisters to New Orleans; in 1830, the Congregation of Our Lady of Mount Carmel took charge of the St. Claude Street School and Convent for free girls of African descent. The Sisters of the Holy Family, all women of African descent, date their founding to 1842.

16. For the best work on Southern women, see Catherine Clinton, *The Plantation Mistress: Woman's World in the Old South* (New York: Pantheon Books, 1982); Ann Firor Scott, *The Southern Lady: From Pedestal to Politics* (Chicago: Chicago University Press, 1970). Jean Friedman explores the lives of Protestant women in the Old South in *The Enclosed Garden: Women and Community in the Evangelical South,* 1830–1900 (Chapel Hill: University of North Carolina Press, 1985).

17. Studies of Catholic sisterhoods and their relationship to the ideal of womanhood focus exclusively on the ideal of domesticity, ignoring the ideal of the Southern woman. For studies that consider Catholic sisters within the realm of domesticity, see Sister Mary Ewens, *The Role of the Nun in Nineteenth-Century America* (New York: Arno Press, 1978), and Joseph Mannard, "Maternity of the Spirit: Nuns and Domesticity in Antebellum America," *U.S. Catholic Historian* 5 (summer–fall 1986): 305-324. Also see James Kenneally, "Eve, Mary, and the Historians: American Catholicism and Women," in *Women in American Religion* (Philadelphia: University of Pennsylvania Press, 1980), edited by Janet W. James.

18. Etienne Rousselon to the editor, publication of the Propagation of the Faith, Lyon, July 16, 1840, no. 2799, Archives de l'Oeuvres Pontifical Missionaire, Lyon, France.

19. Kenneth J. Zanca, ed., in *American Catholics and Slavery, 1787–1866, Anthology of Primary Documents* (New York: University Press of America, 1994, 90.

20. James J. Pillar, *The Catholic Church in Mississippi, 1837–1865* (New Orleans: Hauser Press, 1964), 169–170.

21. Larry Ceplair, ed., *The Public Years of Sarah and Angelina Grimké: Selected Writings 1835–1839* (New York: Columbia University Press, 1989).

22. The New Orleans priest Claude Pascal Maistre, who was a born in France, alone of all the clergy raised a voice for abolitionism. Stephen J. Ochs, *A Black Patriot and a White Priest: André Cailloux and Claude Paschal Maistre in Civil War New Orleans* (Baton Rouge: Louisiana State University Press, 2000).

23. McCants, *They Came to Louisiana*, 27–28.

24. Ibid., 36.

25. Baudier, *Catholic Church in Louisiana*, 428–433.

26. Pillar, *Catholic Church in Mississippi*, 243.

27. Ibid.

28. Sister Eugenie Veglia, "Sisters of St. Joseph of Bourg—New Orleans Province" (master's thesis, Loyola University, New Orleans, Lousiana, 1953), 57. Also see Pillar, *Catholic Church in Mississippi*, 282.

29. Mother Esperance to Mother St. Claude, Bay St. Louis, July 7, 1863, Archives of the Sisters of St. Joseph of Medaille, Cincinnati, Ohio.

30. The General Chapter is the governing body of each community of religious sisterhoods. General chapters are made of the officers of the community and senior sisters elected to sit on the board. Each community has its own constitution, which dictates who is eligible to be elected to sit on a board.

31. The Jesuits were teaching at St. Charles College, which was located next to the Academy of the Sacred Heart in Grand Coteau. The Jesuits were also the spiritual directors of the Sisters of the Sacred Heart.

32. Sister Dorethy McGloin, *Vie de la Reverende Mere*, National Archives of the Sisters of the Sacred Heart (NASSH), St. Louis, Missouri. Mary Blish, R.S.C.J., "Mother Anna Josephine Shannon (1810–1896): Crossing the Lines in the Civil War," in *Religious Pioneers: Building the Faith in the Archdiocese of New Orleans* (New Orleans: Archdiocese of New Orleans, 2004), edited by Dorothy Dawes and Charles Nolan, 40–41.

33. House Journal of Grand Coteau, NASSH.

34. McGloin, *Vie de la Reverende Mere*; Blish, Mother Anna, 42–50.

35. Archives of the Sisters of Mercy, Vicksburg, Mississippi. Sister Mary Denis Maher, *To Bind Up Their Wounds: Catholic Sister Nurses in the U.S. Civil War* (New York: Greenwood Press, 1989), 76.

36. Maher, *To Bind Up Their Wounds*, 37.

37. Steward Brooks, *Civil War Medicine* (Springfield, Ill.: C. C. Thomas, 1966), 76. Also see Maher, *To Bind Up Their Wounds*, 55.

38. Annals of the Civil War, Collection of the Daughters of Charity, Hoaley-Bundschu Library, Avila University, Kansas City, Missouri.

39. Ibid., 347

40. Ibid.

41. Ibid., 347–348.

42. Ibid., 348.

43. Ibid.

44. Sister Theresa Austin Carroll, ed., *Leaves from the Annals of the Sisters of Mercy* (New York: Catholic Publication Society, 1881–1888), 2:63, as quoted in Maher, *To Bind Up Their Wounds*, 136.

45. Annals of the Civil War, op. cit., Lautouradais, Albany, N.Y., December 21, 1866, ADC, 303–304.

46. Annals of the Civil War, op. cit., Larkin, Mobile, December 13, 1866, ADC, 478.

47. Ibid., 479–480.

4

"PUBLIC WOMEN" AND SEXUAL POLITICS DURING THE AMERICAN CIVIL WAR

Catherine Clinton

War produces cultural shifts so dramatic that sexual attitudes, mores, and morality undergo sea changes when nations are under siege. Why should the American Civil War be any different? Yet unearthing evidence on this topic continues to be challenging, for as Civil War scholar Bell Wiley complained, families censored soldiers' letters, and veterans avoided this topic in their reminiscences.[1] A legacy of silence on sexual subjects remained in force for nearly a century after the war.

Regardless of reticence, the Civil War created the largest increase in the sex trade in nineteenth-century America, perhaps the single greatest growth spurt in the nation's history. During the antebellum period, brothels flourished throughout the United States, in bustling port cities as well as rural hamlets. "Blue" guides were published for major cities along the eastern seaboard; New Orleans had its own guide, which ran to several editions.[2] Many women who sold sexual services were affiliated with "houses," but even larger numbers operated independently as "streetwalkers." Evidence indicates that hundreds, perhaps thousands, of nineteenth-century women were involved with a system of concubinage of "kept women" through private contractual arrangements with individual men.[3] Whatever these combined numbers amounted to, they were overshadowed by the figures for those who participated in a more "casual" sex trade.

Poor and wage-earning women frequently sold sexual favors to acquaintances, viewing the transaction as a minor exchange. These women never thought of themselves as professional "prostitutes."[4] "Public women" was a term of contempt for those females who supported themselves *solely* through supplying multiple partners with sex for money, and their lives remain relatively undocumented beyond criminal and court records.[5] Wartime records do not offer much more insight into these women's lives. Yet because of military imperative, soldiers and their commanders comment more frequently on the topic, especially as officers saw prostitutes as a health hazard for their men. In December 1862, an article in the Richmond *Examiner* entreated: "If the Mayor of Richmond lacks any incentive to . . . breaking up the resorts of ill fame in the city, let him visit the military hospitals, where sick and disabled soldiers are received for treatment . . . wrecked upon the treacherous shoals of vice and passion."[6] In 1862, one enterprising madam opened her brothel directly across the street from a hospital run by the YMCA. Females hawking their wares appeared in windows in various stages of undress, trying to entice patients from their beds. The manager of the hospital remonstrated that this activity was interfering with the men's recoveries.[7]

Despite lighthearted stories in local papers about "pox," and references to the "clap" in soldiers' letters, venereal diseases were a serious matter.[8] Three out of five Civil War soldiers died of disease unrelated to battle wounds. Civil War doctors knew venereal diseases debilitated men and added to the risk of soldiers' mortality.[9] They became adept at diagnosing and curing sexually transmitted diseases. A surgeon with the 115th Pennsylvania, near Alexandria, Virginia, described his cure for gonorrhea: "injecting a solution of chlorate of potach, one drachm in eight ounces, every hour for twelve successive hours, and then gradually ceasing its use during the next two or three days by prolonging the interval between each injection."[10] This was an intensive course of treatment. Syphilis also proved entirely curable, as a surgeon with the Seventeenth Massachusetts described his remedy: "Cauterization of the chancre in the first instance, followed by the continuous application of black wash."[11] But treatments were painful and time-consuming, keeping the soldier incapacitated for days—as long as a fortnight from diagnosis to return to duty.

Thus officers were particularly concerned to prevent contact between their soldiers and women who might spread disease. During the Atlanta campaign, Confederate commanders feared the influx of prostitutes into the area. An officer wrote to the post commander in Dalton, Georgia: "Complaints are daily made to me of the number of lewd women in this town."[12] The problem was deemed so extreme that a Confederate officer ordered men to "sweep out" the town. Any woman who could not document her respectability would be expelled. Undocumented females would be confined to the guardhouse, with a diet of bread and water.[13] Individual prostitutes were frequently expelled from army camps. One commander in 1862 proclaimed that all "company laundresses who did not actually wash for the men must be discharged."[14]

Urban centers showcased the problem of prostitutes and the army during wartime. In its 1860 census, Nashville recorded 198 white and 9 mulatto prostitutes.[15] The vice district in Nashville was confined to a neighborhood known as Smokey Row, a riverfront area two blocks wide and four blocks long.[16] Following the federal occupation of Nashville in February 1862, prostitutes increased almost tenfold when thirty thousand federal soldiers crowded into the region. Brothels and cribs multiplied in Nashville, as nearly fifteen hundred female sex trade workers crowded the city streets. By June 1863, Union General R. S. Granger was "daily and almost hourly beset" by the surgeons of the regiments, begging to be rid of "diseased prostitutes."[17]

So the military devised a plan for mass deportation. On July 6, 1863, the provost marshal, Lieutenant Colonel George Spalding, issued an order requiring the "public women" of Nashville to leave town. On July 8, he requisitioned a steamboat, the *Idahoe*, demanding that her captain, John Newcomb, transport the more than one hundred women to Louisville. Spalding failed to provide Newcomb with the guards or the provisions he requested. With a crew of just three, Newcomb was reluctant to proceed, but required to leave. As he sailed away with his cargo of prostitutes, the Nashville *Dispatch* bestowed its blessing: "Wayward sisters, go in peace."

Nearing Louisville five days later, the women were prevented from disembarking by military guards. The ship's captain was ordered to proceed to Cincinnati. Some women were able to make it to dry land; a handful were rescued through the intercession of friends at Newport, Kentucky. The majority remained on shipboard, in legal limbo.

On July 17, the authorities denied the boat safe harbor in Cincinnati, and the captain was forced to weigh anchor across the river from the docks. Finally, after two weeks, orders came from Washington for Newcomb to return with his cargo to Nashville. When the *Idahoe* docked nearly a fortnight later, angry and bedraggled women straggled off. The boat had been completely trashed. The entire enterprise was declared a disaster. The captain sued for damages, as the boat's reputation was injured: it was thereafter known as "the Floating Whorehouse." He finally received compensation of five thousand dollars.[18] This was but a small contretemps, but there were other more serious and sustained imbroglios that confronted the conflicts over women's roles and sexual mores during wartime.

Developments during the Civil War raised issues of sexuality that both civilians and the military wished to handle by turning a blind eye.[19] Yet public debates occasionally erupted when sexually charged issues got into the headlines, despite attempts at containment. What follows are three separate sketches of events that highlight issues involving "public women," illuminating the sexual and political dynamics at play. These case studies suggest ways in which refracted and topsy-turvy images of womanhood created conflict, scandal, and complex intrigue. Sexualized calamities unfolded, as the social fabric was frayed by the threat and reality of military occupation.

The first, most notorious, and most explicit case deals with Union commander Benjamin Butler's occupation of New Orleans. General Butler had been no friend of emancipation when the war broke out. But he had become increasingly hostile to slaveholders as the war progressed. By the time of the capture of New Orleans in April 1862, Butler had zero tolerance for the disrespect secessionists heaped on the federal government and its representatives.

When Butler arrived on the scene in New Orleans, he met with resistance in every quarter. He especially resented the way in which ladies would withdraw from pews in church if a Union man chose to sit nearby, would depart from streetcars if a Yankee boarded, and would gather up their skirts and desert the sidewalk rather than to pass near a federal soldier.

This constant charade was annoying, but did not draw any fire—until a white Southern woman spat into the faces of two officers.[20] As news of this incident circulated, Butler was outraged. He feared that his men would not be able to resist retaliation—unless some appropriate measure was put in place. He decided to take decisive action, with his infamous General Order No. 28, issued on May 5, 1862:[21]

As the officers and soldiers of the United States have been subject to repeated insults from the women (calling themselves ladies) of New Orleans, in return for the most scrupulous non-interference and courtesy on our part, it is ordered that hereafter when any female shall, by word, gesture or movement insult or show contempt for any officer or soldier of the United States, she shall be regarded and held liable to be treated as a woman of the town plying her avocation.[22]

Butler decided that all females in New Orleans who showed insulting behavior toward his men would be treated as "public women": arrested, booked, put in jail overnight, and "fined in front of a magistrate the next morning."

With the fall of New Orleans, patriotic Confederate ladies had adopted a particularly defiant stance. Confederate diarist Julia LeGrand commented: "The *women only* do not seem afraid. They were all in favor of resistance."[23] This resistance had taken an increasingly public and disruptive form, because women had little fear of physical retaliation. But Butler took aim—below the belt. By accusing Southern ladies of being no ladies at all, he was trying to beat them at their own game.[24] Butler suggested that their behavior dishonored Southern civility. They were stepping outside the boundaries of ladyhood, which made them liable for the consequences of their actions—as were "public women."

While Butler's soldiers certainly appreciated the promise of a new regime, the white citizens of New Orleans went on the offensive. The mayor complained that Butler's order provided a license for his men to commit "outrages." A local white girl, Clara Solomon, confided to her diary that she would like to see Butler tied up in ropes by the women of her city—or better yet, sizzling in a frying pan.[25] General Butler's Southern nickname became "Beast Butler." The prostitutes of New Orleans paid their own special tribute, by pasting his portrait on the interior of their chamber pots.[26]

Butler was not just reviled in Louisiana but throughout the Confederacy. Mary Chesnut, wife of a former South Carolina Senator and a member of Jefferson Davis's inner circle, was infuriated by Butler's audacity. She believed that the general should have been concerned about restraining his "brutal soldiery." She feared for her countrywomen, at the mercy of this "hideous cross-eyed beast."[27] Southern newspapers heaped invective, and editors reprinted a poem that used the first letter of his name to begin each line.

> Brutal and vulgar, coward and knave,
> Famed for no action, noble or brave,
> Beastly by instinct, a drunkard and sot
> Ugly and venomous, on making a blot,
> Thief, liar and scoundrel in highest degree,
> Let Yankeedom boast of such heroes as thee,
> Every woman and child shall for ages to come
> Remember thee monster, thou vilest of scum.[28]

Even Lincoln's secretary of state, William Seward, was unhappy with the wording of the order. He regretted that "in the haste of composition, a phraseology which could be mistaken or perverted could be used."[29] Seward, like many others sympathetic to Butler's aims, objected to the ambiguity of Butler's language. Couldn't this lead to soldiers "having their way" with women, rather than just arresting them? Seward was not the only one concerned about this.

Seward was dead wrong to imagine Butler's "haste of composition," however. The order was discussed and dissected word by word before it was sent to the printer. A member of Butler's own staff, a Major Strong, raised objections to Butler's wording, wondering if "some of the troops may misunderstand." He was concerned what might happen if even one man "should act upon it in the wrong way."[30] General Butler was resolute and wanted to move forward with the language as it was: "We are conquerors in a conquered city; we have respected every right, tried every means of conciliation, complied with every reasonable desire; and yet cannot walk the streets without being outraged and spit upon by green [young] girls."[31]

And to Butler's credit, following the order, incidents of insult were precipitously reduced. A northern journalist crowed: "The morals and manners of no class of women in the world were ever so rapidly improved as have been those of the Secession women of New Orleans under the stern but *admirable regime* of General Butler."[32]

There were a few arrests. The women were charged with crimes ranging from displaying Confederate flags (usually replicas on their person) to threatening the life of a soldier. Those found guilty were given light fines and rapidly released. Butler even sent some of the confiscated hand-sewn rebel flags to Massachusetts schoolchildren as souvenirs.[33]

However, one arrest caused widespread publicity. Eugenia Phillips, wife of a former Alabama congressman, was insolent during an interview with a soldier after her detainment on June 30, 1862. She had already been charged with espionage and detained in the District of Columbia in 1861, before her relocation to New Orleans. At this second offense, however minor, authorities were harsh and punitive. She was arrested and, upon conviction, sent into exile. Union authorities transported her to an offshore island, where she was confined to a railroad car. During her ten-week incarceration, she honed her reputation as a rebel by scribbling letters detailing the horrors of her ordeal. When she was released, Phillips fled New Orleans and Butler's grasp. After this escape, her martyrdom increased exponentially. Despite her celebrity, few women wished to follow her example, which suited Butler fine.

Butler did not expect Confederate women to switch allegiance, but he could and did insist that they maintain proper decorum and keep their views private—which was, after all, their designated sphere. Most had vented their fury in letters, in diaries, in parlors, and even in prayer. But when New Orleans women unleashed these feelings in the streets, Butler let it be known that they would be given no better treatment than other "women of the streets," which shocked them into submission.

This image of Southern "women in the streets" leads into the next important incident where the issues of women's place and "public women" intersected dramatically—in the Confederate capital in April 1863.

The streets of wartime Richmond became a kind of complex stage onto which the players were thrust without scripts. Women did not know exactly the outcome or what roles they might play. Unescorted females were always subject to danger on city streets. What was new was the way in which public space was being expropriated shamelessly by "public women," and ladies felt themselves being crowded back into their homes—to knit and roll bandages. Respectable white women needed to prove their refinement and status through confinement and self-sacrifice.

Richmond underwent the same kind of riotous transformation that other urban centers experienced during wartime. Diarist Sallie Putnam reported that "a stranger suddenly transported to the city, without knowledge of preceding facts would have imagined the people in a state of intoxication or insanity."[34] Elizabeth Van Lew, a Union sympathizer in Confederate Richmond, echoed the complaint: " The multitude—the mob—the whopping—the tin pan music and the fierceness of a surging swelling revolution."[35]

When the Confederate capital was moved from Montgomery to Richmond in May 1861, the parade of undesirables began. The local press was crammed full of derelictions and violence: a woman from Lynchburg being found dead drunk in an alley, drunken assaults on brothels (including rapes), slaves "living in improper intimacy" with whites, among other complaints.[36] Headlines became more daring and colorful: "Queer Rollickers" and "Stabbing Affair at a House of Ill Repute."

By May 1862, the Richmond *Examiner* reported: "Fancy women took to the streets and crowded proper ladies off sidewalks."[37] The hurly-burly of illicit activity caused a temporary civic backlash, when the Richmond *Whig* reported:

The *salons* in this city, which for months past have been the popular resort of military officers and others, in pursuit of "creature comfort" . . . will be closed, hereafter until the enemy is driven from the vicinity. The proprietors had a formal meeting last Thursday, and unanimously resolved upon this "suspension of business," finding that the attraction of their establishments had a tendency to allure the officers from their camps, where duty required them to be.[38]

Donations were made to care for those in the military who were sick and wounded, but this patriotic gesture was short-lived. The grog shops and faro houses soon resumed their business, with brothels paying the fines like clockwork, not even bothering to shut down temporarily.

Richmond was overcrowded and vice-ridden, as were most capitals during wartime. Harsh weather and food shortages were testing Richmond residents in the spring of 1863, when a horrible accident added to the city's gloom. The Confederate States Laboratory hired poor women and young girls to work grueling shifts for low pay, filling cartridges with gunpowder. On March 13, the factory blew up, leaving nearly fifty workers dead and twenty more injured by the inferno. A pall fell over the town, as the mayor solicited funds for the victims' families. Over half of those buried were under sixteen.

During this period of mourning, on March 20, the city weathered a ten-inch snowfall. With crops partially ruined, and farmers unable to get their goods to market, fears of starvation arose. The city's limited resources were dwindling, and an atmosphere of panic set in. A group of women from Oregon Hill, a working-class neighborhood southwest of the city, organized a meeting to discuss what was to be done about the high prices and scarcity of food. The women met in a church on the evening of April 1 to formulate a plan. They determined to confront Governor Lechter in person, to demand that food from government warehouses be released to them at government prices. They vowed to threaten the storehouses if their demands were not met.

By eight o'clock the next morning, Easter Thursday, a large crowd of women assembled on the capital steps to offer their petition. Another contingent had gone directly to the governor's mansion to plead in person. The governor spoke to the women at the capital, explaining that although he was sympathetic to their concerns, any attempts to "liberate" goods would be met with police action. Word of his refusal spread like wildfire. The largest mob, restless and resentful, moved into the mercantile district near Twelfth and Cary streets. By nine o'clock, looting and violence had broken out. Merchants locked their stores, but women wielding axes and knives broke in and cleaned out groceries, clothing, and other goods. Police using fire hoses could not prevent the women from plundering the shops.

When Governor Lechter appeared to ask the women to disperse, he took out his watch and promised arrests would begin in five minutes. This cleared the immediate area, but there were gangs of angry women roaming the streets in search of food. More females joined these vengeful brigades with each passing hour. Even President Jefferson Davis ventured outside the Confederate White House to try to calm the masses; reports are mixed as to the success of his negotiations.[39]

By nightfall, peace had been restored, yet throughout Easter weekend, women, some carrying children, wandered the streets begging for food. The YMCA opened its doors and distributed supplies, as did, finally, the government—in the form of bags of rice. The so-called Richmond Bread Riot was over in a matter of hours, but its impact would last longer.

The capital of the Confederacy reeled from this disturbance. The secretary of war forbade reports of the incident in the press, and prohibited telegraphers from transmitting messages even hinting at events. The Richmond papers circumvented this directive by covering the court cases of women arrested for their roles in the riot; over forty women (and twenty-five men) were jailed on April 2. Most of the women were given light sentences, but what is most interesting is the way both the city council and the local press decided to portray these disorderly females.

The Richmond City Council took the position that looters had mainly broken into jewelry stores and clothing shops—undermining the notion that these were poor women seeking bread. Loyal Confederate journals offered counterattacks to the story of Richmond on the brink of starvation. Journalists found their scapegoats by lambasting "Yankees" and "foreigners"—an "outside agitator" school of blame. Richmond papers covering the criminal trials offered sly and insinuating comments on the dress, appearance, and legal counsel of female defendants. As a result, most readers were led to believe these women were *not* the starving indigents painted by those sympathetic to their cause. At worst, readers would assume these women were all too familiar with the courtroom because so many of those caught up in these disturbances were "public women."

Confederate authorities in Richmond in 1863 may have been as guilty of smear campaigns against women as "Beast" Butler had been in New Orleans the year before. In order to salvage the political situation, respectable white Southern men demonized those starving women who had taken to the streets as "women of the streets." The only significant protest previously involving women in Richmond had indeed been a demonstration by "public women," when over three hundred prostitutes mobbed the coroner's office following the brutal murder of one of their own at Alice Hardgrove's brothel on Fifteenth Street. This was less of a riot and more of a rally, but it remained fresh in public memory. The presence of another crowd of angry women just a few months later echoed this earlier incident, and led the civil and military authorities to manipulate the truth about those who raised justified fears concerning dwindling food sources. But like the women of New Orleans before them, the women of Richmond would encounter vicious opposition and retribution.

The final case study involves a much murkier episode in the war's last year. It illuminates the manipulation of gender conventions on opposing sides of the war—the way in which sexuality and innuendo both overlaid and undermined wartime order. Charges of guilt and innocence bounced back and forth during a prolonged period of limbo concerning the fate of a group of Southern white women: mill-workers in Roswell, Georgia, who were captured near the end of the war and took an unsentimental journey from July 1864 until surrender the following spring. The desire to control "disorderly" women remains the connective thread in all three of these cases.

When federal troops arrived in Georgia in the summer of 1864, the Roswell mill-owners were prepared. They flew the French flag over their cotton factories in hopes Union invaders might buy the fiction of their operation being foreign—and therefore neutral. The idea that these factories were exempt from search and seizure was ridiculous, and patently ignored. When Union officers found "CSA" sewn into cloth stored in the mills, they evacuated all workers, mainly women and children, on July 6, 1864.

After all the salvageable cloth had been confiscated, the factories were burnt to the ground. A Union private said: "It did seem at first blush to be a wanton act, to fire those polished machines which filled the building from basement to the top story, after they came to a stand still, but all is fair, it has been stated, in love and war."[40]

On July 7, General William T. Sherman instructed his men to arrest all workers and "let them foot it, under guard, to Marietta, whence I will send them by cars to the North." Well aware what the response would be, Sherman added," the poor women will make a howl."[41] Nevertheless, he insisted upon immediate deportation. The Union troops occupying

Roswell behaved extremely badly. Their commander had to relocate federal camps outside the city limits because they persisted in drunkenness and "making love to the women."

Sherman's order was a harsh demand, and more than half of the mill-working force of eight hundred simply melted into the countryside. They slipped through the pickets, escaping their captors, and made their way to safety. But eventually guards assembled, prepared to lead their charges into exile.

When the four hundred deported mill girls straggled into Marietta, they were not an easy group to manage. The prisoners were confined to a classroom building at the former Georgia Military Institute. An Indiana soldier on guard duty complained: "Some of them are tough and it's a hard job to keep them straight and to keep men away from them. General Sherman said he would rather to try to guard the whole Confederate Army, and I guess he's right about it."[42]

At first, Sherman was clearly moving labor from factories so that they could not reassemble to manufacture. But by the time the workers, mainly women, arrived in Marietta, the reasons for their forced march had shifted. They were instead painted as "troublesome" because *soldiers* sought contact with them. A correspondent for the *New York Tribune* created a highly sympathetic portrait of these Roswell captives: "Four hundred weeping and terrified Ellens, Susans, and Maggies transported, in the springless and seatless Army wagons, away from their lovers and brothers and the sunny south, and all for the offense of weaving tent-cloth and spinning stocking yarn."[43]

Once the news had spread about the torching of the factory town, about the innocent women caught up in war's net, the Roswell drama captured the national imagination. The women's fates were causing concern both North and South, especially as Union captors might allow their men to run wild; for example, the Illinois soldier who said: "[I] just wish they would issue them [the Roswell women] to us soldiers."[44]

Next Sherman decided the detainees had to travel by rail to Kentucky, where on July 21 the first group arrived. These ragtag refugees, most unfortunately, were trans-shipped to Louisville via Nashville. Only a year before, large shipments of "public women" from Nashville to Louisville had caused a public furor. This may have contributed to dredged up memories of previous Union roundups and deportations of "public women."

By August, articles across the country, even in the northern press, were calling this Sherman's "War Against the Women." One New York journalist questioned why "drive four hundred penniless girls hundreds of miles away from their homes and friends to seek livelihoods amid strange and hostile people?"[45]

Even when the Union tried to assist these women, efforts backfired. The Union medical corps tried to draft the Roswell women to take in laundry, or to nurse Yankee wounded—for pay. After these females were advertised in the press as potential servants, a newspaper article fumed that while emancipated slaves were "rioting and luxuriating" in Union camps, white women and children were being "sold into bondage."[46] And this was from a Pennsylvania, not a Confederate, newspaper.

Descriptions of living conditions in Louisville for these Roswell mill-workers confirmed Union indifference to their captive enemy civilians. One survivor's memoir described how two sisters, sixteen and twelve, were housed in a "cavernous stench-filled building" and endured harsh and grinding work in order to provide money for their ailing father.[47]

By August, solicitations appeared in the local paper, as the ladies of Louisville sought donations to supply the needs of these Roswell "refugees." Reports also described an outbreak of typhoid in September. These women prisoners were portrayed as victims, subjected to cruel conditions at the hands of Union captors.

And when the Union government tried to assuage these concerns by putting a woman physician in charge of Roswell women prisoners, this plan failed miserably to improve relations. Dr. Mary Walker, the only female commissioned contract surgeon with the Union army, was brought in to improve care for women at the prison hospital. Walker was a rather eccentric figure within the Union medical corps.[48]

After three months, Southern women from Roswell deeply resented their Yankee female warden, especially the rigid attitude she maintained to keep them in line.[49] They leveled serious charges of maltreatment, and even rioted against her rule. Walker refuted her prisoners' claims, arguing that the incarcerated women were not suffering—in relative terms. Walker confessed that food was not of the highest quality and conditions were Spartan, but she insisted that the women were not in any way given inhumane treatment. Alternately, she suggested they manufactured their complaints because of her enforcement of discipline.

Dr. Walker argued that her unpopularity stemmed from the fact that she prevented familiarity between the male guards and female prisoners, to which previous regimes had turned a blind eye. This was a bold indictment. It again suggested these Roswell women were prone to lewd behavior, tainting them with the brush of impropriety.

Further, Walker confessed that she ignored Confederate women's complaints that guards should hold doors open for them, tip their hats, and render other courtesies. Walker punished women who bellowed rebel songs out loud. She sided against the women and with her own Union guards. But the Louisville commandant failed to support Dr. Walker. Thus her iron rule met with resistance from below and disdain from above. In March 1865, her request for transfer was honored. The next month the war ended, and the remaining Roswell refugees were released from federal custody. They made the long journey home to Georgia in April 1865.

We know the long journey home involved a multitude of changes for men and women following the Civil War. Certainly for enslaved African Americans who had wrenched freedom from owners during the tumult, and promises of emancipation forever after, change was in the air. For white men and women on the homefront, the urgent sense of a return to normalcy was stymied by cultural shifts that seemed to hint at permanent consequences. The loss of an entire generation of young men, half a million North and South, would present a generation of young women with the need for alternatives to what had been a traditional life as a wife. Though many strived for a return to Victorian gentility and traditional sexual roles and standards, in reality too few were able to fulfill this ideal during postwar struggles.

Many women pushed for expanded educational opportunities, as well as pioneering roles in labor and the professions—as an organized women's rights movement focused on suffrage and legal reforms. The more women demanded a presence on the public platform during this era—the social housekeeping of the settlement house movement, the evangelical fervor of the temperance crusade, and the growth and development of women's higher education—the more frenzied campaigns for social and sexual control grew: the legal battles over abortion, the purity crusade, and other late nineteenth-century campaigns. Women who had temporarily assumed roles which had previously been restricted to males, women who had faced adversity and risen to the occasion, were forced back into traditional roles as dependants. Even those who were required by economic necessity to take on wage labor curtsied at the altar of patriarchal hegemony. Traditional sex roles were rigidly reinforced following a brief period of women's agency and achievement.

Women like Eugenia Phillips, who stood up to her federal captors, the Richmond protestors who directly confronted the Confederate government, and Mary Walker, among others, who challenged sex role stereotyping—all of these disorderly women created waves that rocked male prerogatives, undermining status quo antebellum.

Whenever women during wartime put their own priorities forward, governmental authorities responded with blunt force—employing sexual blackmail to stifle dissent. Women in Richmond dared to exert their voices politically, to demand that rulers to share information and resources with civilians. They went so far as to request that government warehouses open their doors to the starving and needy. The response was swift and harsh. Women were arrested, and then treated like "women of the streets." The smear campaign following the Richmond Bread Riot was tactical and effective—if the Confederate government could not conceal the episode from the public, then they would at least spin the incident to make it seem as if "public women" had gone wild.

Ironically, during the battle for the streets in New Orleans following General Butler's order, both North and South seemed to unite on the question of disorderly women. If Confederate women behaved in an unladylike manner, they endangered their status. Of course, there was a thin line of demarcation that separated permissible disgust (crossing the street, changing pews) at coming into contact with the occupying force from improper conduct. Women who crossed that line became impermissible patriots.[50]

Uncovering the complex web of interlocking issues involving race and sex, as well as gender and war, will require a vast army of researchers in twenty-first-century Civil War studies. Exploration of the racial dimensions of wartime sexual violence and many other engaging projects await a new, valiant generation of scholars. Digging deep into available court records and medical corps reports will broaden and deepen our appreciation of sexual matters.

We can begin by exploring campaigns to regulate prostitution, military tribunals of rape cases, and other topics still suffering malignant neglect. We can hope that future work will both investigate and illuminate how sexual dynamics played out for nineteenth-century Americans—and move us toward appreciations of desire, as well as death; of flesh, as well as blood.

NOTES

1. See Bell Wiley, *The Life of Billy Yank* (Indianapolis: Bobbs Merrill, 1951).

2. See, for example, Free Loveyer, *Directory to the Seraglios in New York, Philadelphia and All the Principal Cities in the Union* (New York: Printed and

Published for the Trade, 1859). See also Alecia Long, *The Great Southern Babylon: Sex, Race and Respectability in New Orleans, 1865–1920* (Baton Rouge: Louisiana University Press, 2004).

3. See Patricia Cline Cohen, *The Murder of Helen Jewett: The Life and Death of a Prostitute in Nineteenth-Century New York* (New York: Knopf, 1998), and Dell Upton, ed., *Madaline: Love and Survival in Antebellum New Orleans* (Athens: University of Georgia Press, 1996).

4. See Christine Stansell, *City of Women: Sex and Class in New York, 1780–1860* (New York: Knopf, 1986).

5. Welcome exceptions are Cohen, *Murder of Helen Jewett*, Marilyn Wood Hill, *Their Sisters' Keepers: Prostitution in New York City, 1830–1870* (Berkeley: University of California Press, 1993), and Timothy J. Gilfoyle, *City of Eros: New York City, Prostitution and the Commercialization of Sex, 1790–1920* (New York: Norton, 1992). See also Judith Kelleher Schafer, "Les Nymphs de Pave," unpublished manuscript, forthcoming, a study of women and vice in New Orleans. For legal and reform analysis, see Carol Leonard, *Prostitution and Changing Social Norms in America* (Syracuse, N.Y.: Syracuse University Press, 1979), and Barbara Meil Hobson, *Uneasy Virtue: The Politics of Prostitution and the American Reform Tradition* (New York: Basic Books, 1987).

6. Bell Wiley, *The Life of Johnny Reb* (Indianapolis: Bobbs Merrill, 1943), 57.

7. Ibid., 54. ·

8. See J. M. Jordan to his wife, in Wiley, *Life of Johnnie Reb*, 51.

9. By war's end, of the 259,000 Confederate soldiers dead, 94,000 deaths were attributed to deaths in battle and from battle-related incidents, while 164,000 were caused by disease. Comparable Union numbers were 359,000 dead: 110,000 deaths in battle, 224,000 from disease (the remaining 25,000 were chalked up to suicides and accidents among federal troops). See Stewart Brooks, *Civil War Medicine* (Springfield, Ill.: Charles Thomas, 1966).

10. Brooks, *Civil War Medicine*, 891–892.

11. Ibid.

12. Wiley, *Life of Johnny Reb*, 53.

13. Ibid.

14. Ibid., 52. See also 358: the next year Confederate army regulations required that all four company laundresses had to furnish evidence of their good character to secure employment.

15. The largest brothel in prewar Nashville housed seventeen prostitutes, eight children, and three adult men.

16. Thomas Lowry, *The Story the Soldiers Wouldn't Tell: Sex in the Civil War* (Mechanisburg, Pa.: Stackpole Books, 1994), 77.

17. Ibid., 78.

18. Mary Elizabeth Massey, *Bonnet Brigades: American Women and the Civil War* (New York: Knopf, 1966), 76–78, and Lowry, *Story the Soldiers Wouldn't Tell*, chapter 8.

19. Some Union officers attempted to "regulate" prostitution to clean up disease among the ranks, which was an extremely successful experiment in wartime Nashville and Memphis. See Catherine Clinton, *Public Women and the Confederacy*, Frank L. Clement Lectures, no. 8 (Milwaukee: Marquette University Press, 1999), 27–33.

20. See George Rable, "'Missing in Action': Women of the Confederacy," in *Divided Houses: Gender and the Civil War* (New York: Oxford University Press, 1992), edited by Catherine Clinton and Nina Silber, 140.

21. See Mary Ryan, *Women in Public: Between Banners and Ballots* (Baltimore: Johns Hopkins University Press, 1990), and Rable, "'Missing in Action.'"

22. James Parton, *General Butler in New Orleans: History of the Administration for the Department of the Gulf in the Year 1862* (Boston: Houghton Mifflin, 1868), 327.

23. Rable, "'Missing in Action,'" 138.

24. New Orleans diarists suggested that "true" Southern women would treat Union soldiers with disdain—and not resort to the vulgar rudeness of the lower classes. Massey, *Bonnet Brigades*, 229.

25. Rable, "'Missing in Action,'" 101.

26. Ibid., 101.

27. Massey, *Bonnet Brigades*, 229.

28. Richard M. McMurray, "The Confederate Newspaper Press and the Civil War," *Atlanta History* 42, 1–2 (spring–summer 1998): 69.

29. Parton, *General Butler in New Orelans*, 326.

30. Ibid., 327.

31. Ibid., 328.

32. Massey, *Bonnet Brigades*, 229–230. Despite his success, Butler was relieved of his command in New Orleans in December 1862.

33. Rable, "'Missing in Action,'" 141.

34. Sallie B. Putnam, *Richmond during the War: Four Years of Observation by a Richmond Lady* (New York: G. W. Carleton, 1867), 20.

35. David Ryan, ed., *A Yankee Spy in Richmond: The Civil War Diary of "Crazy Bet" Van Lew* (Mechanicsburg, Pa.: Stackpole Books, 1996), 32.

36. See Catherine Clinton, "Reading between the Lines: Newspapers and Women in Confederate Richmond," *Atlanta History* 42, 1–2 (spring–summer 1998): 19–34.

37. *Richmond Examiner*, May 12, 1862.

38. *Richmond Whig*, June 2, 1862.

39. Clinton, "Reading between the Lines," 31.

40. Michael D. Hitt, *Charged with Treason: Ordeal of Four Hundred Mill Workers during Military Operations in Roswell, Georgia, 1864–65* (Monroe, N.Y.: Library Research Associates, 1992), 18.

41. Hitt, *Charged with Treason*, 22.

42. Ibid., 61

43. Ibid., 89.

44. Ibid., 74.

45. Ibid., 104.

46. Ibid., 125.

47. Ibid., 111. Several prisoners were given the prospect of freedom if they settled in nearby Indiana, but without family or any means of support, most opted to remain in Louisville, waiting out the war, in the hope of returning to Georgia.

48. See chapter 6 of this book, "Mary Walker, Mary Surratt, and Some Thoughts on Gender in the Civil War."

49. Walker's treatment of the Roswell women may be found in Michael Hitt's *Charged with Treason*.

50. For example, the cases of women like Rose Greenhow, whose heroism as a Confederate spy was called into question by rumors of her sexually suspect relationship to Yankee contacts, notably Senator Henry Wilson. See Ann Blackman, *Wild Rose: Rose O'Neale Greenhow, Civil War Spy* (New York: Knopf, 2005).

5

THE OTHER SIDE OF FREEDOM

Destitution, Disease, and Dependency among Freedwomen and Their Children during and after the Civil War

Jim Downs

He found her lying in a ditch a few miles away from a Union camp in Augusta, Georgia. The war had been over for almost a year, yet she lay there in the dirt under the hot August sun as if she were a recent casualty from battle. By the end of war, she certainly was free, but the slow and often unorganized reconstruction of the South did not offer her a clear road to freedom. Instead, as the Bureau agent who discovered her explained, she had been going "from pillar to post and had fallen on her knees."[1]

After finding her lying in the dirt, the Bureau agent brought her to the Freedmen's Hospital in Augusta, Georgia. There, a Bureau physician examined her body and diagnosed her as blind, and then later concurred that her blindness must have resulted from syphilis. While it is difficult to determine the validity of the doctor's diagnosis—as many medical professionals in the nineteenth century associated disease, particularly venereal disease, with social circumstance and morality—questions concerning her condition nonetheless remain. How long she was there before the agent discovered her? How and when did she escape from slavery? If she was, in fact, suffering from syphilis, how was she treated?

While these questions cannot get answered, they challenge our understanding of the Civil War. When we envision the Civil War mainly as soldiers fighting on a battlefield and generals strategizing ways to capture their enemies on the Mississippi, it is difficult to see the freedwoman lying in an abandoned field. Yet, when we imagine the war as a crisis in which the lines were not clearly demarcated between blue and gray; when we recognize that disease killed more soldiers than combat; when we realize that newly emancipated slaves entered an environment pillaged by disease, death, and destruction, we can see her more clearly.[2]

During the Civil War and Reconstruction, there were many women, like her, anonymous and alone, young and old, and often destitute and sick, suffering from the outcomes of war and the abrupt transition to free labor.[3] In Orangeburg, South Carolina, a woman was found lying on cotton bales and suffering from rheumatic fever. It is no wonder that she was lying on burlap-wrapped cotton, as rheumatic fever often causes one's joints to flare up, making walking, even standing upright, a challenge. Lying on the canvas, alone in the middle of a cotton field, she was eventually discovered by a Bureau agent, who concluded she was "feverish" and "unable to work."[4] Miles away from the cotton plantations of South Carolina, in the bustling nation's capital, the story was the same: a Bureau physician found an elderly freedwoman in a hovel suffering from starvation.[5] Government reports, correspondences, and letters like these tell of the hundreds of freedwomen who did not qualify for labor and begged for rations. Some, who had children, congregated around Bureau offices and hospitals hoping to gain a cup of beans, pork, if they were lucky, and, at least, a blanket or a pair of shoes to keep them warm.[6]

Their condition resulted from the wartime policy of employing only the "able-bodied" men. During the Civil War, as thousands of slaves fled to Union lines, General Benjamin F. Butler declared that ex-slaves could enter Union camps as "contraband." And, as historian Barbara J. Fields notes, "contraband" was a term that "left unsettled whether or not such slaves became free," a term that "covered the uncertainty" of their social and legal position.[7] The military continued to capitalize on this uncertainty by enlisting former enslaved men as laborers and then restricting families—particularly unemployed freedwomen and children—to overcrowded and unsanitary camps, depriving them of not only economic and political independence but also adequate clothing, food, and shelter. As a reporter for the *Atlantic Monthly* discovered, the employment of men by the military had unfortunate consequences for freedwomen and children. Addressing the issue of what would happen to freedmen's families after the military transported their husbands and fathers to camps in need of laborers, he wrote: "Here was a new question, and a grave one, on which the government had not yet developed a policy."[8]

Without a policy that provided freedwomen and children with clothing, food, and shelter, thousands women and children, from the eastern shores of Maryland to the southern tip of Georgia and to the banks of the Mississippi, suffered in the transition from slavery to freedom.[9] In January 1862, *Harpers Weekly* reported that over fifteen hundred contraband had arrived at Fortress Monroe, of whom roughly six hundred were women and children without clothing.[10] Drawing from the soldiers' worn and unwanted uniforms, the military provided coats, shoes, and hats for some of the former enslaved men but lacked clothing for other men, as well as *all* the women and children. Similarly, the *Freedmen's Record* later reported, "clothing is their most pressing need, especially for women and children, who cannot wear the cast-off garments of soldiers."[11]

To make matters worse, Congress passed the Second Confiscation Act on July 17, 1862, which formalized Butler's informal practice of allowing fugitive slaves to enter Union camps in exchange for their labor. This policy to employ the "able-bodied" referred only to men, not women.[12] While former enslaved women certainly worked in Union camps as washerwomen, cooks, and domestics, there was no policy that provided for their employment; their labor was often impromptu service, neither regulated nor systematized.[13] Women instead were to gain rations and shelter, and to receive medical care through the support of their husbands' or fathers' employment.[14]

The Union Army, however, barely had adequate resources and supplies to care for their own men, let alone the thousands of freedwomen and children who were in need of support. In the hierarchy of the Union Army, preference was given to the white troops. Black regiments, who were next to receive support, often suffered—as some historians have noted—from insufficient rations, medicine, or other deprivations common to the region in which they were stationed; yet they, at least, registered on the military's radar. The government and the military had a vested interest in the health and well-being of these soldiers, and they assigned medical inspectors, doctors, and nurses to their camps—even if it was less than that was appropriated to white regiments.[15] Trailing behind the Union army were freedwomen and children, who in the military hierarchy were considered nothing more than mere "contraband." According to army officials, women and children harassed Union officers and were a hindrance and a burden to the military's efforts. Their medical needs, in turn, were virtually ignored.[16]

Some military officials attempted to solve this problem by taxing able-bodied men's labor to support women and children.[17] An order from the quartermaster general to the secretary of war stated that a large number of colored men are employed in this District [of Columbia] and in Alexandria as teamsters and laborers at the rate of twenty five dollars per month. In view of the fact that the Government is supporting several hundred women and children of the same class, who are unable to find employment and also furnished medical care, support and attendance, to the sick and helpless, the Secretary directs that you cause five dollars per month to be deducted from the pay of the said color teamsters and laborers . . . to be paid over to a Commissioner who will expend the fund thus accruing for the benefit of the women and children, and as a hospital fund for the sick among the men from whom it is derived.[18]

The program established in Alexandria for freedwomen and children led to the establishment of General Order 46, which provided support for women and children throughout the South. According to General Order 46,

the family of each colored soldier so enlisted and mustered so long as he shall remain in the service and behave well, shall be furnished suitable subsistence, under the direction of the Superintendent of Negro Affairs, or their Assistants; and each soldier shall be furnished with a certificate of subsistence for his family, as soon as he is mustered.[19]

Despite the promise of such support, this policy, nonetheless, failed, since the federal government did not provide enlisted soldiers with their due pay.

The failure to provide adequate support for freedwomen and children impelled many black soldiers to protest the government's mistreatment of their families. Using their newly minted status as soldiers, black men testified in affidavits and filed complaints regarding the poor and sickly condition of freedwomen and children during the war. Their public denouncements against the ways in which the military mistreated their families received national attention, attracting the support of Northern newspapers and benevolent organizations. As a Boston newspaper reported, "the wives of the men are, they say, often refused to almshouses for their color and are reduced to degradation that drives the husbands almost crazy."[20]

In an affidavit submitted to his superiors (later published in the *New York Tribune*), Joseph Miller of Company I of the 124th U.S. Colored

Infantry, stationed at Camp Nelson in Kentucky, testified to the dire and sickly condition of his family, who had followed him to Union lines from the Kentucky plantation where they were enslaved. Once entering the Union camp to enlist in the army, Miller claimed that Edward B. W. Restieaux, his captain, granted him permission for his wife and four children to live in a tent within the limits of the camp. On the evening of November 22, 1864, however, his wife and children were approached by a mounted guard, who ordered them to vacate the premises by early the next morning. Since his seven-year-old son was recovering from an illness and the family had no place to go, they stayed overnight. Abruptly woken by a mounted guard on the freezing morning of November 23, Miller's family was ordered to leave. Miller described the scene in his affidavit:

> I was certain that it would kill my sick child to take him out in the cold. I told the man in charge of the guard that it would be the death of my boy. I told him that my wife and children had no place to go. I told him that I was a soldier of the United States. He told me that it did not make a difference; he had orders to take all out of the camp. He told my wife and family if they did not get up in the wagon he would shoot the last one of them. On being thus threatened my wife and children went into the wagon. My wife carried the sick child in her arms. When they left the tent the wind was blowing hard and cold, and having had to leave much of our clothing when we left our master, my wife, with her little ones, was poorly clad. I followed them as far as the lines. I had no knowledge where they were taking them. At night I went in search of my family. I found them in Nicholasville, about six miles from the camp. They were in an old meetinghouse belonging to the colored people. The building was very cold, having only one fire. My wife and children could not get near the fire because of the numbers of colored people huddled together by the soldiers. I found my wife and family shivering with cold and famished with hunger; they had not received a morsel of food the whole day. My boy was dead. [21]

Miller then stated that his boy had died when the family got off the wagon and arrived at the "colored meetinghouse." After spending the night at the boarding house with his family, Miller left the next morning for Camp Nelson, carrying his dead son so he could give him a proper burial. Making it safely behind Union lines did not protect Miller from the excruciating pain and sadness he must have felt that day. Alone on the cold walk back to Camp Nelson, carrying his son beneath the Kentucky sky, Miller certainly was free, but the federal government's failure to uphold their part of their agreement had devastating effects for him and his family. Where the horizon met the outline of the camp site— where weeks before, the sight of Union troops and blazing bonfires had represented freedom for the Miller family—Miller buried his son. Miller would eventually continue his service in the army, only to be haunted by thoughts of his wife and three remaining children huddling by a fire, hoping to gain a morsel of food to eat.[22]

Two weeks after the Miller family's expulsion from the camp, E. D. Townsend, the assistant adjutant general at Camp Nelson, wrote to the quartermaster general in Washington, D.C., telling of the "large number of colored women and children that accumulated at Camp Nelson." He then explained that many of them were the wives of the "colored soldiers and that there will be much suffering among them this winter unless shelters are built and rations issued to them."[23]

In addition to the pleas made by black soldiers and sympathetic military officials, Northern benevolent workers serving in the South, mostly as teachers, became major advocates for the development of a policy to meet the health needs of freedwomen and children. As J. C. Maxwell explained to his readers in the *Christian Recorder*, "men best fitted for work followed the army, digging trenches." The freedwomen and children, however, were "obligated to remain in the rear and support themselves." He went on to say that women and children should not be ignored; rather, they "demand in unmistakable language, our immediate concern."[24] Alerting his readers to the deplorable condition of freedwomen and children in the postwar South, Maxwell tugged on his readers' middle-class, Christian sensibilities in order to form freedmen's aid societies. He further explained:

There are thousands of them at Fortress Monroe, Hilton Head, Cairo, and other places; and although the Government supplies them with food, they are in want of other necessities that sustain life. Winter is hard by, and they must have blankets and comfortable clothing, or they will perish and die to our utter shame. They are now no longer brutes and chattels, but women and children; and if we do not stretch forth our arms to their relief, the curse is upon our head.[25]

Advertisements calling for volunteers to travel to the South to help former enslaved women and their children appeared in politically progressive newspapers, like the *Weekly Anglo African* and the *Liberator*. The New England freedmen's aid societies and the more religiously oriented groups, such as the Quakers, also published reports and advertisements in their monthly bulletins.[26]

Former abolitionists heeded the call and went to the South to help newly emancipated slaves.[27] As agents for the freedpeople, they alerted military officials to the needs of freedwomen and children in the camps. Initially, their intervention was met with resistance by military and government officials. In southern Illinois, Laura Haviland, a benevolent worker, became an advocate for a freedwoman who attempted to get medical assistance for her dying son. The captain justified ignoring the woman's appeal because, as he told Haviland, "I don't know whether it is so or not; they get up all sorts of excuses."[28] Hours later, Haviland learned that the woman's child had died, and then, on behalf of the woman she approached the Captain to see if the child could receive a proper burial. Recalling, years later, in her diary, what the freedwomen had said to her, Haviland quoted the mother using dialect: "Oh, Missus, it 'pears like I can't leave him so; they leave him here tonight, an' dess wharf-rats are awful. Da eat one dead chile's face all one side off, an' one of its feet was gnawed off. I don't want to leave my chile on di bare groun'."[29]

Fearing that the government would—as the mother predicted—not properly bury her child and that wharf rats would eat the body of the dead baby, Haviland approached the captain a second time. "What is the difference," said the captain, "if that child shouldn't be buried this afternoon, or whether wharf-rats eat it or not?" Infuriated by the captain's attitude, Haviland said, "You promised to have it buried this afternoon . . . and I told the poor woman that it was done. . . . I see no other way to hold you to that promise, for I shall meet her on the island, I must report to her." Reproaching Haviland for her sympathetic attitude, the captain told her, "You won't allow such things as these to break your heart, after being in the army a little while and seeing our soldiers buried in a ditch, with no other than a coffin or winding sheet than the soldier's dress."

While the captain ultimately made the necessary arrangements for a coffin to be made for the freedwoman's son, many military officials during the war did not view the conditions of freedwomen and children as different from the conditions endured by Union soldiers. The military understanding of health and sickness as a byproduct of the gritty reality of war life only further invigorated benevolent associations' claims that they needed to be in the South and serve the freedpeople.

Consequently, benevolent associations established offices throughout the South, starting mostly in major cities and then expanding their efforts to rural locales. Northern white women, from New York, Philadelphia, and Boston, most of whom were abolitionists, arrived in the South under the guise of being teachers, to help improve the conditions of freed slaves. In Lambertville, New Jersey, Sarah Gage learned of the suffering condition of freedmen from her friends in Philadelphia and subsequently organized a Freedmen's Home Relief Association of Lambertville. After a few months of meetings and fundraising, Gage left her small town and traveled to Beaufort, South Carolina, to establish a school and assist the freedpeople.[30]

As teachers, the military provided benevolent reformers with access to the Union camps and allowed them to interact with the freedpeople— as education, according to federal officials, would provide former slaves with the tools to become independent wage earners. With this access, freedmen's aid societies encouraged these women to investigate the living and health conditions of former slaves. Benevolent women, throughout the South, soon discovered countless freedwomen and children who were being forced to live in abandoned, filthy buildings plagued by disease, suffering from lack of proper nutrition and medical care.[31]

Consequently, these Northern teachers began to advocate for the military to extend relief and provide better living conditions for former slaves. An agent for the Rochester Ladies Anti-Slavery Society, Julia Wilbur arrived in Alexandria, Virginia, where the small Washington, D.C., suburb had been transformed into a hospital station for Union soldiers. After visiting the former bank, which was converted to a sick ward filled with beds for soldiers, Wilbur then made her way near the "Old Capital Prison," where former slaves, criminals, and vagrants were kept. Overwhelmed by the devastation and sickness of Alexandria, she wrote in her diary that evening: "What a place I have found. How can I stay here? It is too uncomfortable to sit and write."[32] Yet, Wilbur did stay in Alexandria and continued to write. Unlike military officials in Alexandria, who not only neglected the condition of former enslaved women and children but also refused to enter their living quarters, Wilbur did not shy away from the overcrowded, disease-ridden places that could "prove contagious and fatal." Instead, she willingly entered them. "I went in to the oldest tenement, I saw," she wrote in her diary. She found "3 women and 13 children. . . . Old women lying in damp places." Turning to one of her fellow reformers, she pleaded that they bring bedding to the women "to keep them from sleeping on the ground." Later that day, she returned to the "slave pen."[33] There, "in one room with one window," she discovered "20 women and children, some of them sick." Lying on the bare damp floor, "only few could get near the small fire. . . . I had to leave. . . . It was horrible! I went to other room until I felt sick. I had to leave."[34]

After Wilbur left the slave pen, she did not allow the images she observed to quickly fade from view. Though still new to Alexandria, she wrote a letter that evening to the provost marshal of Alexandria, asking for barracks to be built for the contraband. Wilbur's call for adequate shelter was in line with nineteenth-century understandings of disease and contagion. Overcrowded living spaces were often equated with sickness. With this understanding, physicians and medical authorities attempted to cure health crises by improving the physical environment in which afflicted people lived. From concerns about proper ventilation to whitewashing rooms with lime to encouraging proper hygiene, medical authorities and reformers in the mid–nineteenth century moved away from an understanding of illness as a sign of socioeconomic status and morality.[35] Yet the majority of Union physicians and military officers during the Civil War viewed sickness among emancipated slaves as the result of their physiological inferiority and inherent vulnerability to disease.[36] As a reporter for the *Nation* observed:

> There has been considerable speculation as to the effect of freedom upon the physical condition of the former slave. By many it is thought that his ultimate fate will be that of the Indian, and for this opinion there seems to be some ground. That mortality and disease are largely on the increase cannot be doubted: of this fact I am assured by leading physicians, and the statistics would seem to confirm this statement.[37]

By investigating the living conditions and then calling for adequate housing, Wilbur refuted the popular theories and understandings about the causes for sickness and disease. She, like a growing number of physicians and reformers, understood sickness in relation to one's environment and, as a result, fought hard to improve the living conditions of freedwomen and children in Alexandria. "Women and children are sick and dying, not for want of necessary for food, but for want of suitable shelter from this cold storm," Wilbur explained in 1862. "Could barracks be built for them at once so that we could have them move together & a physician and medical stores be provided for them, I think we can get supplies of clothing and bedding from the North, & they can be made comparatively comfortable for the winter."[38]

Relentlessly advocating for military officials to take seriously her claims about the living and health conditions of freedwomen, Wilbur reminded the provost marshal, the leading government official in Alexandria, that Army generals gave her the right "to act as a matron, visitor, advisor, and instructor to these poor women." She then chided the provost marshal for having done nothing to assist the women and children since she had informally informed them of their suffering condition. "And, as a result," she wrote, "on this wintry morning, I have presumed to appeal to the President of the U.S. on behalf of suffering humanity."[39]

After learning that Wilbur had written to the president, the provost marshal, who months before had ignored first requests for the construction of new barracks, forwarded Wilbur's request to the military governor of Alexandria. Although Wyman agreed to the construction of barracks because of the "increasing population" of contraband in the town, he only gave authority "to build cheap barracks," in order for the contraband to be "subjected to the necessary supervision and control."[40]

General Heintzelman, who ultimately received these requests, refused to build even temporary barracks because—like many government and military officials during this period—he feared that such places would make the former slaves dependent on the government for support. He argued: "If we build temporary barracks they will soon be filled. Now there are a number of Contrabands in this vicinity, who are supporting themselves. When they learn that the government will feed and shelter them, they will flock to Alexandria."[41] He further stated that the freedmen "would spend their wages, and leave the women and children a tax on the government." Heintzelman's fear that providing women and children with shelter would only incite dependency led to no solution for homeless freedwomen and children. In fact, Heintzelman callously said, "What shall be done with these people, beyond temporary expedients, I have not the time to consider."[42]

Despite Heintzelman's attitude, Wilbur continued in her fight to attain adequate living quarters for former slaves. After numerous debates between city government and military officials, adequate barracks were finally constructed for freedwomen and their children, four months later in February 1863.[43] In the meantime, Wilbur had been joined by Harriet Jacobs, author of *Incidents in the Life of a Slave Girl*, who, with the help of the New York Society of Friends, provided clothing, money, and medical assistance to support women and children in Alexandria. With the assistance of the New York Friends and her relentless letter-writing campaigns, Wilbur eventually forced military officials to consider more closely the living conditions of freedwomen and their children.[44]

Yet Wilbur's efforts in Alexandria only provided a temporary solution. By the end of the war, the number of newly emancipated slaves stood at four million. If the military's concern for freedwomen and children during the war was abysmal, after the war, they had even less of a stake in the welfare of freedpeople. Military officials wanted to return home and to leave the South to forget the conditions and casualties of war. Benevolent organizations that had been individually organized and separated by seemingly nuanced political and religious ideologies recognized the need to unite to provide organized support for the health conditions of freedwomen and children. At their first annual meeting in 1865, they decided to approach Congress for both financial and administrative support to aid freedpeople.[45]

Thomas Elliot, a U.S. congressman from Massachusetts, agreed to represent their cause and introduced legislation to Congress that would provide assistance to former slaves in their transition from slavery to freedom.[46] Despite a number of qualms on the congressional floor, Congress ultimately passed a bill on March 3, 1865, that established the Bureau of Refugees, Freedmen, and Abandoned Lands, commonly known as the Freedmen's Bureau.[47] This organization, whose main purpose was to assist the freedpeople in their transition from slavery to freedom, offered a number of different services. The Bureau established schools throughout the South; mediated labor disputes between former slaveholders and slaves; and distributed abandoned land. The Medical Division, although ostensibly created to provide medical services to freedmen and white refugees, responded largely to the condition of those who were not employed, namely freedwomen and children.

In short, the Medical Division responded to the effects caused by the sudden and often unorganized transformation of the South into a free labor economy. The federal government's emphasis on the benefits of free labor overlooked the ways in which the creation of this new economic system simultaneously created the category of dependency, referring to those who did not fit into the labor force, namely freedwomen and children.[48] At the end of the war, military officials transported black men to regions in need of workers, leaving their families without the economic means to support themselves.[49] This process of literally "carrying off" able-bodied male laborers to plantations created a crisis of dependency. When the able-bodied men were taken away to work as woodcutters and gravediggers on Craney Island, Virginia, a Northern teacher reporting to the American Freedmen's Inquiry Commission described the island as a "Government Poor House," "a desolate and exposed place."[50]

The sudden transition to free labor not only involved Bureau agents literally "carrying off" able-bodied male laborers but also included the ways former slaveholders and Bureau agents drafted employment contracts. Favoring family and kinship networks within freedmen's communities, Bureau agents and planters often negotiated employment contracts with the male heads of household.[51] As part of these networks, freedwomen had the opportunity to withdraw from the labor force and devote their efforts to household duties—including growing food and rearing their children. Or, depending upon their location and the economic condition of their family, they could enter the work force as active participants in the burgeoning sharecropping enterprise.[52] These freedwomen had the structure and the support of their families to endure both the crises of the emancipation and the challenges of the new free labor system.

Many freedwomen, however, were searching for lost family members, looking for work, or following migration patterns, and, as a result, they were temporarily outside of these kin networks. As a benevolent worker in New Berne, North Carolina, explained to her sponsors in Boston, "where there are men in the family, they get along quite nicely; for they work at the trades, etc. . . . but as often is the case, I find a woman with six or eight children to care for, some of them sick, perhaps, and an old grandmother perfectly unable to take care of herself."[53] Without a family association, it was difficult to find employment. An eighteen-year-old freedwoman, whom we only know as "Hannah," was abandoned in a rural part of South Carolina, because the freedpeople with whom she was traveling through the town "were not interested in her."[54]

Despite offering support to displaced white men or women, who were also looking for lost family members and employment, local, state, and charitable institutions systematically denied assistance to dependent freedwomen. Many freedwomen were forced to take refuge in deserted barns or nearby hovels; the *Montgomery Daily Ledger* reported that a freedwoman died in an abandoned dump cart after giving birth to her child. Hours later, the newspaper reported, hogs came along and ate the infant.[55] Throughout the South, thousands of unemployed freedwomen faced similar, albeit less graphic, conditions.[56] The *Richmond Dispatch* reported a freedwoman found dead of starvation on the streets of the city.[57]

As freedwomen and children attempted to adjust to the challenges of a free labor economy, smallpox tore throughout the South in 1863–1866, worsening their already vulnerable position. Throughout the war, smallpox plagued both the Confederate and Union armies; due to the constant movement of military forces and the unsanitary conditions of camps, the disease easily spread throughout the South.[58] Without adequate resources or protection from this virus, freedwomen and children were the most vulnerable to these outbreaks. When smallpox first rolled through the Mississippi valley in the winter of 1863–1864, freedwomen and children perished at higher rates than both black men and white men and women, accounting for roughly 75 deaths a day.[59] When smallpox made its way north to Richmond, Virginia, in 1866, more freedwomen and children applied for assistance than any other demographic group.[60] When the epidemic reached Washington, D.C., women and children continued to outnumber any other group in need of vaccination or assistance.[61] As Lucy Chase, a Northern teacher serving in Virginia, reported, "they were dying as they died at Hampton by hundreds and thousands. Every woman will say she lost three or more children."[62]

Outbreaks of smallpox, in particular, devastated freedwomen and children because of their migratory conditions and their lack of employment and access to medical treatment. Working as washerwomen, cooks, and domestics offered freedwomen an alternative to the plantation labor force, but in many cases it encouraged their migratory status and subsequently exacerbated their displacement, making them particularly vulnerable to outbreaks of the virus. When the smallpox epidemic hit the area surrounding Raleigh, North Carolina, in February 1866, two freedwomen "walked twenty-two miles" to get rations and support. The unexpected cold weather, combined with the outbreak of smallpox in the state capital, however, depleted the Bureau's supply reserve. After discovering that even the Bureau office had "only empty barrels and boxes" and "nothing of real service to offer," the women wept.[63]

On plantations, like the Butler plantation in Georgia, former slaves could quarantine those suffering from the virus to isolated sick houses or pest homes.[64] Such measures prevented further infection of the virus, but unemployed freedwomen who were not part of plantation economies were ultimately more vulnerable to the virus.[65] Beyond quarantine as a defense against the virus, employed former slaves also had the opportunity to receive vaccinations on their plantation. Throughout the postwar South, planters negotiated contracts with freedpeople that stipulated medical care would be provided, but former slaves would be charged the expense of vaccination or medical treatment.[66] Although this often proved costly, it provided protection against the virus for those employed.[67]

Without vaccination, many freedpeople relied on homeopathic remedies to ward off the virus. From covering the body with tar to isolating afflicted family members to a remote location, freedpeople devised ways to prevent the virus from spreading within their communities.[68] The devastation that the smallpox epidemic produced was not, however, limited to only those freedwomen who remained unemployed. In fact, reports indicate that smallpox infected an estimated forty-nine thousand freedpeople from June 1865 to December 1867.[69] That unemployed freedwomen remained the most infected with the virus reveals the extent to which disparities developed as a result of the adjustment to free labor— which privileged the employment of able-bodied men.

By early 1867, the smallpox epidemic began to dissipate, but the larger economic problems that caused freedwomen to remain most vulnerable to sickness and disease continued. In reports and correspondences among federal authorities, dating from 1865 to 1869, freedwomen outnumbered freedmen in terms of illness. From accounts of venereal disease in North Carolina in 1867 to cases of destitution throughout the postwar South to reports of insanity, Bureau doctors documented that the overwhelming majority of afflicted freedpeople in the South were freedwomen.[70] Because freedwomen did not easily fit into the new labor force, their illnesses were more conspicuous to Bureau doctors and agents, who traveled throughout the postwar South and reported on the conditions of the freedpeople.

In many, if not all of these reports, freedwomen appear in these records as inhibiting the federal government's plan to rebuild the economy and organize the labor force. Of the many afflictions reported, cases of insanity among freedwomen best illustrate this point. From reports of "an insane freedwoman" running frantically through the streets of Charleston, South Carolina, to accounts of an "insane colored woman" disturbing the otherwise quiet life of New Berne, North Carolina, Bureau doctors and agents received dozens of requests to take charge of these afflicted freedwomen, who lacked a place in the new economy of free labor.[71] In Columbia, South Carolina, Bureau officials described "a violent insane Negro woman" who had recently arrived in town, while officials in Washington, D.C., referred to one nameless freedwoman as "Dummy."[72]

That freedwomen disproportionately outnumbered freedmen throughout the accounts of insanity is by no means coincidental.[73] Unlike freedmen, who could have been easily placed into a labor gang and transported to a plantation, freedwomen, because of their displacement from the labor force, migrated from town to town in search of temporary employment and shelter. Walking under the hot sun, surviving the drama of war and emancipation, and living without subsistence more than likely caused many freedwomen to appear to Bureau agents as unstable.[74] The dire conditions endured by displaced freedwomen often resulted in medical and government officials perceiving them to be wayward, demented, and, in many cases, insane. In South Carolina, for example, a Bureau physician diagnosed Jeanette Small, a freedwoman living in Charleston, as "idiotic" and suffering from "starvation." In addition, in Washington, D.C., a Bureau agent described Bettie Bell as "blind" and "insane."[75]

While Bureau physicians continued to report on cases of insanity among freedwomen, throughout much of the federal government's records, freedwomen simply appeared as "dependent and destitute." The Freedmen's Bureau attempted to solve this problem by establishing almshouses, modeled after Northern asylums, for destitute freedwomen and orphanages for their children, providing temporary refuge, clothing, and rations. Outside of Washington, D.C., for example, military officials converted a former Union hospital into the Lincoln Hospital for Women. Lincoln Hospital treated freedwomen ranging in ages from fourteen to eighty-two. Doctors diagnosed the women with contagious afflictions, such as fever, smallpox, dysentery, but also noted a handful of cases of freedwomen suffering from blindness, old age, and malnutrition.[76]

The Bureau, however, did not construct these institutions because they adopted a more humanitarian policy toward newly emancipated slaves but rather because the sickly and destitute condition of freedwomen and children threatened the sanctity of the federal government's objective of Reconstruction. Creating separate homes and providing medical assistance for destitute freedwomen facilitated the federal government's objectives of developing a labor force in the South. Once freedwomen and children were literally taken away from the abandoned plantations, forced to leave their makeshift hovels and stick-built homes, the government could then more easily clear the land to grow cotton.

Despite even the economic motivation undergirding the establishment of these almshouses for destitute freedwomen, the Medical Division of the Freedmen's Bureau, during its four-year tenure in the South, only established a few of these homes for destitute women. While freedwomen certainly represented the majority of the patients at the roughly forty hospitals that the Bureau constructed after the war, these institutions were unable to adequately and effectively handle the challenges of freedwomen's health. Although presented with cases ranging from infant mortality to malnutrition to everyday aches and pains, the Bureau's efforts dealt primarily, if not exclusively, with contagious diseases. Furthermore, the rhetoric of free labor obscured the actual health conditions of freedwomen.

Outside the Bureau hospitals, within the freedpeople's community, former enslaved women who had served as caretakers on plantations attended to freedwomen's medical conditions.[77] Yet records documenting the private aspect of freedwomen' illnesses within their homes and inside their communities are largely nonexistent. Contagious diseases, like smallpox, or even afflictions such as insanity consistently made their way into government reports and public record, because these disorders produced visible manifestations or gave rise to public health crises. Smallpox created noticeable sores on one's body, while cases of insanity created public outbursts. The visibility of these illnesses simultaneously and unwittingly obscured the private and hidden aspects of freedpeople's health.

To understand the private matters of freedwomen's health requires one to move beyond the public sphere. Inside their homes, freedwomen suffered from the mere exhaustion of the war and the challenges of adjusting to the unfamiliar and new demands of free labor. Visiting and often teaching classes at night, Northern teachers entered into freedpeople's homes and offered a more vivid portrait of their conditions. "In every family there is the languor and weakness of convalescence," wrote teacher Laura Towne from the Sea Islands in 1868, for nearly every individual has been severely ill with fever, and they have not recovered spirits or care for anything."[78] Towne's description of the actual "spirits" of the freedpeople provides a rare insight into the actual conditions of the freedpeople that was often lost in the Bureau's medical reports, which consisted largely of charts and tables. Visiting a family in Maryland, a Northern teacher reported meeting the mother of the household who was "afflicted with a disease of the spine and suffers constantly from physical pain."[79]

C. E. McKay, a Northern teacher stationed in Baltimore, Maryland, discovered a boardinghouse operated by a freedwoman "when a young colored boy" approached her and announced that "Miss Downs wants you to come see her." Located in an alley in a deserted part of the city, Downs opened her home to destitute children and freedwomen. She also rented out rooms in her home to local boarders, and then used the money, along with some cash she earned as a washerwoman, to buy medicine for the orphans in need. After visiting the boardinghouse, McKay wrote to her Northern association in order to send funds to support Downs's efforts.

"A part of this [Downs's income] has to be expended in medicines for one of the little orphans, who is dropsical, her head and neck swelled to an unnatural size, and her arms and legs slender as pipes."[80] Downs's boardinghouse represents one of the many efforts within the black community to provide support and medical assistance for those in need. The term *dropsical*, which McKay explained, was a common way nineteenth-century observers described a swelling that was a result of excessive accumulation of serous fluid in tissue. Such a condition would not alarm medical authorities but certainly elicited the sympathy and concern of those within the freedpeople's communities.

By 1868, freedpeople's communities gained the strength and support to assist freedwomen and children. In the years between slavery and freedom, from roughly 1862 to 1867, disease and the deprivation of war prevented many freedpeople from helping those most in need in their communities. Many freedwomen, as a result, suffered from the unexpected problems of emancipation. Benevolent organizations desperately attempted to respond to these problems by distributing clothes, providing food, and constructing hospitals for those who were set apart as dependent and outside of the labor force. More important, benevolent organizations alerted federal officials to the need for governmental intervention. The federal government's establishment of the Freedmen's Bureau attempted to help freedwomen in the transition from slavery to freedom but failed to solve the larger economic problems that caused their dependency. In fact, Bureau physicians' constant reporting that women and children suffered more from illness than any other demographic group unwittingly suggested that if free labor was not working, it was clearly a result of freedwomen—lying in abandoned fields, disturbing peaceful communities, and, most of all, not working.

ACKNOWLEDGMENTS   I am grateful to Elizabeth Blackmar, Eric Foner, Jennifer Fronc, and Jennifer Manion, who read earlier drafts and versions of this essay and provided insightful advice and valuable criticism.

NOTES

1. A. J. Rebuis to Surgeon J. W. Lawton, August 13, 1866, Letters Received, Augusta, Georgia, microfilm (hereafter M) 1903, roll (hereafter R) 49, Bureau of Refugees, Freedmen, and Abandoned Lands (hereafter BRFAL), Record Group (hereafter RG) 105, National Archives (hereafter NA).

2. Three out of five men died from disease unrelated to battle during the Civil War; for more information on this, see Paul E. Steiner, *Disease in the Civil War: Natural Biological Warfare in 1861–1865* (Springfield, Ill.: Charles C. Thomas), 1968. Ira Berlin, Joseph P. Reidy, and Leslie S. Rowland, *The Black Military Experience* (New York: Cambridge University Press, 1982), 633–655. Frank R. Freemon, *Gangrene and Glory: Medical Care during the American Civil War* (Madison, N.J.: Fairleigh Dickinson University Press, 1998), 221–228.

3. Testimony by a Surgeon at Freedmen's Village, Washington, D.C., January 9, 1864, Freedmen and Southern Society Project, University of Maryland.

4. Henry Root to W. R. Dewitt, September 21, 1865, Orangeburg, S.C., BRFAL, RG 105, e. 2979, Chief Medical Officer, Letters Received, 1865–66.

5. H. N. Howard to O. H. Howard, September 11, 1867, Subordinate Field Offices and Subassistant Commissioner (SubDistrict 1) Register of Letters Received, Washington, D.C., M 1902, R 20, BRFAL, RG 105, NA; James E. Yeatman, "A Report on the Condition of the Freedmen of the Mississippi, Presented to the Western Sanitary Commission" (St. Louis, n.p., 1864), 2–3, and Report of the Western Sanitary Commission for the Year Ending June 1, 1863 (St. Louis, n.p., 1863), 24–25, both Western Sanitary Commission reports, Massachusetts Historical Society (hereafter MHS).

6. Brig. General C. C. Washburn to Hon. E. M. Stanton, September 6, 1862, W-1251 1862, Letters Received, RG 107 [(L-18]); A.A.Q.M.B.O. Carr to Capt. F. S. Winslow, July 24, 1862; Mansfield French to Salmon P. Chase, January 6 1863, Abraham Lincoln Papers, Library of Congress. L.Thomas, Adjutant General, to General Meigs, September 27, 1862, RG 92, Consolidated Quartermaster Files, filed under "Contraband Camps," box 399, NA.

7. Barbara J. Fields, "Who Freed the Slaves?" in *The Civil War* (New York: Knopf, 1990), edited by Geoffery Ward, 178–179.

8. "The Contrabands at Fortress Monroe," *Atlantic Monthly*, November 1861, p. 637.

9. For women in Virginia and the Upper South, see Col. George H. Hall to Major James Rainsford, September 18 1863, Unentered Letters Received, ser 2594, Dept. of the MO, RG 393, pt. 1 [C-130]. *Freedom*, ser. 2, doc. 85; Official Records, ser. 1, vol. 22, pt. 2, p. 450. Both are quoted in Ira Berlin, Steven F. Miller, Joseph P. Reidy, and Leslie S. Rowland, *Freedom, Wartime Genesis of Free Labor: The Upper South* (New York: Cambridge University Press, 1993), 578–579. Testimony of Ladies Contraband Society before the American Freedmen's Inquiry Commission, [December 2, 1863], filed with O-328 1863, Letters Received, ser. 12, RG 94 [K-209], quoted in Berlin, Miller, Reidy, and Rowland, *Freedom*, 584. For women in Arkansas, Tennessee, and Vicksburg, Mississippi: Yeatman, "A Report on the Condition of the Freedmen of the Mississippi," 2–3, Report of the Western Sanitary Commission for the Year

Ending June 1, 1863 (St. Louis, n.p., 1863), 24–25. Also for women in the Mississippi valley, see Ira Berin, Thavolia Glymph, Steven F. Miller, Joseph P. Reidy, Leslie S. Rowland, and Julie Saville, *Freedom: The Wartime Genesis of Free Labor; The Lower South* (New York: Cambridge University Press, 1990), 210, 659, 665, 677–670. *Harper's Weekly*, p. 18, January 11, 1862. For women in North Carolina, see Mrs. C. E. McKay, *Stories of Hospital and Camp* (Philadelphia: Claxton, Remsen and Haffelfinger, 1876), 167–168.

10. *Harper's Weekly*, January 11, 1862, p. 18.

11. *Freedmen's Record*, February 1865, MHS, 26.

12. While there has been a recent proliferation in the study of women and gender during the Civil War and Reconstruction, historians have not explored the ways the Second Confiscation Act legally established a gender asymmetry through the deployment of the "able-bodied policy." This policy continued throughout Reconstruction to permit the hiring only of men as laborers. The term *able-bodied* originated in the antebellum North in legal and social discourse surrounding the employment the urban poor. See Michael Katz, *In the Shadow of the Poorhouse* (New York: Basic Books, 1996). For studies of gender during Reconstruction, see Laura Edwards, *Gendered Strife and Confusion: The Political Culture of Reconstruction* (Urbana: University of Illinois Press, 1997), Noralee Frankel, *Freedom's Women: Black Women and Families in Civil War Mississippi* (Bloomington: Indiana University Press, 1999), Leslie Schwalm, *A Hard Fight for We: Women's Transition from Slavery to Freedom in South Carolina* (Urbana: University of Illinois Press, 1997).

13. Maj. General John A. Dix to Hon. Edwin M. Stanton, December 13, 1862, D-77 1862, Letters Received Irregular, RG 107 [L-99], and Excerpts from Vincent Colyer to Hon. Rob. Dale Owen, May 25, 1863, filed with O-328 1863, Letters Received, ser. 12, RG 94 [K-84], as quoted in Berlin, Miller, Reidy, and Rowland, *Freedom: The Wartime Genesis of Free Labor: The Upper South*, 127, 138-139.

14. Capt. Murray Davis to Col. James A. Hardie, December 3, 1864, Letters Received, ser. 15, RG 159, Freedmen's Village, Washington, D.C. [J-2], Freedmen and Southern Society Project, University of Maryland. Joseph P. Reidy, "Coming from the Shadow of the Past: The Transition from Slavery to Freedom at Freedmen's Village, 1863–1900," *Virginia Magazine of History and Biography* 95, 4 (October 1987): 203–428.

15. Berlin, Reidy, and Rowland, *Black Military Experience*, 633–655; Andrew K. Black, "In the Service of the United States: Comparative Mortality among African-American and White Troops in the Union Army, *Journal of Negro History* 76, 4 (autumn 1994): 317–333.

16. General Orders, no. 46, Head Quarters, Dept. of Virginia and North Carolina, December 5, 1863, vol. 52, VaNC, General Order Issued, ser. 5078,

Dept. of Virginia and North Carolina and 18th Army Corps, RG 393, pt. 1 [C-3062], as quoted in Berlin, Miller, Reidy, and Rowland, *Freedom,* 174.

17. General Orders, no. 46, Head Quarters, Dept. of Virginia and North Carolina, December 5, 1863, as quoted in Berlin, Miller, Reidy, and Rowland, *Freedom,* 174.

18. Thomas to Meigs, September 27, 1867, quoted in Berlin, Miller, Reidy, and Rowland, *Freedom,* 270.

19. Ibid., 85–109.

20. Clipping, Edward Wilkinson Kinsley Papers, Perkins Library, Duke University. Edward Wilkinson Kinsley was a major supporter of the enfranchisement of blacks later in the South. During the Civil War, he used his status as a commanding leader in the Colored Regiment to voice the concerns of black soldiers. His letters to his family members express his concern for providing the wives and children of black soldiers with improved assistance.

21. Miller's affidavit was published in the November 28, 1864, issue of the *New York Tribune*; however, this article was found in the Quartermaster's Consolidated Reports, filed under "Negro," at the National Archives. It seems that the condition of women and children and, in particular, the tragedy that faced the Miller family attracted a great deal of attention. RG 92, box 727, Quartermaster Consolidated File, NA.

22. I have not yet been able to locate Miller's pension file. I read through by the pension lists at the National Archives organized by troop and name and was unable to locate his file, but the date and the filing of the affidavit suggests that he remained on duty for a year.

23. E. D. Townsend to Quartermaster General, December 2, 1864, RG 92, box 72, Quartermaster Consolidated Collections, file 75, filed under "Negroes," NA.

24. November 6, 1862, *Christian Recorder.*

25. Ibid.

26. "Volunteers Wanted," March 1, 1862, *Weekly Anglo African, Liberator,* March 7, 1862, *Anglo African,* March 22, 1862.

27. National Freedmen's Relief Association, May 1863, MHS, and *American Freedmen's Bulletin* 11, 6 (May 1866), MHS. On the Quakers, see Philadelphia Friends Annual Meeting Reports, 1863–1865, Haverford College.

28. Laura S. Haviland, *A Woman's Life-Work; Labors and Experiences* (Chicago: Waite, 1887), 246.

29. Haviland, *Woman's Life-Work,* 246–247.

30. Sarah Gage Journal, George Gage Papers, Manuscript Division, Perkins Library, Duke University.

31. Maria R. Mann to "Elisa," February 10, 1863; Maria Mann to "Miss Peabody," April 19, 1863, Maria Mann Papers, Library of Congress. Also

on Mann's work see Report of the Western Sanitary Commission, July 1, 1863, 24–25. Testimony of Ladies Contraband Society before the American Freedmen's Inquiry Commission, [2 December 1863], filed with O-328 1863, Letters Received, ser. 12, Rg 94 [K-209] as quoted in Berlin, Miller, Reidy, and Rowland, *Freedom*, 584; National Freedmen's Relief Association, May 1863; and *American Freedmen's Bulletin* 11, 6 (May 1866). On the Quakers, see Philadelphia Friends Annual Meeting Reports, 1863–1865.

32. Julia Wilbur Diary (microfilm), November 5–10, 1862, Alexandria Historical Society, Alexandria, Virginia.

33. In regard to the reference to the slave pen, antebellum Alexandria was a major station in the interstate slave trade. Before buyers and auctioneers bid on slaves, they were often kept in a slave pen located on Duke Street in Alexandria. During the war, the pen became a holding cell for slaves who migrated to northern Virginia.

34. Julia Wilbur Diary, November 6, 1862.

35. For reformer's concern for personal hygiene, see Lydia Marie Child, *Freedmen's Book* (Boston: Fields, Osgood & Co., 1869); for military understanding of a clean environment, see Robert Reyburn, "Type of Disease among Freed People of the United States," in New York Academy of Medicine, New York, and, for example, Kipps to Robinson, October 12, 1866, Office of Staff Officers, Surgeon, Letters Sent, vol. 1 (31), Alabama, September 7, 1865–July 21, 1865, R 8, RG 105, BRFAL, Alabama Microfilm, NA.

36. B. B. French to Hon. Edwin M. Stanton, February 13, 1862, F-187 1862, Letters Received, RG 107 [L-12], as quoted in Berlin, Miller, Reidy, and Rowland, *Freedom*, 262–263; *Nation*, August 15, 1872, 105.

37. "Negro Mortality at the South," *Nation*, August 15, 1872, 105.

38. Julia Wilbur to Abraham Lincoln, November 7, 1862; Capt. John C. Wyman to Brig. General John P. Slough, November 24, 1862, filed with W-1263 1862, Letters Received, ser. 12, RG 94 [K-55], as quoted in Berlin, Miller, Reidy, and Rowland, *Freedom*, 276–277.

39. Wilbur to Lincoln, November 7, 1862, as quoted in Berlin, Miller, Reidy, and Rowland, *Freedom*, 276–277.

40. Captain John C. Wyman to Brig. Genl. Jno P. Slough, October 21, 1862, and endorsements, enclosed in Qr. Mr. General M. C. Meigs to Hon. E. M. Stanton, December 13, 1862, "Alexandria, Va," Consolidated Correspondence File, ser. 225, Central Records, RG 92 [Y-226], as quoted in Berlin, Miller, Reidy, and Rowland, *Freedom*, 268–269.

41. Ibid., 278–279.

42. General Heintzelman endorsement, Wyman to Slough, November 24, 1862, as quoted in Berlin, Miller, Reidy, and Rowland, 277.

43. Lewis McKenzie to Honl. E. M. Stanton, September 19, 1862, enclosed in Brigdr. Genl. Jno. P. Slough to Hon. E. M. Stanton, September 25, 1862, S-91 1862, Letters Received Irregular, RG 107 [L-179]. Wyman to Slough, October 21, 1862, and endorsements, enclosed in Qr. Mr. General M. C. Meigs to Hon. E. M. Stanton, December 13,1862, as quoted in Berlin, Miller, Reidy, and Rowland, *Freedom*, 268–269.

44. Harriet Brent Jacobs, "Commentary," *National Anti-Slavery Standard,* March 26, 1864, April 16, 1864.

45. O. O. Howard, *Autobiography of Oliver Otis Howard* (New York: Baker & Taylor, 1907), 194–201, L. P. Brockett, *Heroines of Rebellion* (Philadelphia: Hubbord Bros., 1908), 186, Yeatman, "Report on the Condition of the Freedmen of Mississippi," 16. This was also the beginning of the Freedmen's Inquiry Commission. See Freedmen's Inquiry Commission Papers, Widener Library, Harvard University.

46. *Second Annual Report of the New England Freedmen's Aid Society* (Boston: Published at the Office of the Society, 1864), 10.

47. Howard, *Autobiography*, 194–201.

48. Robert Dale Owen to Abraham Lincoln, August 5, 1863, Abraham Lincoln Papers, Library of Congress.

49. *Second Annual Report of the New England Freedmen's Aid Society,* 37–38; Davis to Hardie, December 3, 1864.

50. Lucy Chase, before the American Freedmen's Inquiry Commission, [10 May 1863], as quoted in Berlin, Miller, Reidy, and Rowland, *Freedom,* 150–153.

51. In fact, Bureau agents advocated for freedwomen "to stay home." Men were to go out to work, while women were "to take care of the household." Address Given at Arlington Cemetery, Daniel A. P. Murray Collection, 1807–1919, Library of Congress; John Eaton, *Grant, Lincoln, and the Freedman: Reminiscences of the Civil War* (New York: Longman, Green & Co., 1907), 34.

52. This idea does not contradict Jacqueline Jones's argument that emancipated women withdrew from the labor force in favor of being homemakers. Jones's research, much like Steven Hahn's new work on former slaves, charts the experience of those who were part of family or kin networks. My analysis examines what happened to those who were not, albeit temporarily, part of these associations. The constant reporting by military officers, government officials, physicians, and even the Northern press tells of the hundreds of freedwomen and children who were left without support. It is my position that these women and children were displaced because they were outside of the kin, and by extension, labor networks. Jacqueline Jones,

Labor of Love, Labor of Sorrow: Black Women, Work and the Family from Slavery to the Present (New York: Vintage Books, 1985); Steven Hahn, *A Nation under Our Feet* (Cambridge, Mass.: Harvard University Press, 2003).

53. *Freedmen's Record*, January 1, 1866, MHS.

54. Daniel Freedmen and W. H. Redish to General Scott, October 12, 1866, Orangeburg, South Carolina, e. 3314. Letters Sent, Letters, General Orders, and Special Orders Received and Endorsements Sent and Received, RG 105, NA. Steve Hahn demonstrates how kin networks benefited African Americans politically, but economically the story is a bit different. Hahn, *A Nation under Our Feet* (Cambridge, Mass.: Harvard University Press, 2003).

55. *Montgomery Daily Ledger*, October 12–13, 1865, p. 3, as quoted in Howard N. Rabinowitz, *Race Relations in the Urban South 1865–1900* (Urbana: University of Illinois Press, 1980), 131.

56. Combining local Bureau records in which at least two hundred freedwomen in any given area are unemployed and without access to rations; I have tallied thousands who were in what the Bureau defined as dependent or destitute condition. In the *American Freedmen*, General O. O. Howard published his report on the number of rations and stated that roughly seven million rations were provided to freedpeople from June 1865 to May 1866. See *American Freedmen*, included in *Pennsylvania Freedmen's Bulletin*, September 1866, Library Company of Philadelphia, p. 91.

57. *Richmond Dispatch*, October 4, 1865, October 17, 1865, as quoted in Rabinowitz, *Race Relations in the Urban South*, 131.

58. Jacob Gilbert Forman, *The Western Sanitary Commission; A Sketch of Its Origin, History, Labors for the Sick and Wounded of the Western Armies, and Aid Given to the Freedmen and Union Refugees, with Incidents of Hospital Life* (St. Louis: Published for the Mississippi Sanitary Fair), 14–15. On the state of Union camps, also see O. A. Judson to Abbott, July 18, 1863, Washington, e. 5412, Miscellaneous Records, 1861–1869, box 7, RG 393, Continental Army, NA. "Health in the Hospitals," *Atlantic Monthly*, November 1861, pp. 718–730. Katherine Prescott Wormeley, *The Sanitary Commission of the United States Army: A Succinct Narrative of Its Works and Purpose* (New York: United States Sanitary Commission, 1864), 42–43. Thomas T. Ellis, *Leaves from the Diary of an Army Surgeon: Or, Incidents of Field, Camp, and Hospital Life* (New York: Bradburn, 1863), 312.

59. *Second Annual Report of the New England Freedmen's Aid Society*, 37–38.

60. U.S. Senate, *Laws in Relation to Freedmen*, 39th Cong., 2nd sess., Senate executive doc., no. 6, 164.

61. Ibid., 26.

62. Testimony of Miss Lucy Chase before the American Freedmen's Inquiry Commission, May 10, [1863], field with O-328 1863, Letters

Received, ser. 12, RG 94 [K-68], as quoted in Berlin, Miller, Reidy, and Rowland, *Freedom,* 154.

63. *Freedmen's Journal* 2, 3 (March 1866): 57.

64. For references to the sick house on the Butler plantations, see Butler Family Papers, 1771–1900, Historical Society of Pennsylvania, Philadelphia. Also see Catherine Clinton, *Fanny Kemble's Civil Wars* (New York: Simon and Schuster, 2000), 204–205. While Clinton notes the resistance that some freedwomen expressed toward the sick house, this does not run counter to the idea that former slaves would have used such a home in order to prevent the further spread of smallpox, which plagued thousands of freed slaves in the region from 1864 to 1866. For more on the smallpox epidemic in South Carolina, see U.S. Senate, *Laws in Relation to Freedmen,* 114.

65. For more on the Butler plantation, see Clinton, *Fanny Kemble,* and Butler Family Papers, 1771–1900.

66. "Agreement between Baskerville and Betty, a Negro Family," December 25, 1865, "Agreement between Mason and Baskerville, December 25, 1865," "Agreement of Hands with R. Baskervill for the year 1866," signed November 24, 1865, MSS1B2924a 1669–1685, "Agreement, 1867 and 1868," "Hands Agreement, 1868," Baskervill Family Papers; "Contracts," Allen Family Papers, Buckingham County, Virginia, January 1866–January 1868, MSS1AL546c, microfilm; "Isaac Claiborne, January 17, 1866, Amelia County," Harvie Family Papers, MSS 1H2636c2844, "Amelia Burton," Harvie Family Papers, MSS 1H2636a2841, Virginia Historical Society, Richmond.

67. "Agreement between Charles J. Haskell and Freedmen and Freedwomen on Alston Plantation," July 21, 1865, sec. 24, MSSSIC1118a 731–732, January 1, 1866, sec. 43, MSS 1c1118a8881, Cabell Family Papers, Virginia Historical Society.

68. U.S. Senate, *Laws in Relation to Freedmen,* 79–80; Register of Patients at Smallpox Hospital and Weekly Reports of Sick and Wounded Volume (163), R 49, Georgia, BRFAL, NA; U.S. Senate, *Laws in Relation to Freedmen,* 110–111; Alexander Augusta to Caleb W. Horner, June 2, 1866, Savannah, Lincoln Hospital, Letters Sent, vol. 1 (354), December 1865–January 1868, M 1903, R 85, BRFAL, NA.

69. *Weekly Anglo African,* January 18, 1862.

70. Report of Hon. T. D. Elliot, chairman of the Committee of Freedmen's Affairs, U.S. House of Representatives, March 10, 1868 (Washington, D.C.: Government Printing Office, 1869). These statistics only tell part of the story. Records of Union physicians in the field suggest that the numbers in their specific jurisdictions were, in fact, much higher. Due to the countless number of freedpeople in need of medical assistance, many Bureau doctors claimed to be unable to keep accurate records. Furthermore, the statistics

regarding the number of afflicted freedpeople only represent those whom doctors encountered. In rural regions, places in which the Freedmen's Bureau did not establish a medical presence, the number of those infected with the virus went unreported.

71. Monthly Report of Sick and Wounded Refugees and Freedmen, June 1867, July 1867, Charlotte Freedmen's Hospital, 1867–1868, BRFAL, RG 105, North Carolina, e. 2587, box 32.

72. A. G. Brady to J. K. Fleming, June 1, 1866, New Berne, North Carolina, e. 2535, Letters Sent, BRFAL, RG 105.

73. Inventory, May 15, 1868, Columbia, South Carolina—1866–67, e. 3170, Letters Sent, BRFAL; for Washington, D.C, see Beebe to Roger, February 2, 1867, Subordinate Field Offices, Local Superintendent for Washington and Georgetown Correspondences, Letters Sent, vol. 1 (77), July 15, 1865–September 10, 1867, M 1902, R 13, BRFAL, RG 105.

74. For South Carolina, see J. V. DeHanne to Greese, June 18, 1867, Office of Staff Officers, Surgeon-in-Chief, Letters Sent and Register of Letters Received, September 1865–July 1867, vol. 52 (R 26), BRFAL, RG 105, NA; Pelzer to Hogan, January 16, 1868, Charleston, S.C., Letters Sent, e. 3132, September 1867–1869, BRFAL, RG 105; Pelzer to Lockwood, May 28, 1868, Charleston, S.C., Letters Sent, e. 3132, September 1867–1869, BRFAL, RG 105; for North Carolina, see Chase to C. A. Cilley, June 21, 1866, p. 52, Raleigh, N.C., e. 2535, Letters Sent, BRFAL, RG 105; for Washington, D.C., see Register of Patients in Female Ward of Lincoln Hospital, 1, July 1866–March 22, 1867, Consolidated Weekly Reports of Sick and Wounded Freedmen, R 19, M1902, BRFAL, RG 105.

75. Historian Lynette Jackson makes a similar argument in her study of medicine and gender in twentieth-century Africa. See Jackson, "Narratives of 'Madness' and Power: A History of Ingutsheni Mental Hospital and Social Order in Colonial Zimbabwe, 1908–1959" (Ph.D. diss., Columbia University, 1997).

76. Pelzer to Hogan, January 16, 1868; Beebe to Rogers, December 14, 1866, Subordinate Field Offices, Local Superintendent for Washington and Georgetown Correspondences, Letters Sent, vol. 1 (77), July 15, 1865–10 September 1867, M 1902, R 13, BRFAL, RG 105.

77. Lincoln Hospital for Women, Washington, D.C., Bureau Records, RG 105; Women's Asylum, South Carolina Inventory, RG 105; Women's Asylum, Louisiana Annual Reports, 1866, RG 105, NA.

78. For a brilliant analysis of the work of enslaved women as caretakers and healers in the antebellum South, see Sharla Fett, *Working Cures: Healing, Health, and Power on Southern Slave Plantations* (Chapel Hill: University of North Carolina Press, 2002).

79. *Pennsylvania Freedmen's Bulletin*, February 1868, Library Company of Philadelphia, p. 6.

80. *Freedmen's Record*, May 1868, New England Freedmen's Association, MHS, pp. 78–79.

81. Ibid.

6

MARY WALKER, MARY SURRATT, AND SOME THOUGHTS ON GENDER IN THE CIVIL WAR

Elizabeth D. Leonard

The study of gender and the Civil War has come a long way in the last two decades. Back in the late 1980s, graduate students might take otherwise fascinating graduate seminars on the war that nevertheless completely ignored women's involvement in, and their experience of, that crucial event. In a parallel manner, equally fascinating graduate seminars on women in American history omitted virtually all references to the Civil War. Fortunately, as readers of this collection of essays clearly know, many fine scholars have been busy over the last twenty years adding significantly and expertly to our knowledge and understanding of the intersection of gender (and of women specifically) and the American Civil War.[1] I hope that I, too, have contributed some valuable insights, and in the essay that follows I will ponder anew the more salient ones.

A fundamental question late twentieth-century scholars of women and the Civil War have attempted to answer is, simply, what sorts of contributions did women make to the war effort on both sides of the front, and what were the long term implications for gender conventions of women's wartime activities? For example, my first book—*Yankee Women: Gender Battles in the Civil War*, published in 1994—focused on two individual Northern women who represented much larger categories of Union women's Civil War service: Sophronia Bucklin, a nurse who served under the auspices of the Union army's superintendent of women nurses, Dorothea Dix; and Iowa's Annie Wittenmyer, a leader in soldiers' (or sanitary) aid, first at the state and then at the national level.[2] *Yankee Women* also explored the wartime career of Dr. Mary Edwards Walker, who, in contrast with Bucklin and Wittenmyer, occupied a position all her own: she was the only woman during the entire four years of the war to receive a contract as a civilian surgeon from the Union army's medical establishment.

The stories of Bucklin and Wittenmyer direct us to the thousands (even tens of thousands) of nurses and aid activists they represented, without whose labor and commitment in both the North and the South, I would argue, the Civil War could not have continued. These women's stories also suggest the Civil War—especially as it dragged on—permitted a noticeable, if temporary, expansion of Victorian notions of what constituted "appropriate" behavior, at least for Northern white women of the middle class. As a result, nurses like Bucklin and aid activists like Wittenmyer were able to overcome much of the resistance they experienced early in their wartime service from observers who at first interpreted their contributions to the Union war effort as "unladylike"—and therefore unacceptable—intrusions upon the public (read "male") sphere of war. At the same time, Dr. Mary Walker's story vividly indicates that the wartime flexibility with regard to gender that was evident in the stories of Bucklin and Wittenmyer was by no means limitless.

One of a very few women in the mid–nineteenth century to have completed an M.D. degree (Walker graduated from Syracuse Medical College in 1855), in the fall of 1861 Walker left her admittedly not terribly successful private medical practice behind in central New York, determined to apply her skills and training to the care and healing of the mounting numbers of sick and wounded soldiers at the front. Once she reached Washington, D.C., Walker consistently refused to be assigned to a military hospital as a woman nurse. Indeed, although she preferred a genuine military surgeon's commission, she refused to accept anything *less* than a civilian surgeon's contract, both of which were privileges (and forms of recognition) hitherto reserved exclusively for men. Even while she stubbornly awaited official acknowledgment of her ability and training, Walker donated her services to the Union army as a volunteer physician, going wherever she saw a need for her labor, and steadily earning herself the gratitude of the soldiers, whose medical needs she proved capable of meeting with as much skill as any of her male peers, and sometimes with even more compassion.

Nevertheless, only in the final full year of the war, when absolute emergency unexpectedly overlapped with Walker's relentless persistence, did the army's medical brass decide to heed the numerous recommendations arriving from officers in the field regarding Walker's good work among their men. In January 1864, upon the sudden death of the Fifty-second Ohio Infantry's assistant surgeon, Dr. A. J. Rosa, the army medical establishment rather grudgingly tapped Walker as his replacement. Having at last received her coveted surgeon's contract, Walker spent the remainder of the war first with the Fifty-second Ohio and then—after being captured by Confederate pickets while on an errand beyond camp lines—as a prisoner of war in Richmond's infamous Castle Thunder from April to August 1864. After her release from prison, Walker was transferred for most of the war's final months to a federal military prison for women located in Louisville, Kentucky, where she was the surgeon in charge.

In general, women nurses and aid activists such as Bucklin and Wittenmyer progressively accumulated laurels for their work on behalf of the men in blue (and sometimes in gray). Moreover, with virtually no enduring harm to their reputations as "proper Victorian ladies," the vast majority of Civil War nurses and aid activists managed to stretch the boundaries of acceptable behavior for women like themselves by effectively persuading observers and male coworkers that the work they were performing was, in fact, nothing more than traditional women's work in a nontraditional setting. (It hardly damaged their case, either, that they also proved themselves essential to the progress of Union and Confederate arms.) In contrast, throughout the war, Dr. Mary Walker remained in many people's eyes a deeply controversial and, in some cases, even a deeply reviled figure, despite her passionate and unwavering commitment to the soldiers' medical care, because she flatly and explicitly (and often quite testily) rejected the unspoken expectation that she should balance her practical challenges to Victorian ideals about gender with at least the appearance of fundamental conformity.

But such was not her nature. Indeed, in addition to attending medical school, Walker also boldly divorced her philandering husband and then remained single (and economically independent) for the rest of her life. Perhaps most shocking of all, however, was Walker's disdain for standard Victorian codes of dress. Instead of a conventional hoopskirt and yards of undergarments, at the time of the Civil War, Walker chose slacks and a knee-length "jacket" (really a short dress), laying the foundation for her lifelong activism in the cause of women's dress reform. In the end, then, the wartime experiences of the proud and irascible Dr. Mary E. Walker (as she signed all of her letters, even those she wrote to family members) indicate that, although Victorian Americans were quite capable of temporarily adjusting their gender standards if necessity and expediency demanded it, they had little tolerance for women who rejected outright the basic premise that their wartime intrusions into the public sphere were nothing more than femininity redirected, and only "for the duration." True, Walker got her surgeon's contract, but her year and a half of service as an army surgeon yielded her far more public criticism than praise (unlike the laudatory comments of those who directly received or observed the benefits of her medical care). Furthermore, although Mary Walker is often celebrated today as the first and only woman to have received the Congressional Medal of Honor, the medal was "awarded" to her not as a way of honoring her wartime contributions but as a way of placating her at the war's end. Once federal government officials decided to refuse Walker's repeated requests to remain on staff as an army surgeon, they terminated her surgeon's contract, gave her the admittedly rather generous consolation prize of the Medal of Honor (which, along with the medals given to almost a thousand soldiers, was subsequently revoked), and sent her on her way.[3]

Walker, of course, was pleased to receive the Medal of Honor, but that does not alter the fact that she was frustrated and deeply saddened by her dismissal from military service. Still, war's end gave way to the predictable return of prewar notions about gender and proper behavior, and by far the majority of Northern middle-class women who had devoted their energies to nursing and sanitary aid returned to their homes and resumed, in essence at least, the lives they had left behind when they headed for the front. (Many undoubtedly expected, in vain, that Walker would do the same.) Meanwhile, individuals such as Frank Moore, Linus P. Brockett, and Mary C. Vaughan set about recording for posterity the contributions of Northern women to the Union war effort. Significantly, in their massive histories published just after the war, these authors omitted Mary Walker's story entirely, while enthusiastically and at great length telling the tales of heroic women who, like Sophronia Bucklin and Annie Wittenmyer, had dedicated themselves (and in some cases had given their very lives) to the support and care of the soldiers as nurses and aid activists.[4] According to these and many subsequent historians, only women like Bucklin and Wittenmyer had done *true* woman's work, after all—the sort of work that was worthy of commemoration—though they had undertaken that work in the unusual and unfamiliar public context of the Civil War.

Now, given the fact that historians such as Moore and Brockett and Vaughan spared not one page, not even a paragraph, for Walker (although the story of her bold and uncompromising advance on the male sphere of Civil War doctoring was by no means unknown to her contemporaries), at first glance, it seems somewhat surprising that these early writers devoted any space at all to the contributions of a number of seemingly even less "conventional" Civil War women than she. But they did, including such fondly remembered Union army "daughters of the regiment" as Annie Etheridge and Kady Brownell, as well as a number of women who were engaged in espionage, and even some who disguised themselves as men and were subsequently "found in the ranks, fighting as common soldiers," in Moore's rendering, either for love, or adventure, or because of a "hallucination that victory and deliverance would come to the war-burdened land only by the sacrifice of their lives."[5]

If the inclusion of such women initially seems strange in light of the complete exclusion of Mary Walker, it must be understood, however, that early histories of women's involvement in the Civil War functioned in a variety of different ways. In part, they served to enforce, implicitly and perhaps not even consciously, certain limits on the expectations Civil War women might have for postwar changes in their social status, and for their civil and political rights, on the basis of their wartime activities. And thus, although Moore and the others were pleased to celebrate a wide range of contributions women had made to the North's war effort, I would argue that Walker was somehow understood to be an "unfit" example, because although she gave generously of her time, energy, and skills to the Union cause, she simultaneously demanded something that was both impossible and unforgivable: to be considered a man's equal. And one suspects that at some profound level, observers of women's contributions to the Union's Civil War effort such as Moore and Brockett and Vaughan feared that offering official, public praise to even one fiercely independent woman doctor (divorced and in trousers, no less!) for her medical contributions on the battlefield could have long-lasting implications for the transformation of postwar gender relations, in a way that commemorating the donated labor and abundant good will of other women—even women soldiers who temporarily disguised themselves as men in order to do a "man's job"—would not.

I would argue that "properly" dressed (and behaved) women nurses and aid activists, or women traveling with the army as cooks, laundresses, and morale boosters, or women who transformed their purported talent for gossip into the standard tool of an effective spy—indeed, even women masquerading as men in order to enlist—simply failed to provoke the sorts of wartime and postwar gender anxieties that Mary Walker's story did. Sadly, the same sort of apprehension seems to have been shared even by prominent suffragists Susan B. Anthony and Elizabeth Cady Stanton, who, though drawn to unusual (but determinedly "feminine") characters, for example, Victoria Woodhull, actively distanced themselves after the war from Walker, despite her demonstrated commitment to the vote for women.[6] All this leads one to wonder whether things might not have gone just a bit more smoothly for Walker if she had made the decision early in her public life to assume a thoroughgoing male identity, as women who chose to enlist as soldiers did by necessity, at least for a period of time. Then, at least, she might have won the sympathy of those who thought they "understood" her, who thought that what she really wanted was to *be* a man, not just to enjoy the same rights and opportunities as one, though this was not, in fact, true in her case. As it turns out, Walker's very refusal to adopt such a tactic when she believed she should not have to earned her the enduring sympathy of very few.

Which brings me to the bumper sticker a student once gave me, that confidently declares "Well-behaved women rarely make history" but in fact offers at best a partial truth. For my own research suggests that while the best behaved women (i. e., those who conform most completely to the gender standards of their time and social position) may not often "make history," still a woman's chances of making it into the history books in a positive light, at least during the latter half of the nineteenth century, were generally higher if she behaved "pretty well" than if she behaved "badly," in the sense of pushing too hard against the relevant standards of her day. In this particular sense, one could argue that Dr. Mary Walker did indeed behave "badly," with the result that her story—not to mention her unique contributions to the history of Civil War medicine—was for many decades omitted from the record. As late as the 1960s, Walker's first biographer, Charles Snyder, could not quite bring himself to treat her with much respect. Snyder's book about her life, entitled *Dr. Mary Walker: The Little Lady in Pants*, denigrated many of his subject's accomplishments and challenged her on almost every front.[7]

In contrast with Walker, however, Civil War women aid activists and nurses for the most part behaved "well," or at least well enough—even the bolder ones, like Mary Ann "Mother" Bickerdyke, Clara Barton, and, one could add, Annie Wittenmyer, who herself ruffled quite a few feathers along the way, especially during the period when she was struggling to resist the long arm of the male-dominated United States Sanitary Commission and maintain her control over sanitary affairs in Iowa.[8] Such women's behavior was, overall, good enough to win them praise and honor, even though they were subsequently expected to return to more thoroughgoing "feminine" roles after Appomattox. It is also worth noting that, perhaps ironically, despite postwar yearnings for the return to a presumed prewar gender balance, such women's thoughtful concessions to (and careful manipulation of) Victorian notions of "appropriate" female behavior during the war ultimately had lasting progressive effects for American women. For not only did these women's stories fill the pages of both early and subsequent histories of women's Civil War service but also, more to the point, they ended up altering gender norms in the long term by paving the way for Northern middle-class American women after the war to expand the scope and social impact of the various humanitarian endeavors in which they had already been engaged during the antebellum period.

A good example of this is the 1874 creation of the first great national women's organization, the Women's Christian Temperance Union (WCTU; Annie Wittenmyer was its founding president). Moreover, right around the same time it was founded, less than a decade after Appomattox, the nation began to establish its first real nursing training schools, which honored women's nursing efforts during the war by actively recruiting women students. In contrast, although Syracuse Medical College and a few others had accepted a small number of women applicants in the mid–nineteenth century, and had granted them M.D. degrees (most notable among these was Dr. Elizabeth Blackwell), medical schools in the United States did not begin accepting women students in significant numbers for another hundred years.[9]

These are some of the insights on gender and the Civil War that Mary Walker's story provides, though certainly there is room for a good deal more research on the details and the meaning of her wartime experience, the cultural significance of her exclusion from the early historical record, and the suggestion that adopting a male identity might have spared her much of the criticism—even ridicule—she experienced throughout her life for pushing so hard against gender norms.

But what of another Mary, namely Mary Surratt, the middle-aged, Maryland-born widow and mother of three grown children who, in the spring of 1865, owned a boardinghouse on H Street in Washington, D.C., where John Wilkes Booth, her younger son John Surrat Jr., and several other passionate Southern nationalists met on occasion in to formulate a plan to kidnap the president of the United States and hold him hostage for the release of Confederate prisoners of war?[10] As it turns out, on April 17, 1865, three days after the initial failed abduction plot gave way to Abraham Lincoln's assassination, Mary Surratt and several other members of her household were arrested and confined in Washington's Old Capitol Prison. From there she was transported a few days later to what was called the Old Arsenal Penitentiary, where she was joined by other prime suspects in the assassination case, including David Herold, George Atzerodt, Lewis Thornton Powell, Samuel Mudd, Michael O'Laughlen, Samuel Arnold, and Edman Spangler. Mary Surratt's son John—also a key suspect, and the primary link between her and the assassination scheme—had left Washington for Canada some days before Booth shot the president.

About three weeks after her arrest, and after having been interrogated repeatedly by the authorities (to whom she adamantly denied any involvement in or knowledge of the murder plot), in early May 1865, Mary Surratt—along with Herold and the others—was put on trial before a panel of nine military commissioners Of her male codefendants, at least six were undeniably associated in one way or another, and to different degrees, with Booth and his evolving plot against Lincoln. Most, indeed (unlike Surratt herself), had already confessed some level of complicity, at least in the kidnapping plot. As for Booth himself, he never made it to trial, having been killed at the time of his capture on April 26, twelve days after the murder, by an eccentric soldier named Boston Corbett who was acting without orders.

In any case, over the course of the next six weeks or so, the commissioners—all of whom were Union army officers—as well as the chief prosecutor (Judge Advocate General Joseph Holt) and his assistants, the eight defendants, and their attorneys were joined by a shifting crowd of curious spectators for several hours each day (except Sundays) in the stifling heat of a courtroom specially designated and refitted for the purpose on the second floor of the Old Arsenal Penitentiary. Together they heard an abundance of testimony from literally hundreds of witnesses, some more reliable than others.

Numerous witnesses, of course, were called to speak on behalf of the accused, and witnesses summoned by Mary Surratt's lawyers diligently emphasized her Christian (Catholic) devotion, her kindness, honesty, and generosity and—not least of all—her good mothering, which presumably precluded any possibility that she could have committed a crime of this sort, or even permitted her fugitive son to do so. Witnesses for the prosecution, however, steadily—if not always intentionally or even accurately—wove Mary Surratt and the other defendants ever more tightly into a web of conspiracy that extended far beyond Booth and his plans first to abduct and ultimately to kill Abraham Lincoln. The purported conspiracy that Holt and his prosecutors thus "revealed" to the public and the officers of the court reached south to Richmond and north to Montreal. And at its center was none other than the Confederacy's president, Jefferson Davis. According to Holt's grand theory, Davis and his leading minions, along with a host of lower level operatives like Booth, had plotted together from the beginning of the war to destroy the Union by methods both fair (honest, honorable warfare between opposing groups of uniformed soldiers on the battlefield) and viciously foul (engaging in brutal, "irregular" warfare against civilian targets, depriving Union prisoners of war of the most basic means of survival, poisoning Northern water supplies, assassinating government leaders). Key to the prosecution's case, in other words, was the idea that the assassination of Lincoln was by no means an isolated act committed by Booth and his local coconspirators. Rather, Lincoln's murder was simply one particularly gruesome and tragically successful example of the Confederacy's odious agenda spanning the past four years. It was a theory that struck a deeply resonant chord among Northerners stunned by the timing of Lincoln's death, seemingly at the moment of the Confederacy's capitulation, and it is a theory that even today has committed adherents.[11]

Although this grand theory was the foundation upon which Holt organized his overall trial strategy, in the immediate moment his primary task was to prove Mary Surratt and the other seven prisoners at the bar guilty of conspiracy with Booth to kill the president. The trial continued into late June, during which time the national press kept its readers' attention focused on the drama as it unfolded within the Old Arsenal Penitentiary's steamy courtroom. Newspapers from Maine to Virginia, and points further south and west, reprinted each day's testimony and provided as well an ample supply of analysis, opinion, and invective, the one not always distinguishable from the other. Notably for a modern reader, reporters seem to have experienced a complete lack of restraint with regard to the terminology they employed in referring to the defendants: they clearly did not feel bound by the current convention of describing the accused—up to the point that a guilty verdict is finally handed down from the bench—as "allegedly" having committed an "alleged" crime. Instead, even before the trial began, the press freely identified Mary Surratt and her codefendants as, simply, the "conspirators" and the "assassins," the "murderers" who had plotted with Booth and, by extension, with Jefferson Davis.

Even more worthy of remark in the context of this discussion, however, is the fact that virtually from the moment of Mary Surratt's arrest on April 17—which was in fact the product of official suspicions aroused primarily by her son's involvement with Booth and the Confederate "underground" rather than her own—the press and the Northern public seemed eager to condemn her. As such, Mary Surratt appeared in press accounts not just as a boardinghouse-keeper who might be presumed to have known something about the evil designs being worked out under her roof but as an active participant in the planning process. Indeed, news stories routinely depicted Mary Surratt not just as a willing partner in the scheming but in fact as a leader, second only to Booth, and in some accounts, actually at the helm giving him orders. Hardly atypical was the *Philadelphia Inquirer*'s May 11 description of her, even before the trial had moved into the testimony phase, as a "female fiend incarnate" and the "'mater familias' of these criminals."[12]

Clearly many in the press as well as in the Northern public at large already felt as certain of Mary Surratt's guilt as they did of Booth's, and were utterly determined to exact deadly revenge against her. Significantly, these were attitudes that Chief Prosecutor Holt, his assistants in the courtroom, and most, if not all, of the nine military commissioners shared. And in the end, this widely held and inelastic presumption of Mary Surratt's guilt, both within the confines of the courtroom and without, combined with a good supply of circumstantial evidence against her to pose an obstacle that her defense attorneys found themselves hard pressed to overcome. On June 30, the commissioners made it official: they declared Mary Surratt and her seven male codefendants guilty. The court then sentenced four of the convicted (Mudd, O'Laughlen, Arnold, and Spangler) to prison; they condemned Mary Surratt and the others to death by hanging. On July 5, President Andrew Johnson approved all eight verdicts and sentences,[13] and by the early afternoon of July 7, Mary Surratt, David Herold, Lewis Powell, and George Atzerodt were dead, bringing to a close, the *Philadelphia Inquirer* commented, the "last scene of the terrible tragedy of the 14th of April."[14]

I first came upon Mary Surratt's story when I was doing research on women engaged in espionage and resistance activities during the war, including a large number of Confederate women offenders against the citizens, soldiers, and government of the United States, whom the Union identified as "troublemakers" but who nevertheless routinely escaped what might be considered appropriate punishment for their deeds. Even those who were arrested and convicted for their crimes still typically endured penalties that could hardly be deemed harsh, regardless of how the women themselves later described their sufferings at the hands of the federal government and its soldiers.[15] Indeed, despite the existence of military regulations that stipulated the same stern punishment for women traitors as for men, and despite General Benjamin F. Butler's famous, angry "Woman

Order" of May 1862, issued in response to troublesome female Confederates in Union-occupied New Orleans, in practice the worst penalty that countless "she-rebels" received during the war was a prison sentence of a few weeks or months. Far more often a symbolic slap on the wrist, such as banishment deeper into the Confederacy, was thought sufficient, though in practice it was rarely, if ever, effective. It seems that, despite abundant evidence to the contrary, federal and military officials were simply unable fully to come to terms with the concept of a woman (particularly a middle-class, white woman) being capable of instigating and carrying out actual—and, especially, violent—criminal activity. Officials struggled mightily, too, with the idea of holding a woman fully responsible for her misdeeds in the way they would hold a man responsible for his. At least when it came to white, middle-class women traitors against the nation, federal and military officials' responses continued to be shaped by a powerful combination of Victorian chivalry and the long legal tradition of men being held to account for "their" women's transgressions rather than the women themselves.[16]

Clearly the case of Mary Surratt developed in a very different manner, however. For whereas most Confederate "she-rebels" typically suffered relatively mildly (if at all) for their treasonable activities against the Union, Mary Surratt, in contrast was promptly arrested, jailed, tried, convicted, and hanged, making her the first woman executed by the federal government since its inception in 1789. Even if she was guilty of some degree of involvement in Booth's scheme—it was pretty clear she had not pulled the trigger—why was Mary Surratt's case handled so differently from those of other women who had actively supported the Confederate cause before her? Why was she made to suffer the ultimate punishment, especially when a good portion of the circumstantial evidence against her could be read as more contrived than compelling?

Perhaps it was predictable: after all, the gravity of the crime with which Mary Surratt was associated far exceeded that of any crime with which the federal government had previously charged a Confederate woman, such as carrying contraband materials and documents across military lines, engaging in acts of sabotage, conveying information gathered surreptitiously from the enemy to Confederate military officials, spitting on Union soldiers, or dumping chamber pots on their heads. Perhaps on this basis alone one can understand how the relative lenience most U.S. government and military officials had displayed throughout the war toward women rebels, and their uncertainty about how to punish them, could give way so dramatically to absolute intolerance and a desire for revenge, especially given how thoroughly Lincoln's assassination shattered and betrayed the relief and optimism most Northerners had enjoyed following the surrender of General Robert E. Lee at Appomattox on April 9, 1865. One could argue persuasively, too, that the fury generated by Lincoln's murder heaped upon Mary Surratt's head four full years of accumulated, but insufficiently expressed, anger many Northerners and government officials felt toward Confederate women and their active support for the Southern cause.[17]

But there is more to be learned about gender and the Civil War from Mary Surratt's story than this. For although federal officials and the Northern public at large seem to have been positively reckless with delight at having the opportunity, on this one occasion, to set gender conventions completely aside and march Mary Surratt directly to the gallows, for many the enthusiasm dissipated almost immediately once the deed was done. The desire for revenge against Confederate women that had gripped the hearts of so many Union officials and Northern citizens in the spring and early summer of 1865 lasted, in fact, only as long as it took to take that revenge, and then ambivalence and remorse set in with gusto.

This was not true for all who had wished to see Mary Surratt hanged, of course. Among those who remained unflinchingly committed to the view that Mary Surratt got what she deserved was Judge Advocate General Holt, whose more general resentment of the women who had thrown their weight behind the Confederate cause endured until his death in 1894. But there were many others who raised their voices in protest, or horror, almost from the instant the drops were knocked out from under the scaffolding that was hastily built for Surratt, Herold, Atzerodt, and Powell in the Old Arsenal Penitentiary courtyard.[18] Suddenly, gaps in the circumstantial evidence against Mary Surratt that had previously seemed insignificant became, in many people's eyes, proof of the government's own vengeful conspiracy against her, a poor, innocent Catholic woman who had loved her son and his wayward friends and could not possibly have been expected to derail their dastardly plot. Rumors (and in some cases, verifiable stories) about the government's refusal to deny Mary Surratt the most basic forms of last-minute mercy became the subject of enraged speculation: was it true that Mary Surratt's priest had been refused access to the Old Arsenal on the day before her execution? And how could Holt and President Johnson have deprived her weeping daughter, Anna, the privilege of a final hearing on her mother's behalf? Word in the popular press that several of the military commissioners had approved Mary Surratt's conviction and then argued for clemency in her case added strength to the wave of remorse that swelled in the immediate aftermath of her death at the hands of the federal government. It was as if Northerners in large numbers were sickened by their own bloodlust for a woman scapegoat, and at the same time simply could not believe that the government had actually enforced its own declared regulations with regard to female traitors. As early as July 18, less than two weeks after the execution, the *New Haven Register* joined in a growing chorus of popular sentiment to the effect that Mary Surratt's hanging was "nothing less than murder."[19]

What can we possibly learn about gender and the Civil War from Mary Surratt's story? Perhaps this: that as was the case with Dr. Mary Walker, Mary Surratt in her own way fundamentally challenged many Victorians' willingness to accept with equanimity the ways the Civil War threatened to alter common notions about gender. In the immediate aftermath of Lincoln's death, Mary Surratt came in many minds to represent the host of women who had gone too far—in this case, too far in opposition to the Union—in their Civil War work. And whereas tolerance for what would otherwise be considered "unladylike" behavior (by spies and saboteurs as much as by nurses and aid activists) had been the rule during the war, so long as certain conventions were observed, now that the war was over and Lincoln was dead, all bets were off. After the war, women like Mary Surratt and Mary Walker had to be put in their place, one way or another.[20]

In Mary Surratt's case, however, the effort to put her "in her place" had lethal effect. And as tempers began to cool and a swift and relatively painless reunion of the North and South increasingly came to seem desirable,[21] the notion that the poor widow and mother Mary Surratt had been dealt an unnecessarily cruel and vengeful blow gained more and more adherents. In the end, it seems, although Victorian Americans were flexible in their tolerance for changes in the gender system when necessity temporarily required them to be, they had their limits. Those limits, in turn, could be expressed in a variety of ways: by exclusion from the historical record, for example, by public ridicule, or by more tangible kinds of harsh personal punishment. Still, if Mary Surratt's story is any guide, the limits Victorian Americans sought to impose on women's pressure on the gender system were limited in their own way: many people, it appears, did not have the stomach for the government's killing of a woman who transgressed, or for the severe and irrevocable violation of gender traditions that irrevocable act represented, in and of itself.

NOTES

1. See, among numerous examples, Jeanie Attie, *Patriotic Toil: Northern Women and the American Civil War* (Ithaca, N.Y.: Cornell University Press, 1998); DeAnne Blanton and Lauren M. Cook, *They Fought Like Demons: Women Soldiers in the American Civil War* (Baton Rouge: Louisiana State University Press, 2002); Catherine Clinton, *Harriet Tubman: The Road to Freedom* (New York: Little, Brown, 2004); Catherine Clinton and Nina Silber, eds., *Divided Houses: Gender and the Civil War* (New York: Oxford University Press, 1992); Drew Gilpin Faust, *Mothers of Invention: Women of the Slaveholding South in the American Civil War* (Chapel Hill: University of North Carolina Press, 1996); Michael Fellman, *Inside War: The Guerrilla Conflict in Missouri during the American Civil War* (New York: Oxford University Press, 1989); Judith Giesberg, *Civil War Sisterhood: The U.S. Sanitary Commission and Women's Politics in Transition* (Boston: Northeastern University Press, 2000); Nell Irvin Painter, *Sojourner Truth: A Life, a Symbol* (New York: Norton, 1996); George C. Rable, *Civil Wars: Women and the Crisis of Southern Nationalism* (Urbana: University of Illinois Press, 1989); Jane E. Schultz, *Women at the Front: Hospital Workers in Civil War America* (Chapel Hill: University of North Carolina Press, 2004); Leslie Schwalm, *A Hard Fight for We: Women's Transition from Slavery to Freedom in South Carolina* (Urbana: University of Illinois Press, 1997); Lyde Cullen Sizer, *The Political Work of Northern Women Writers and the Civil War, 1850–1872* (Chapel Hill: University of North Carolina Press, 1993); Elizabeth R. Varon, *Southern Lady, Yankee Spy: The True Story of Elizabeth Van Lew, a Union Agent in the Heart of the Confederacy* (New York: Oxford University Press, 2003); Wendy Hammand Venet, *Neither Ballots nor Bullets: Women Abolitionists and the Civil War* (Charlottesville: University Press of Virginia, 1991); and LeeAnn Whites, *The Civil War as a Crisis in Gender: Augusta, Georgia, 1860–1890* (Athens: University of Georgia Press, 1995).

2. Elizabeth D. Leonard, *Yankee Women: Gender Battles in the Civil War* (New York: Norton, 1994).

3. For a fuller discussion of Mary Walker during and immediately following the war, see Leonard, *Yankee Women*, 105–157.

4. Linus P. Brockett and Mary C. Vaughan, *Women's Work in the Civil War: A Record of Heroism, Patriotism, and Patience* (Philadelphia: Zeigler, McCurdy, 1867); and Frank Moore, *Women of the War: Their Heroism and Self-Sacrifice* (Hartford, Conn.: S. S. Scranton, 1866).

5. Moore, *Women of the War*, 529. These daughters of the regiment and women soldiers, along with numerous other women who served the Union and Confederate armies in supporting roles as regimental nurses, cooks, laundresses, and sutlers, in the late 1990s joined women spies and resistance

activists as the focus of my second book, *All the Daring of the Soldier: Women of the Civil War Armies* (New York: Norton, 1999).

6. Leonard, *Yankee Women*, 165–166.

7. Charles McCool Snyder, *Dr. Mary Walker: The Little Lady in Pants* (New York: Vantage Press, 1962; reprint, New York: Arno Press, 1974).

8. Leonard, *Yankee Women*, 51–103.

9. Ibid., 191.

10. The story of Mary Surratt, the other key Lincoln assassination conspirators, and the ways the assassination and its aftermath shaped Reconstruction are the subject of my third book, *Lincoln's Avengers: Justice, Revenge, and Reunion after the Civil War* (New York: Norton, 2004).

11. See, for example, William A. Tidwell, James O. Hall, and David W. Gaddy, *Come Retribution: The Confederate Secret Service and the Assassination of Abraham Lincoln* (Jackson: University of Mississippi Press, 1989).

12. *Philadelphia Inquirer*, May 11, 1865. For a fuller discussion of Mary Surratt within the context of the trial, see Leonard, *Lincoln's Avengers*, 118–122. See also my essay on Mary Surratt in Joan Cashin, ed., *The War Was You and Me: Civilians in the American Civil War* (Princeton, N.J.: Princeton University Press, 2002), 286–309.

13. As it turns out, five of the commissioners signed a clemency plea for Mary Surratt, on the basis of her age and sex, which Johnson ignored. See Leonard, *Lincoln's Avengers*, 266, 270–273, 297–300.

14. *Philadelphia Inquirer*, July 8, 1865.

15. For the stories of such women—Belle Boyd, Rose O'Neal Greenhow, Eugenia Phillips, Antonia Ford, and others—see Leonard, *All the Daring of the Soldier*, 21–97. See also Curtis Carroll Davis, *Belle Boyd in Camp and Prison, Written by Herself* (New York: Thomas Yoseloff, 1968), and Rose Greenhow, *My Imprisonment, and the First Year of Abolition Rule at Washington* (London: Richard Bentley, 1863).

16. As mentioned earlier, Dr. Mary Walker spent most of the last months of the war as surgeon in charge at a Louisville, Kentucky, military prison for women. I think it is telling that federal officials put a woman for whom they had uneven amount of respect in charge of a group of women prisoners, who in this case were, incidentally, overwhelmingly from hardscrabble backgrounds. In my mind it demonstrates, at least to some extent, federal officials' failure to take seriously either the prisoners—who seem to have enjoyed a great deal of freedom during their incarceration (one observer described the place at the time of Walker's arrival as "no better than a brothel")—or Walker herself. (For an expanded treatment of this, see Leonard, *Yankee Women*, 142–149.)

17. See Leonard, "Mary Surratt and the Plot to Assassinate Abraham Lincoln," in Cashin, *War Was You and Me*, for a fuller discussion of this argument.

18. For a fuller discussion of the upsurge of popular sympathy for Mary Surratt following her execution, see Leonard, *Lincoln's Avengers*, 142–146.

19. *New Haven Register*, July 18, 1865.

20. It bears noting that Judge Advocate General Joseph Holt played a major role in the federal government's assault on both women after the war: he was chief prosecutor in the conspiracy trial that led to Mary Surratt's conviction and execution; and it was he who wrote the lengthy legal brief for President Johnson outlining the many reasons why Mary Walker should be dismissed from military service. (See Leonard, *Yankee Women*, 152–155.) Although Mary Surratt could not forgive Holt from beyond the grave, recent research I have done in Holt's papers surprisingly indicates that Holt and Mary Walker managed to develop a cordial and even friendly relationship toward the end of his life, periodically corresponding with one another and greeting each other warmly when they met on occasion in Washington. (See Mary E. Walker to Joseph Holt, August 16, August 20, August 27, September 28, and December 20, 1890, container 88, Joseph Holt Papers, Library of Congress.)

21. Some, like Holt and Secretary of War Edwin Stanton, clung to their fervor for justice against the Southern Confederacy, but more generally across the North (and particularly in light of Andrew Johnson's evolving policy toward the errant South in the summer and fall of 1865), a mood in favor of forgiveness began to take hold.

7

EMBATTLED MANHOOD
AND NEW ENGLAND WRITERS,
1860–1870

John Stauffer

Emerson captured the temper of the times. "War is a realist," he wrote in his journal in 1862; "[it] shatters everything flimsy & shifty, sets aside all false issues, & breaks through all that is not [as] real as itself." Antebellum notions of manhood, which for Emerson encompassed idealism, were among those "flimsy & shifty" things that, like the nation itself, would be transformed by war. For war, "like its own cannonade, comes crushing in through . . . walls that have stood fifty or sixty years as if they were solid." Emerson felt sure that manhood and the country would be revitalized: "War disorganizes, but it also organizes; it forces individuals & states to combine & act with larger views."[1]

While Emerson acknowledged a crisis of manhood during the war, Nathaniel Hawthorne suggested its relation to fiction. While futilely trying to complete three novels during the war, he summed up his plight in a letter to a friend in 1862:

> I feel as if the great convulsion were going to make an epoch
> in our literature as in everything else (if it does not annihilate
> all), and that when we emerge from the war-cloud, there will be
> another and better . . . class of writers than the one I belong to.

Hawthorne was, of course, referring to male writers. Before the war he had felt compelled to defend himself against "a d——d mob of scribbling women." But the mob of scribbling women had not silenced (or emas-culated) him as a writer in the way the war did. The war would spawn a new epoch, with a new class of male writers, and there would be no place for him or his writings in it. His chosen genre, the romance, would no longer be an appropriate mode for representing life: romantic thoughts could not "assume life" in the midst of a civil war; they were drowned out by the sound of the "cannon [and the] smell [of] gunpowder." The new epoch would require hard, firm, strong men who could face reality head-on.[2]

The Civil War writings of Emerson and Hawthorne point to a crisis of manhood among Northern white men from 1860 to 1870. This cri-sis coincided with a dwindling of literary output among New England men who had been prominent and prolific writers before the war. Dur-ing the same decade, however, women's writings burgeoned: "Woman has now taken to her pen . . . and is flourishing it with a vengeance," wrote a *Frank Leslie's Illustrated* journalist in 1863. In contrast to their New England male counterparts, Harriet Beecher Stowe and Louisa May Alcott were extremely productive during the 1860s, and jubilant about being treated as part of a *national* class of writers. The war inspired Alcott "to free my mind": "I've often longed to see a war," she added, "and now I have my wish. I long to be a man." With men under attack, women could fill their shoes.[3]

The Civil War created a battleground over the meaning of white man-hood that was still raging in 1869, when Stowe published "The True Story of Lady Byron's Life" in the *Atlantic Monthly*, followed by *Lady Byron Vindi-cated* in 1870. In these works Stowe attacked Lord Byron, accusing him of incest with his half-sister, among other sins, and championing her friend Lady Byron as one of Europe's great intellectuals and literary figures. The male backlash was virtually unprecedented in American literature. The-*Atlantic*, which catered primarily to literary men, lost fifteen thousand subscribers in the immediate wake of Stowe's article. Oliver Wendell Hol-mes likened the "Byron Whirlwind" to the worst windstorm to hit Boston in fifty years, which coincided with Stowe's *Atlantic* article and caused considerable damage. Throughout the country, newspaper and magazine editors excoriated Stowe. As her brother Henry Ward Beecher put it, "the papers are venomously excited." Lord Byron had long been viewed as a symbol of the male liberator and freedom fighter par excellence. For numerous male readers, to attack Byron, as Stowe did, was tantamount to attacking the mass of Northern men who had fought in the war to save their nation. In response they called her story "revolting and obscene";

they impugned her "disgusting" motives; they didn't "believe the story at all"; or they argued that Lady Byron was insane.[4]

Stowe's attack on Byron was perfectly timed, for it came during an era of embattled manhood: 620,000 men had lost their lives; women were battling for political and social rights; manhood increasingly required martial virtues, which seemed inconsistent with the profession of letters; and women's writings—both in quality and quantity—put men on the defensive. The male outrage against Stowe was part of the process of vindicating one's own manhood.[5]

The male backlash against Stowe also reflected changes in literature and culture. The backlash was "a symptom of the polarization of literature along gender lines" that became especially prominent after the war, according to Joan Hedrick. Stowe's attack on Lord Byron occurred at the end of a decade in which concepts of manhood were in a state of transition and would ultimately become codified in the 1880s by proponents of American realism and an embrace of masculine virtues. This transformation of culture, along lines of gender, began with the war; and it is highlighted in the work of prominent New England writers, from Stowe, Alcott, Emerson, and Hawthorne to John De Forest and Lydia Maria Child. As their writings reveal, a crisis of manhood during the war led to a backlash against feminine virtues and a masculinization of culture after the war.[6]

Emerson's attitudes toward women changed almost as soon as war broke out. Throughout the 1850s he defined himself as a woman's-rights man. At an 1855 woman's rights convention, he argued for female suffrage and thought his doctrine of self-reliance "would be sooner carried in the state if women voted." But, like many female suffragists, he also argued for equal but different spheres for women. Women "are more delicate than men," he told his female audience, "delicate as iodine to light,—and thus more impressionable." In their differences, women complemented men: "Man is the will, and Woman the sentiment." And "in this ship of humanity, Will is the rudder, and Sentiment the sail: when Woman affects to steer, the rudder is only a masked sail." Women powered society, Emerson was saying, but men held the reins.[7]

With the onset of war, Sentiment had lost its power, and men needed to find their own source of energy. Sentiment was associated with femininity, and shaped morality. But war required force, not sentiment and morality. Emerson said as much in his journal: "'Tis not so much that you are moral, as that you are genuine, sincere, frank, & bold," he wrote in September 1861. "I *do not approve* [of] those who give money, or give their voices for liberty, from long habit, & the feminine predominance of sentiment." He did approve of "the rough democrat who hates Garrison, but detests these Southern traitors." The moralists and the abolitionists "will go in the right way, but they are devoured by sentiments, like premature fruit ripened by the worm." Emerson had not abandoned morality. "The only incorruptible thing is morals," he wrote in May 1865. "But morals must be fresh & perfect every day," not rotting. The war demanded a new, masculine morality, one that placed less emphasis on Sentiment, and more on will and fate, which were for Emerson masculine concepts.[8]

Emerson advocated total war and the total "subjugation of the rebel country." In fact, he was distressed at General Grant's terms of surrender in April 1865, which he considered too lenient, and thought that Lee should be convicted of treason. He saw war as an opportunity to "stifle our prejudices" and achieve equality of condition for all *men*, including "an equal vote in the state" for blacks, "and a fair chance [for blacks] in society." While in the 1850s he had advocated equality and suffrage for women, now he sought them for black men. In 1869 he refused a request to write an article endorsing women's suffrage. Equality itself had become a masculine concept, and anyone refusing to fight for it, or compromise with it, was effeminate and morally corrupt. Bullets had replaced the ballot during the war, and would, Emerson hoped, lead to justice and the ballot for men alone. In such an environment, there was no place for feminine timidity. He said as much in August 1862, when he excoriated General McClellan for refusing to fight, concluding that "some strong-minded president of the Woman's Rights Convention" could as easily lead the Army of the Potomac. With men under siege, those who betrayed feminine traits, and refused to fight, were traitors to their sex and to the Union.[9]

War clarified one's masculine character. "It is no respecter of respectable persons," Emerson wrote. "Respectability" had become a mark of feminine shame. He liked Lincoln in part because of the president's coarseness and his lack of refined "taste," which betrayed manliness. Emerson wanted men to become "coarse, manly, [and] not polite." In 1864 he approvingly described the rise of "muscular Christianity," a phrase that emerged in the 1850s to attack the perceived effeminacy of the Church of England and gained currency in America with Thomas Wentworth Higginson. Muscular Christianity in America countered feminine morality and the feminine qualities of the Protestant church. Although the American version of muscular Christianity did not begin to flourish until the 1880s, and coincided with the rise of masculine literary realism, the Civil War sowed the seeds of both movements. And Emerson, always an astute observer of trends and cultural patterns, treated rugged masculinity as compost in a war that would yield a bountiful, new harvest.[10] War itself became for him an apt metaphor of life, in which homosocial relations took the form of a battlefield code. To survive the war, men needed to shed their sentiments and become hard, coarse, and robust, terms that Emerson used repeatedly to describe the culture of war.[11]

"Emerson is breathing slaughter like the rest of us," Hawthorne wrote a friend in late 1861. He was responding to Emerson's lecture "American Nationality," in which Emerson purportedly declared: "War destroys an effete aristocracy to supply its place with the men of the day; it removes all present foundations and land-marks to make room for newer and better." These newer and better foundations were for Emerson manly rather than effete and effeminate. But Hawthorne, too, considered the strength and vigor brought by the war to be a good thing. For a brief period, the war had a "beneficial effect" upon his spirits, which had been "flagging woefully before it broke out."[12]

But Hawthorne, unlike Emerson, understood the costs of war and of a newly masculinized society. Despite his periodic claims that the war was reviving his spirits, he wrote little and was often "mentally and physically languid," as he put it, until his death in 1864. He repeatedly suggested that the war would serve as a death blow to the romance as a commercially viable genre. "The war continues to interrupt my literary industry; and I am afraid it will be long before Romances are in request again, even if I could write one." The transformation of literature coincided with a makeover of culture and society: "You will live to see the Americans another people than they have hitherto been; and I truly regret that my youth was not cast in these days, instead of in a quiet time." Romance, which had fueled Hawthorne's writings, would be replaced by a martial culture. "Military notoriety will be the measure of all claims to civil distinction," he predicted in "Chiefly About War-Matters," which he published in the *Atlantic Monthly* in 1862: "One bullet-headed general will succeed another in the Presidential chair; and veterans will hold the offices at home and abroad, and sit in Congress and the State legislatures, and fill all the avenues of public life."[13]

A strain of cynicism ran through Hawthorne's writings during the war. Despite his claims that war could be regenerative, he longed for peace and a negotiated settlement. If there had to be a war, he wrote an English friend, old men rather than young should be required to fight and die, since old men "already had their natural share of worldly pleasures and life's enjoyments." He repeated these sentiments in "Chiefly About War-Matters." But he also advocated peace, even at the cost of letting the Confederacy remain a separate nation: "Amputation seems to me much the better plan, and all we ought to fight for is, the liberty of selecting the point where our diseased members shall be lopt off." The Confederate states were diseased, not because they were slave states but because they had seceded. Emancipation was not a war aim for Hawthorne; although he considered slavery a sin, he was relatively unconcerned about it as a matter of federal policy. In fact, throughout the war, he continually wondered "what we are fighting for, or what definite result can be expected." These questions fueled his desire for peace and his cynicism.[14]

John William De Forest was preoccupied with the role of manhood in American life. During the war he wrote two nonfiction narratives, one a record of his war experiences, the other an account of his duties as an officer during Reconstruction. In 1867 he published one of the great novels of the Civil War, *Miss Ravenel's Conversion: From Secession to Loyalty*, a loosely autobiographical book based on his wartime experiences. All three books focus on new meanings of manhood.[15]

For De Forest, the Civil War was as much a conflict over Northern and Southern masculinity as it was about slavery and political conflicts. *Miss Ravenel's Conversion* highlights the sectional differences of masculinity, personified by the two male protagonists. Edward Colburne is the moral hero of the tale; he is "one of nature's noblemen," but, unlike James Fenimore Cooper's Natty Bumppo, who enjoyed the same appellation, Colburne has been feminized by New England society. He comes from "New Boston," a thinly veiled description of New Haven and Yale College during the war era; and, like De Forest himself, Colburne is bookish, temperate, and sentimental—noble traits, but misunderstood in a culture of war.

Most of New Boston's men are sorry specimens of manhood. They are either mere boys, "blessed with immortal youth, or rather childhood"; or they are professors, "men of the world" who have a "pleasant cerulean tint." Both types of men are thin and pale, lack muscle, and seem incapable of fighting the battles of life. Colburne bucks this trend by keeping fit, physically as well as mentally. In college he had been one of the best gymnasts and oarsmen. And he maintained his physique on the "swinging-bars and racing shells," and so became one of the few manly men of the region. He fits the description of "primitive masculinity" articulated by Thomas Wentworth Higginson in a series of essays in the *Atlantic Monthly* beginning in the late 1850s, which stressed physical strength and fighting prowess through harnessing male instincts. When Higginson, in his 1861 essay "Gymnastics," instructs his readers, "Don't go to the Chess-Club; come with me to the Gymnasium," it is as though he wrote for Colburne, who heeded his advice.[16]

But Colburne's masculinity pales in comparison to that of Lieutenant-Colonel John Carter, a Virginian and West Point graduate who, though a Union officer, remains a Southerner in his essential character. Carter is very strong, very good-looking, and very athletic. His physique suggests the paragon of an Anglo-Saxon warrior: "A little above the middle height, he [had] a full chest, broad shoulders, and muscular arms, brown curling hair, and a monstrous brown mustache." Add to these a "straight" nose and "dimpled" chin, "brown eyes at once audacious and mirthful, and a dark rich complexion," and he "made one think" of "years of sunburnt adventure." Carter also enjoys a "gigantic" social status, for he is a direct descendent of an "old Colonial blue blood" family of Virginia.[17]

Colburne is socially as well as physically inferior to Carter. When he first meets Carter, he feels himself "shrink to grasshopper mediocrity." And when he volunteers, he serves as a captain in Colonel Carter's regiment. His men are "limited in number and not martial nor enthusiastic in character." Although Colburne is proud of his biceps, they pale in comparison to Carter's, who had built up his massive chest and arms through "sword exercises," as he tells Colburne.[18]

Colburne and Carter compete for more than bicep size; they vie for the affections of Lillie Ravenel, who was raised in New Orleans and moved to New Boston with her father in the wake of secession. Lillie remains loyal to her South and to Southern masculinity. Like "most Southern women," she liked men who liked to fight, and "respected a man the more for drawing the sword." Although Colburne falls in love with her, she prefers "more masculine men." She is "fascinated" by Carter's "masculine maturity," and becomes enamored with "his bronzed color, his monstrous mustache, his air of matured manhood." She liked him even more for being thirty-five years old rather than a mere boy. And she felt proud of Carter, in part because she feared him: she knew that he would lord over and "govern" her. Despite Colburne's "youth, modesty, and Puritan education," which promised "much beauty and usefulness," "there was something powerfully magnetic in" Carter's "ardent nature, which found its physical expression in that robust frame, that florid brunette complexion, those mighty mustachios, and [his] darkly burning eyes." Lillie marries him.[19]

But Southern masculinity, though powerful, is fraught with corruption, for Carter is also a drinker and philanderer. Although Lillie does not know the specific nature of his dark side when she marries him, she realizes that he is less than pure, which she initially found endearing: his wickedness was an aspect of his masculinity; and he was "simply more masculine than most men."[20]

The heart of the novel involves Lillie Ravenel's conversion. It is both political and gendered in nature: she converts to the Union cause, and to an appreciation of virtuous Northern manhood, specifically the kind Colburne displays. Her conversion begins in the South; she and her father return to New Orleans following the Union occupation of the city, where both Carter and Colburne are stationed. While there, Lillie begins to question the martial ideal of Southern manhood. When her husband is promoted to brigadier-general and ordered to return to the field of battle, Lillie, now pregnant, urges him not to fight. "My darling, you want to make a woman of me," Carter responds. When Lillie discovers her husband's infidelity, she flees to New Boston. Her preference for Northern society occurs in the immediate wake of her realization that Southern manhood is deeply flawed. "I like it [the North] so much better," she says after returning to New Boston. As the narrator summarizes, "Providence" guides Lillie's conversion from Southern to Northern society and her awakening to virtuous manhood, as well as the overthrow of slavery and the North's victory over the South. At the novel's end, Lillie marries Colburne, and together they raise their son—from her marriage to Carter—to become a virtuous and brave Northerner.

Colburne has also been transformed by the war. He has become more combative and ruthless toward his enemies, which is one reason why Lillie is now attracted to him. "The old innocence of the peaceable New England farmer and mechanic had disappeared from these war-seared visages and had been succeeded by an expression of hardened combativeness, not a little brutal." By the war's (and the novel's) end, Colburne has acquired "the patience of a soldier, and a soldier's fortitude under discouragement. He is a better and stronger man for having fought three years, out-facing death and suffering. Like the nation, he has developed and learned his powers." He is part of a new breed of "citizen-soldier," able to brave the "flame of battle for his country" and "earn his own living."[21]

Carter, meanwhile, dies a martyr for his lost cause of Southern manhood. He attempts to reconcile his sin of infidelity by fighting courageously, and seeks renewed love with Lillie. But his corrupt manhood remains unchanged. The reconciliation of Southern manhood with Northern virtue is, in De Forest's rendering, impossible.

Although De Forest does not develop the theme, he links Southern manhood with slaveholding, and suggests that reconciliation between North and South is impossible unless the South changes its attitudes toward blacks and manhood. Colburne's *perceived* femininity resembles that of blacks: both lack the "physical courage" of Southern white men, but are in moral courage "sublime." Colburne recognizes that the *perception* of femininity can mask true valor. He and his black comrades fight extremely well; and he comes to view blacks not only as crucial to the Union cause but as fellow citizens. Lillie ultimately converts to Colburne's beliefs about slavery and blacks; she champions black freedom and citizenship, which Carter can never do. The message of the novel seems clear: reconciliation between North and South depends upon a conversion to virtuous Northern manhood, which also leads to an embrace of black freedom and citizenship. Southern men must follow Lillie's lead: they must relinquish their corrupt Southern manhood and become faithful husbands; in so doing, they will learn how to treat blacks as citizens, capable of self-government, and of fighting the battles of life.[22]

In Emerson, Hawthorne, and De Forest, then, we see three different variants of a new conception of manhood. For Emerson, the war highlighted the need for martial virtues and an abandonment of sentiment. In the wake of war, morality itself has been masculinized. Hawthorne is more ambivalent. Although he, like Emerson, considers the masculinization of culture to be superior to sentimentalism and romance, he feels that this new form of manhood will lead not to utopia or the good life. Instead it will lead to "bullet-headed" generals, untold sacrifices, and a far greater proclivity for bloodshed. De Forest distinguishes between Northern and Southern manhood; while the former is superior, it is not without its genteel, feminine qualities. But, fortunately, the war accelerates Northern combativeness and martial vigor, resulting in a healthier mixture of physical strength and moral fortitude coupled with virtue that constitutes the essential ingredients of the redeemed nation's manhood.

As a writer and independent woman, Louisa May Alcott came of age with the Civil War. *Hospital Sketches* (1863) launched her career, and *Little Women* (1868) immortalized her. Both books are war novels, the one a fictionalized account of her experience as a nurse during the war, the other a story of how women live at the homefront when the men are away fighting. What is especially striking about both books is the degree to which Alcott's female protagonists become, in effect, men. Perhaps more than any other writer of the era, Alcott understood the crisis of manhood caused by the war; and she transforms herself and her leading characters into masculine women for profit, opportunity, and the good of society. Whereas Lillie Ravenel learns to love and appreciate Northern manhood, Alcott and her characters become like men in order to vanquish their enemies, redeem their nation, and assert their independence.

From the outset of *Hospital Sketches*, Alcott masculinizes her first-person persona, Nurse Periwinkle, and the other women who serve the war effort. When she decides to become a nurse, she says that she has "enlisted," refers to other nurses as "soldiers," and speaks of them coming home on "furlough." She describes the woman who helped her find a position as "Miss General." "I turned military at once," she acknowledges,

> called my dinner my rations, saluted all new comers, and ordered a dress parade that very afternoon. Having reviewed every rag I possessed, I detailed some for picket duty while airing over the fence; some to the sanitary influences of the wash-tub; others to mount guard in the trunk; while the weak and wounded went to the Work-basket Hospital, to be made ready for active service again.

It is the language and outlook of a soldier training for war.[23]

Although Nurse Periwinkle is not allowed to fight in the same way men do, she is nevertheless as capable of martial vigor, courage, and sacrifice as men. "If I never come back," she tells her family stoically, "make a bonfire of" my things. While traveling to the village depot, she revises a line from a popular soldier's song "The Girl I Left Behind" by singing: "The town I left behind." The town has become the equivalent of a female lover. And although she cries as she leaves for the front, she does so in private, and maintains that "the soldier who cries when his mother says 'Good bye' is the boy to fight best and die bravest when the time comes, or go back to her better than he went." There is a levity and humor to Alcott's masculine language of war, which cloaks her seriousness about martial women: she is only half in jest when she says that she wishes she were a man. She really does want to fight and believes herself as capable in war as men.[24]

Alcott's war is as much against incompetent men as it is against slavery and the South. In ways that resemble De Forest's Colburne, Nurse Periwinkle plays the role of a virtuous man to defeat a more corrupt form of manhood. The men with whom she comes in contact are "fat" and "easy" or "loitering" and "lounging," "penned in a row like colts at a Cattle Show." She uses the term "boy" with "scornful emphasis to denigrate young men who shirk their duties." And she identifies herself with the virtuous and noble male hero, Christian, of *Pilgrim's Progress*.

Like Emerson, Alcott acknowledges that sentimentality can be dangerous, even fatal, in war. Although Nurse Periwinkle is kind and affectionate to her friends, she is unforgiving to her enemies, and quickly ascertains whether or not someone is friend or foe. In the process, her own manly character is clarified. She dispenses with the Christian and sentimental doctrines of forgiving one's enemies and of avoiding profanity. When confronted with a wounded Southern soldier, she "resolved to put soap in his eyes, rub his nose the wrong way, and excoriate his cuticle generally" if she were forced to wash him. Like hardened soldiers, Nurse Periwinkle has a "taste for ghastliness," and concludes that strong alcohol is better medicine for the wounded than the Chaplain's homilies. These are not the pieties of "true womanhood," which before the war had emphasized moral and spiritual purity.[25]

Jo March, the hero of *Little Women*, forsakes her femininity and becomes the breadwinner of her family. In this she resembles Nurse Periwinkle and Alcott herself. Jo is a tomboy and wants to fight in the war. She also loves books, but not as a way to retreat into a domestic sphere; rather, her bookishness is a source of empowerment and a means to write and earn a living. Jo is Alcott's alter ego: while Jo sells her hair for money, Alcott has her "head shaved," as she notes in her journal. Indeed Alcott refers to herself as "Jo" in her journal. And after reading the proofs of *Little Women* (part 1), she notes: "It reads better than I expected. Not a bit sensational, but simple and true, for we really lived most of it."[26]

In shedding her femininity, Jo becomes a productive member of her family and of society. She sells her hair for twenty-five dollars, and thus sells part of herself to support her family, much as she sells another part of herself—her intellectual capital through writing—to add value to the family. Jo and Alcott both become intellectuals through the process of shedding the physical signs of femininity. After cutting her hair, Jo becomes boyish and brainy, the man of the family; she acquires a public voice and thus cultural power, and eagerly participates in the wartime economy. Alcott accomplishes much the same thing in the process of writing and publishing *Little Women*. Jo (and Alcott) view their masculinization as the means to achieve gender equality. Meg lacks Jo's stoicism and martial discipline, and easily succumbs to sentimentality. Jo hates Meg's femininity and her sentimental desire to marry: "She's got such a soft heart," Jo says distressingly of Meg: "it will melt like butter in the sun if any one looks sentimentally at her." Jo sees Meg as heading down the road, if not to hell, then to marriage. She wants to marry Meg herself, to keep "her safe in the family" and protect her from the corrupt influences of sentimentality. Alcott and her protagonists (especially Nurse Periwinkle and Jo) become, like De Forest, citizen-soldiers of sorts, able to face the "flame of battle" for their "country" and "earn [their] own living."[27]

Alcott writes within the tradition of the sentimental novel, but scorns feminine sentimentality. This is why Jo's marriage to the German professor Bhaer in the second part of *Little Women* (1869) seems so shocking, a cheapening of Jo's independence and tenacity. Laurie would have been a better match. He is, in everything from name to disposition, more of a girl than Jo; and because of such gender-bending, theirs is one of the few male-female friendships of equals in Civil War culture. Alcott seems aware of the problems of marriage. Immediately after beginning the sequel, she wrote in her journal: "I won't marry Jo to Laurie to please any one." But when Jo marries Professor Bhaer, she becomes feminized and relinquishes her persona as an artist and entrepreneur. Fortunately, Alcott did not follow suit.[28]

Alcott suggests that with men under attack, women should become soldiers on the homefront. Part of her pathbreaking representations of soldier-women stemmed from her age. Almost thirty years younger than Emerson and Hawthorne, Alcott was part of the first generation of realist writers—including Rebecca Harding Davis, Mark Twain, Bret Harte, William Dean Howells, and Albion Tourgée—who were born in the 1830s and came of age as writers with secession and war. They were still comparatively young during the war, and their identities—as men, women, and writers—were still developing and in a state of flux. It was thus easier for Alcott (and, to a lesser extent, her peers) to refashion her understanding of masculinity and create heroic, masculine female characters. While Emerson and Hawthorne advocated a martial ideal for men, Alcott led the way in transforming the representations and roles of women.[29]

Harriet Beecher Stowe sometimes cast her female protagonists as men, though much less frequently than did Alcott. In "A True Story of Lady Byron's Life," she likens Lady Byron to a man. "Lady Byron, though slight and almost infantine in her bodily presence, had the soul not only of an angelic woman but of a strong, reasoning man." Stowe's Lady Byron has the mind and soul of a man, and through strength of character and intellect she "formed the personal acquaintance of many of the very first minds of England." In vindicating Lady Byron and condemning Lord Byron, Stowe resembles Alcott, attacking masculine culture by casting her heroine as male.[30]

Stowe's rendering of a female protagonist as a "strong, reasoning man" was comparatively rare, however. Like her contemporary Lydia Maria Child, she typically embraced the martial ideal only for men, and only as a means to vanquish slavery. Both women were contemporaries of Emerson and Hawthorne (Child was fifty-nine years old in 1861, Stowe fifty), and thus had more difficulty transcending the sentimental and feminine ideals under which they had lived for most of their lives. As a result, as masculinity became embattled, Stowe and Child increased their attack against it as a way to achieve freedom for women and blacks—both of whom were widely seen as feminized and subordinate to the abilities of men.[31]

Child attacks manhood in her most popular work during the war, *Correspondence between Lydia Maria Child and Gov. Wise and Mrs. Mason, of Virginia*. The book collected her correspondence with Governor Henry Wise of Virginia and Mrs. Margaretta Mason, the wife of Virginia senator James Mason, following John Brown's capture at Harpers Ferry. Appearing in 1860, after most of their correspondence had circulated in newspapers, it sold three hundred thousand copies, "a record figure," and had enormous influence. While Child opposed Brown's use of violence, in one sense her book legitimated Brown's militant actions by helping to mobilize the North for war against slavery.[32]

At the same time, however, Child denigrates Southern masculinity while also preferencing femininity over martial manhood in the North. She condemns the "drunken master, overseer, or patrol" for going "into the negro cabins, and commit[ting] what outrages he pleases, with perfect impunity." She makes it clear that she cannot "sympathize" with Brown's methods of "murder, robbery, and treason" to "advance the cause of freedom." But she considers him "brave" and in need of female nurturing: "He needs a mother or sister to dress his wounds, and speak soothingly to him." In a letter to Mrs. Mason, Child summarizes her views of Brown, noting that his motives would be "righteously judged by Him who knoweth the secrets of all hearts," adding: "Men [John Brown in particular], however great they may be, are of small consequence in comparison with principles; and the principle for which John Brown died is the question at issue between us." For Child, opposition to slavery (the "principle") is more important than John Brown (the man). It is an ironic statement, for it defies the abolitionist belief that all humans are sacred and more important than principle or positive law. By affirming principles over men (specifically John Brown), Child downplays the role of Northern masculinity as a means to end slavery. Indeed, the book emerged out of her desire to go to Virginia to nurse Brown and infuse him with her feminine virtues.[33]

It is also ironic that Child invokes such moral certainty in her quest to create order out of the chaos of a nation divided by slavery. As Louis Menand has noted, "moral certainty of any kind can lead" more easily to chaos and bloodshed than to order. When the war came, Child believed that the chaos and bloodshed would lead to a new dispensation, a heaven on earth. She refused to compromise with the sin of slavery, which reflected her embrace of principles over men, and viewed slavery itself as a state of war, a horrific form of social chaos that needed rectifying. "Much as I deprecate civil war," she wrote in February 1861, "I deliberately say even *that* is better than compromises of principle." In the wake of the Revolutionary War, reformers were willing to compromise with their principles in order to achieve order. After the Civil War, and culminating with the emergence of pragmatism, reformers increasingly concluded that "moral certainty" was something they "should sacrifice a little of in exchange for order." As a result, the price of reform in the United States, from the 1880s until at least World War I, was "the removal of the issue of race from the table." But Child refused to sacrifice her sense of moral certainty. "I grow more radical" as I "grow older," she wrote in 1866. Her reputation declined after the war.[34]

Moral certainty was also gendered: it meant an adherence to principle, and tended toward emasculation. By contrast, the social order urged by pragmatists was masculine, as highlighted by William James in "The Moral Equivalent of War" (1910), which applied martial virtues to society. For James, "the horrors" of war made life fascinating: "War is the *strong* life; it is life *in extremis*. . . . Militarism is the great preserver of our ideals of hardihood, and human life with no use for hardihood would be contemptible." James, the great proponent of pragmatism, sought a "moral equivalent of war" without the concomitant bloodshed. He extended Emerson's notion that morality should be masculine; for him, it should affirm "intrepidity," "discipline," and "hardihood" as a way to test one's inner strength. "Martial virtues must be the enduring cement" of morality.[35]

The rise of pragmatism, beginning in the 1880s, coincided with a new masculinist ethos and the rise of literary realism, which similarly embraced a masculinization of culture. But affirmations of a martial ideal and the attack on sentimentalism were already in place in 1870, especially by a new generation of writers. While Emerson and Hawthorne understood that the Civil War would create a new, realistic, and masculine form of representation, De Forest partly attributed the war to a crisis of gender, while also lauding its effect on Northern men. Alcott, whose reputation, unlike Stowe's and Child's, did not decline in the post-bellum era, saw the war as a means to reconcile men and women, North and South, by creating manly women and womanly men. She attacked the corrupt influences of masculinity, especially men's efforts to control, govern, and exploit women, by creating masculine women. In a sense, she borrowed from her war experiences and affirmed a battlefield code, becoming like the enemy in order to subdue him. Long before James's famous essay, Alcott articulated a moral equivalent of war for women. But it was a code that her older comrades, Stowe and Child, could not conform to.[36]

NOTES

1. *The Journals and Miscellaneous Notebooks of Ralph Waldo Emerson*, vol. 15, 1860–1866, edited by Linda Allardt and David W. Hill (Cambridge: Harvard University Press, 1982), 299, 353, reprinted in Louis P. Masur, ed., *The Real War Will Never Get in the Books: Selections from Writers during the Civil War* (New York: Oxford University Press, 1993), 134, 138. Masur's *Real War* is a superb collection of writings, which led me to this essay. On Emerson's notions of manhood, see David Leverenz, *Manhood and the American Renaissance* (Ithaca, N.Y.: Cornell University Press, 1989), 1–71, 192. Leverenz argues that the ideology of manhood among American Renaissance writers was "a compensatory response to fears of humiliation." For Emerson, those fears related to his antebellum emphasis on idealism.

2. Nathaniel Hawthorne to Horatio Bridge, February 13, 1862; Hawthorne to Francis Bennoch, October 12, 1862, in *The Centenary Edition of the Works of Nathaniel Hawthorne*, vol. 18,*The Letters, 1857–1864*, edited by Thomas Woodson, L. Neal Smith, and Norman Holmes Pearson (Columbus: Ohio State University Press, 1987), 427, 501, reprinted in Masur, *Real War*, 161, 177. On Hawthorne and "scribbling women," see Michael Davitt Bell, "Conditions of Literary Vocation," in *The Cambridge History of American Literature*, vol. 2, *1820–1865*, edited by Sacvan Bercovitch (Cambridge: Cambridge University Press, 1995), 89.

3. *Frank Leslie's Illustrated*, October 10, 1863, quoted in Elizabeth Young, *Disarming the Nation: Women's Writing and the American Civil War* (Chicago: University of Chicago Press, 1999), 7; Louisa May Alcott to Alfred Whitman, May 19, 1861, in *The Selected Letters of Louisa May Alcott*, edited by Joel Myerson and Daniel Shealy (Boston: Little, Brown, 1987), 65, reprinted in Masur, *Real War*, 19.

4. Harriet Beecher Stowe, "The True Story of Lady Byron's Life," *Atlantic Monthly*, September 1869, pp. 295–313; Stowe, *Lady Byron Vindicated: A History of the Byron Controversy, From Its Beginning in 1816 to the Present Time* (London: Sampson Low, Son, and Marston, 1870); Frank Lentricchia, Jr., "Harriet Beecher Stowe and the Byron Whirland," *Bulletin of the New York Public Library* 70, 4 (April 1966): 218–228, quotations from 228, 221, 222; Joan D. Hedrick, *Harriet Beecher Stowe: A Life* (New York: Oxford University Press, 1994), 353–370, quotations from 363–365; Mark A. DeWolfe Howe, *The Atlantic Monthly and Its Makers* (Boston: Atlantic Monthly Press, 1919), 49–50; Paul Baender, "Mark Twain and the Byron Scandal," *American Literature*, 30, 4 (January 1959): 467–485. On Byron's popularity in America as a male liberator and freedom-fighter, see William Ellery Leonard, *Byron and Byronism in America* (1905; republished, New York: Gordian Press, 1965); Andrew Elfenbein, *Byron and the Victorians* (New York: Cambridge University Press, 1995), 3–89; Northrup Frye, *Fables of Identity: Studies in Poetic Mythology* (New York: Harcourt Brace, 1963), 188–189; John Stauffer, *The Black Hearts of Men: Radical Abolitionists and the Transformation of Race* (Cambridge, Mass.: Harvard University Press, 2002), 60–62.

5. Hedrick, *Harriet Beecher Stowe*, 353–370; Lentricchia, "Harriet Beecher Stowe and the Byron Whirland," 218–228.

6. Ibid., 370. My choice of dramatis personae and their writings stems from their influence in New England from 1860 to 1870. See Lawrence Buell, *New England Literary Culture: From Revolution through Renaissance* (Cambridge: Cambridge University Press, 1986); and Alice Fahs, *The Imagined Civil War: Popular Literature of the North and South, 1861–1865* (Chapel Hill: University of North Carolina Press, 2001).

In developing the essay, I have relied more generally on the following: Catherine Clinton and Nina Silber, eds., *Divided Houses: Gender and the Civil War* (New York: Oxford University Press, 1992); Nina Silber, *The Romance of Reunion: Northerners and the South, 1865–1900* (Chapel Hill: University of North Carolina Press, 1993); Silber, *Daughters of the Union: Northern Women Fight the Civil War* (Cambridge: Harvard University Press, 2005); Catherine Clinton, *The Other Civil War: American Women in the Nineteenth Century* (New York: Hill and Wang, 1984), 72–97; Shirley Samuels, *Facing America: Iconography and the Civil War* (New York: Oxford University Press, 2004); Lyde Cullen Sizer, *The Political Work of Northern Women Writers and the Civil War, 1850–1872* (Chapel Hill: University of North Carolina Press, 2000); Gerald F. Linderman, *Embattled Courage: The Experience of Combat in the American Civil War* (New York: Free Press, 1987); Thomas H. O'Connor, *Civil War Boston: Home Front and Battlefield* (Boston: Northeastern University Press, 1997); Elizabeth Young, *Disarming the Nation: Women's Writing and the American*

Civil War (Chicago: University of Chicago Press, 1999); Elizabeth D. Leonard, *Yankee Women: Gender Battles in the Civil War* (New York: Norton, 1994); Kim Townsend, *Manhood at Harvard: William James and Others* (New York: Norton, 1996); Fahs, *Imagined Civil War.*

7. Ralph Waldo Emerson, "Woman: A Lecture," in *The Works of Ralph Waldo Emerson*, edited by James Elliot Cabot, vol. 11, *Miscellanies* (Boston: Houghton Mifflin, 1878), 337–339. See also Lawrence Buell, *Emerson* (Cambridge, Mass.: Harvard University Press, 2003), 270–287; Richard F. Teichgraeber III, "'Our National Glory': Emerson in American Culture, 1865–1882," and David S. Reynolds, "'A Chaos-Deep Soil': Emerson Thoreau, and Popular Literature," in *Transient and Permanent: The Transcendentalist Movement and Its Contexts*, edited by Charles Capper and Conrad Edick Wright (Boston: Massachusetts Historical Society, 1999); Len Gougeon, *Virtue's Hero: Emerson, Antislavery, and Reform* (Athens: University of Georgia Press, 1990), 250–336.

8. Joel Porte, ed., *Emerson in His Journals* (Cambridge, Mass.: Harvard University Press, 1982), 496, 527. Emerson acknowledged the fatefulness of war: "Everything must perish except that which must live. Well, this is the task before us, to accept the benefit of the War" (506). Emerson had become an abolitionist in the 1850s, and championed John Brown's raid on Harpers Ferry, borrowing the words of his friend Mattie Griffith to say that Brown would make the gallows like the cross. See John Stauffer, *The Black Hearts of Men: Radical Abolitionists and the Transformation of Race* (Cambridge, Mass.: Harvard University Press, 2002), 37.

9. Porte, *Emerson in His Journals*, 507, 504; Hedrick, *Harriet Beecher Stowe*, 361, 465.

10. Ibid., 506, 511, 515; Clifford Putney, *Muscular Christianity: Manhood and Sports in Protestant America, 1880–1920* (Cambridge, Mass.: Harvard University Press, 2001), 1–3, 22–25.

11. In many respects, Emerson's writings during the war anticipated William James's famous essay at the end of the century, "The Moral Equivalent of War." See James, "The Moral Equivalent of War" (1910), in *William James: The Essential Writings*, edited by Bruce Wilshire (Albany: State University of New York Press, 1984), 349–361.

12. *Works of Nathaniel Hawthorne*, vol. 18, 422–423.

13. Ibid., *Letters, 1857–1864*, 427, 379, 421; Hawthorne, "Chiefly about War-Matters," *Atlantic Monthly*, July 1862, p. 45.

14. *Works of Nathaniel Hawthorne*, vol. 18, *Letters, 1857–1864*, 381, 388, 412, 420–421, 455, 461; Hawthorne, "Chiefly about War-Matters," 51.

15. On De Forest, see James H. Croushore, ed., *John William De Forest, A Volunteer's Adventures: A Union Captain's Record of the Civil War* (New Haven: Yale University Press, 1946); De Forest, *A Union Officer in Reconstruction,*

edited by James H. Croushore and David Morris Potter (Baton Rouge: Louisiana State University Press, 1997); James A. Hijiya, *J. W. De Forest and the Rise of American Gentility* (Hanover, N.H.: University Press of New England, 1988); James F. Light, *John William De Forest* (New York: Twayne, 1965); John Limon, *Writing after War: American War Fiction from Realism to Postmodernism* (New York: Oxford University Press, 1994), 59–65, 79–83; Daniel Aaron, *The Unwritten War: American Writers and the Civil War* (New York: Knopf, 1973), 164–180; Edmund Wilson, *Patriotic Gore: Studies in the Literature of the American Civil War* (1962; reprint, New York: Norton, 1994), 669–742; and Thomas H. Fick, "Genre Wars and the Rhetoric of Manhood in Miss Ravenel's Conversion from Secession to Loyalty," *Nineteenth Century Literature* 46 (March 1992): 473–494. *Miss Ravenel's Conversion* did not sell well when it was first published, owing primarily to the fact that Americans were not yet ready to read about the carnage of war. On this point, see Alan Trachtenberg, *Reading American Photographs: Images as History, Mathew Brady to Walker Evans* (New York: Hill and Wang, 1989), 71–118; Fahs, *Imagined Civil War*, 287–310.

16. John William De Forest, *Miss Ravenel's Conversion: From Secession to Loyalty* (1867; reprint, New York: Holt, Rinehart and Winston, 1962), 19, 34–35, 38, 199; Thomas Wentworth Higginson, "Gymnastics," *Atlantic Monthly*, March 1861, p. 133; E. Anthony Rotundo, *American Manhood: Transformations in Masculinity from the Revolution to the Modern Era* (New York: Basic Books, 1993), 222–239, quotation from 223; Leverenz, *Manhood and the American Renaissance*, 4, 73, 98–100, 108–134.

17. De Forest, *Miss Ravenel's Conversion*, 20, 22, 28, 84.

18. Ibid.

19. Ibid., 19, 26, 80, 193, 223.

20. Ibid., 194.

21. Ibid., 194, 257, 397–398, 462, 484–485.

22. Ibid., 290.

23. Louisa May Alcott, *Hospital Sketches*, edited by Alice Fahs (Boston: Bedford, 2004), 53–56. I have benefited immensely from Fahs's introduction and notes to this edition. Alcott uses the same masculine, martial tone in her journals: "I was ready, and when my commander said "march!" I marched. Packed my trunk, and reported in B[oston] that same evening." See *The Journals of Louisa May Alcott*, eds. Joel Myerson and Daniel Shealy, associate editor, Madeleine B. Stern (Boston: Little, Brown, 1989), 110. On Alcott, see also Young, *Disarming the Nation*, 69–108; Martha Saxton, *Louisa May Alcott: A Modern Biography* (1977; reprint, New York: Noonday Press, 1995), 239–268; Judith Fetterley, "Little Women: Alcott's Civil War," *Feminist Studies* 5 (1979): 369–383; Karen Halttunen, "The Domestic Drama of Louisa May Alcott," *Feminist Studies* 10 (summer 1984): 233–254.

24. Alcott, *Hospital Sketches*, 53–56. Alcott's use of humor resembles that of Mark Twain, who "wanted to belong, but . . . also wanted to laugh from the outside." Twain and Alcott used humor to make their scathing social critiques palatable to large audiences. See Justin Kaplan, *Mr. Clemens and Mark Twain: A Biography* (New York: Simon and Schuster, 1966), 17.

25. Alcott, *Hospital Sketches*, 64, 69, 73, 74.

26. *Journals of Louisa May Alcott*, op. cit., 166; *The Selected Letters of Louisa May Alcott,* edited by Joel Myerson and Daniel Shealy (Boston: Little, Brown, 1987), 91–92.

27. Alcott, *Little Women* (1868; reprint, New York: Penguin Books, 1989), 203.

28. *Journals of Louisa May Alcott*, op. cit., 167.

29. Alcott was born in 1832, Rebecca Harding Davis in 1831, Mark Twain in 1835, Bret Harte in 1836, William Dean Howells in 1837, and Albion Tourgée in 1838.

On these first-generation realists, see Richard H. Brodhead, *Cultures of Letters: Scenes of Reading and Writing in Nineteenth-Century America* (Chicago: University of Chicago Press, 1993), 69–106; Edwin H. Cady, *The Road to Realism: The Early Years, 1837–1885, of William Dean Howells* (Syracuse, N.Y.: Syracuse University Press, 1956); Paul Abeln, *William Dean Howells and the Ends of Realism* (London: Routledge, 2005); Margaret Duckett, *Mark Twain and Bret Harte* (Norman: University of Oklahoma Press, 1964); Gary Scharnhorst, *Bret Harte* (New York: Twayne, 1992); Jean Pfaelzer, *Parlor Radical: Rebecca Harding Davis and the Origins of American Social Realism* (Pittsburgh: University of Pittsburgh Press, 1996); Sharon M. Harris, *Rebecca Harding Davis and American Realism* (Philadelphia: University of Philadelphia Press, 1991); Hedrick, *Harriet Beecher Stowe*, 346, 350–351; Otto H. Olsen, *Carpetbagger's Crusade: The Life of Albion Winegar Tourgée* (Baltimore: Johns Hopkins University Press, 1965). On masculinity in realism, see Michael Davitt Bell, *The Problem of American Realism: Studies in the Cultural History of a Literary Idea* (Chicago: University of Chicago Press, 1993), 31–34, 131–148, 192–204; Fahs, *Imagined Civil War*, 311–318; Helen M. Cooper, ed., *Arms and the Woman: War, Gender, and Literary Representation* (Chapel Hill: University of North Carolina Press, 1989); Alfred Habegger, *Gender, Fantasy, and Realism in American Literature* (New York: Columbia University Press, 1982).

30. Stowe, "The True Story of Lady Byron's Life," *Atlantic Monthly*, September 1869, p. 305.

31. George M. Fredrickson, *The Black Image in the White Mind: The Debate on Afro-American Character and Destiny, 1817–1914* (1971; reprint, Middletown, Conn.: Wesleyan University Press, 1987), 97–129; Ann Douglas, *The Feminization of American Culture* (1977; reprint, New York: Anchor Books,

1988), 80–120. Child was born in 1802; Emerson in 1803; Hawthorne in 1804; Stowe in 1811; De Forest in 1826; Alcott in 1832.

32. The correspondence began when Child wrote John Brown and Governor Wise proposing to go to Virginia to nurse Brown's wounds. Brown told her not to come, suggesting instead that she raise money for his "bereaved family." See Caroline Karcher, *The First Woman in the Republic: A Cultural Biography of Lydia Maria Child* (Durham, N.C.: Duke University Press, 1994), 419–420; Louis Ruchames, ed., *John Brown: The Making of a Revolutionary* (New York: Universal Library, 1969), 139–140. Child was enormously prolific during the war, publishing ten books or pamphlets between 1860 and 1870.

33. Carolyn L. Karcher, ed., *A Lydia Maria Child Reader* (Durham, N.C.: Duke University Press, 1997), 243; *Correspondence between Lydia Maria Child and Gov. Wise and Mrs. Mason, of Virginia* (Boston: American Anti-Slavery Society, 1860), 3–4, 7, 14, 18, 20; Karcher, *First Woman of the Republic*, 416–418.

34. Louis Menand, *The Metaphysical Club: A Story of Ideas in America* (New York: Farrar, Straus and Giroux, 2001), 369–375, quotation from 374; Menand, "John Brown's Body," *Raritan* 22, 2 (fall 2002): 59; Karcher, *First Woman of the Republic*, 442, 532, 531, 533. Child's exact statement in 1866 reads: "They say people grow more conservative as they grow older; I grow more radical" (532).

35. George M. Fredrickson, *The Inner Civil War: Northern Intellectuals and the Crisis of the Union* (1965; reprint, Urbana: University of Illinois Press, 1993), 217–238. James, "Moral Equivalent of War," 73–148; Townsend, *Manhood at Harvard*.

36. Leverenz, *Manhood and the American Renaissance*, 1–8, 72–107; Fahs, *Imagined Civil War*, 316–318; Hedrick, *Harriet BeecherStowe*, 369–370; Howe, *Atlantic Monthly and Its Makers*, 49–50; Bell, *Problem of American Realism*, 11–38; Limon, *Writing after War*, 32–83; Richard Slotkin, *The Fatal Environment: The Myth of the Frontier in the Age of Industrialization, 1800–1890* (New York: Atheneum Press, 1985), chap. 1.

8

SEXUAL TERROR IN THE RECONSTRUCTION SOUTH

Lisa Cardyn

Contrary to the implication of much recent popular and scholarly discourse, terrorism is not an artifact peculiar to contemporary, or even modern, life, but a phenomenon with a long and sanguine history that has been intermittently subject to suppression and neglect.[1] This is emphatically true of the history of *sexual* terror, a mode of violation that categorically subsumes many of the impediments constraining historical research on terrorism and sex crime generally, notably the incentives for concealment common to perpetrator and victim alike and the relative paucity of witness testimony that both reflects and reproduces the disproportionate number of assaults committed to those successfully prosecuted. Moreover, sexualized violence is often overlooked in discussions of terrorism, a casualty of dated preconceptions of what counts as "terror" and what does not.[2] At the same time, the problem of sexual violence in warfare has been widely regarded as incidental, a mere byproduct of armed conflict itself the traditional province of men. Notwithstanding the myriad terminological, ideological, and political factors that have obscured its recognition, there is compelling evidence that the American South was an arena of vigorous sexual combat from slavery through the Civil War and Reconstruction, when it was avidly pursued by white supremacist groups throughout the region.

When the peace treaty was signed at Appomattox Courthouse, four years of bitter internecine strife were resolved in favor of the Union. Or so it appeared. There remained a vast population of disaffected whites who refused to accept defeat, some of whom contrived to effect a more congenial outcome through extralegal means. Founded by a motley assortment of disgruntled former rebels, the original Ku Klux Klan, along with its many vigilante counterparts, relied on terrorism to advance its aims. Klan terror assumed disparate shapes—from the storied nightriding of disguised bands on horseback to cryptic threats, barbarous assaults, and, not infrequently, murder.[3] Among the most striking features of these offensives was their pervasively sexualized character. Yet however bewildering some of their tactics might seem, their intentions were perfectly transparent. Concisely put, "[t]error and terrorism aim to frighten and, by frightening, to dominate and to control."[4] And that is precisely what the nightriders meant to do.

While students of Reconstruction have explored various facets of klan violence, none has previously canvassed the full spectrum of *sexualized* violence in its historical specificity, leaving unresolved important questions about the conjunction of sex, violence, terror, and traumatization. As historians have persuasively demonstrated, sexuality was a critical site upon which the complex and convoluted social and political conflicts of the era were waged, one that must be excavated and analyzed as part of a remarkably robust and resilient system of repression.[5] Examining the myriad sexual valences of these acts—their ubiquity, intensity, and ideological coherence, undertaken as they were within a racial patriarchy that normalized forced sex and compulsory procreation—likewise establishes sexualized violence as a prominent feature of the postwar Southern landscape. Given the klans' dubious distinction as the post-bellum period's foremost practitioners, their reign stands as a signal historical episode in which sex was deployed as an instrument of terror.

Resounding throughout these events is the indefeasible legacy of slavery and civil war. Just as slave-owners and their minions had used sexual violence and coercion to exercise mastery over their human chattel, habits in which some soldiers and civilians are known to have indulged during the years the Confederacy held sway, klansmen too ravaged their prey in an effort to traumatize, and thereby control, freed black communities and those allied with them.[6] Violent sex was in each instance a performance of dominance by its perpetrators and a harshly lived reality for its victims. Animated by unbridled vengeance and hate, the klans' objectives were in the end mainly instrumental—thus sex became an essential component in their campaign to reinstantiate white male supremacy in its antebellum form, replacing the legal infrastructure of slavery with illicit supports of their own making.

With the Ku Klux Klan as its prototype, this essay provides a brief introduction to the structure, functions, and objectives of post-bellum white supremacist organizations and the circumstances that were prone to incite their wrath. Nightriders, preoccupied with conduct they deemed socially, politically, or sexually verboten, surveilled the countryside for transgressors, upon whom sexualized punishments were routinely inflicted. Serving as the effective "military arm of the Democratic party,"[7] they engaged in whipping, rape, lynching, genital mutilation, and other tortures aimed at compromising the stability, resolve, and selfhood of the newly freed slaves, while punishing their white "accomplices" as traitors to their race, denying them the privileges of color that would otherwise have accrued. Insights from the growing field of trauma studies help to illuminate the significance of the klans' reign for the individuals, families, and communities most directly impacted. Much like the trauma of slavery touched those beyond its immediate grasp, so the imprint of klan terror has persisted in collective memory, contributing in intangible, yet nonetheless meaningful, ways to the perpetuation of racial and gender subordination. The enduring consequences of sexualized violence for the freedpeople, their white sympathizers, and subsequent generations underscore the confounding potency and elusiveness of historical trauma and the daunting obstacles to its resolution.

Debate about the role of sexual violence in klan terror began before the nightriders abandoned their robes. Arguing for the defense in one of South Carolina's 1871 Ku Klux Klan trials, Cyrus Melton used a familiar courtroom ploy to vindicate his client: refuting guilt through emotive invocation of the heinousness of the crime alleged. With studied disbelief, he queried, "Was ravishing helpless women a part of this conspiracy?"[8] There was, of course, but one acceptable response to a proposition so presumedly outlandish. And so Melton proceeded to embellish his rhetorical question, appealing to the loftiest ideals of Southern white manhood, endeavoring to portray as somehow fabricated or fantastical sexual assaults against freedwomen that were in truth startlingly commonplace.

> We have had here, from women, details of the most disgusting character, put forward for the purpose of showing from this act that ravishing women was one of the purposes of this organization. Now, I ask you, do you believe it, and that there did exist upon the face of God's earth an organization which would have among its purposes that of committing these gross outrages upon helpless women?[9]

By accident or design, counsel grievously exaggerated the manly righteous-
ness of the order, for the KKK and its imitators resorted not just to rape but
to a diverse range of sexual violations for strategic advantage. On behalf of
the prosecution, Daniel Chamberlain rejected these fallacious claims:

> [M]y eloquent friend asked yesterday, if, when they are ravishing
> women, and whipping women, if they are still pursuing Radical-
> ism? I answer, yes, yes. When they whipped Mary Robertson it
> was to make her tell where her husband was; when they ravished
> [Harriet] Simril, it was to punish her as well as to gratify their lusts,
> and to punish her because she would not tell where her Radical
> husband was. . . . Its general and constant purpose was the terror-
> izing of colored people by injuring them; by injuring their families
> until they shall have paid the penalty for their Radicalism, and be
> deterred from voting at future elections.[10]

Whereas Melton had depicted the "ravishing" of freedwomen as an unin-
tended, even regrettable, outgrowth of klansmanship, Chamberlain identified sexual violence as an integral part of the entire enterprise. More
than that, it was in retrospect among its most starkly defining features.

Of the thousands of attacks staged by the Reconstruction-era klans,
whipping was by far the most widespread. Klansmen exercised little
restraint in the administration of racial justice, imposing brutal lashings
on men, women, and children of all ages and colors that resulted in scores
of deaths and countless more serious injuries. Chastisement had been a
central feature of slave life, one that white Southerners on the whole were
demonstrably unwilling to forsake. While it would be an overstatement
to assert that all of these attacks were unambiguously sexual in nature, it
is fair to say that even the most unexceptional klan whippings often bore
a perceptibly sexualized cast.[11] Emblematic of this pattern are the innumerable floggings that contain some deliberately unnamed element with
vaguely yet palpably sexual overtones. Otherwise reticent witnesses managed to communicate a great deal through discreet silences, measured
pauses, and carefully chosen words. Thus, for instance, when an officer
of the Freedmen's Bureau recalled a raid in which the victims were "taken
from their beds at night and severely whipped and *shamefully* bruised,"[12]
it was likely not the violence alone that was "shameful" but its implied
sexualization.[13]

There are many more explicit examples of the klans' affinity for sexualized whipping. Although these attacks varied considerably in their par-

ticulars, they were skillfully designed to destroy enemies of the prewar status quo. This purpose was readily apparent when, in the midst of a nighttime offensive, klansmen came upon the daughter of a freedman with whom they had some trivial grievance and promptly set about punishing her in her father's stead. Unsated by the lashing, they ordered her to dance, recasting the hapless woman as the evening's entertainment.[14] Hannah Travis, an ex-slave intimately familiar with the ways of the Klan, told an almost identical incident in which the nightriders dragged a pregnant woman out of bed, demanding that she dance as her husband plaintively looked on.[15] A front-page article in the *New-York Tribune* derided the vigilantes who participated in such cruel exhibitions, ridiculing the "chivalrous gentlemen" who "pulled negro women from their beds and made them dance naked for the amusement of the spectators, beating the victims with ramrods to quicken their steps, and forcing them to submit to other outrages too revolting for description."[16]

Some attacks were more overtly sexual still. Thomas Settle, Jr., who sat on North Carolina's high court for much of the period, recounted an episode in which klansmen "took a young negro man who was in the house that night and whipped him, and compelled him to go through the form of sexual intercourse with one of the girls, whipping him at the same time," all of this in the presence of the girl's father.[17] In other cases, freedmen who had themselves been scourged were ordered to whip one another, as klan members orchestrated the proceedings.[18] So it was with a former slave in South Carolina who was obliged to turn the lash against one of his fellows while his assailants, seemingly intoxicated by the scene of mastery reasserted, persisted in compulsively lashing him.[19] Whatever the constituents of a given raid, klan members were rarely content to inflict just physical pain, but endeavored to exacerbate their enemies' debasement. Zealous perpetrators and approving bystanders were complicit in creating the voyeuristic atmosphere that was a hallmark of these encounters. When victims danced, feigned sex acts, or went through the motions of flagellation, they were performing their own subjugation, to satisfy the specular and the sexual needs of klansmen determined to restore the privileges of white masculinity over the bodies of their former slaves.

The category of whipping that is perhaps most indisputably sexualized involved forcibly stripping victims prior to or during a klan offensive.[20] Revived from slavery days, this disciplinary technique was calculated to shame a threatening "other" into abject submission.[21] Although whites desperate to maintain control over the region's African American population no longer had the force of law to sustain them, they had ready access to customery modes of coercion and the resources needed to apply them. An especially egregious example of this reliable style of punishment is manifest in a salacious klan attack against a Georgia freedwoman, Mary Brown, together with a number of her friends and relatives. As one of the women described it,

> [t]hey had a show of us all there; they had us all lying in the road, Mary Brown, Mary Neal, and my next youngest daughter. They had us all stripped there, and laughed and made great sport. Some of them squealed the same as if they were stable horses just brought out.[22]

Underscoring the intrinsic voyeurism of this onslaught, another witness remarked, "they had a powerful show; you never heard the like."[23] Spectacles of this sort were evidently not unusual. According to the recollections of a former slave whose testimony was recorded by the Works Progress Administration, young women were favored targets of stripping and whipping by the klans.[24]

For decades prior to the Civil War, critics of the South's "peculiar institution" decried the constant vulnerability of female slaves to rape and other forms of sexual abuse. White abolitionists were acutely aware of the gravity of the situation, and regularly cited the sexual exploitation of bondswomen as one of the slavery's greatest wrongs.[25] Clergymen, including some Southerners, also entered the fray to condemn what was commonly termed the "licentiousness" of bondage.[26] Though they ordinarily foregrounded the peril this posed to their fellow whites, critics nevertheless exposed a fundamental iniquity of slave life: the nearly total vitiation of sexual consent. When white jurists and legilators excluded those in bondage from the protection of the criminal law of rape, they denied them ownership and control of their bodies, and consequently perpetuated their corporeal subjugation.[27] Nor did emancipation release them from white men's thrall; indeed, they may have been more susceptible to sexual encroachment in what was called freedom.[28] Whether or not such a shift in actuality occurred, the record of klan violence amply confirms that former slaves remained vulnerable well after the institution's juridical demise.[29] But these avowed white supremacists did not confine themselves to molesting women of the supposedly inferior race; while victims were predominantly black, white women also suffered their depredations.[30]

Nightriders' engagement in the practice of terroristic rape was a matter of public record for most of the klans' existence. Witnesses at various Reconstruction-era tribunals confronted the issue directly. Essic Harris, a North Carolina freedman, had this to say to his congressional interlocutor:

Q: I understood you to say that a colored woman was ravaged by the Ku-Klux?

A: Yes, sir.

Q: Did you hear of any other case of that sort?

A: Oh, yes, several times. *That has been very common.* The case I spoke of was close by me, and that is the reason I spoke of it. It has got to be an old saying.

Q: You say it was common for the Ku-Klux to do that?

A: Yes, sir. They say that if the women tell anything about it, they will kill them.[31]

Although murderous threats issued to those who dared disclose these crimes would have naturally been dissuasive, some women accepted the risk inherent in speaking openly of their rapes. Besides the numerous governmental commissions that investigated reports of Southern atrocities,[32] black as well as mainstream newspapers included occasional articles chronicling similar assaults.[33] Despite this history of at least modest public recognition,[34] the terroristic rape of women, particularly black women, has seldom been accorded the attention it merits both as a blunt instrument for the assertion of racial, gender, and class dominance and as an agent of pervasive traumatization in the years following the Civil War. Yet, crucial as it is that these events be apprehended as part of an intricate web of oppression, their implications for individual victims cannot be ignored. As Catherine Clinton has incisively stressed, these women were not mere "symbols of their race, but persons subjected to torture."[35]

In the early weeks of 1866, the *Loyal Georgian* reported the ominous descent of five disguised men upon the home of Chandler Garrot, "a *colored* man," where "each violated the person of his wife, a *colored* woman."[36] Freedpeople required no assistance to understand the intimation that white men would continue to employ terror to surmount the color line they so vigorously guarded when it suited their aims. Appearing as a witness at the South Carolina Ku Klux Klan trials, Harriet Simril offered this unadorned sketch of her own ravaging:

Well, they were spitting in my face, and throwing dirt in my eyes
. . . and after awhile they took me out of doors, and told me all
they wanted was my old man to join the Democratic ticket; if he
joined the Democratic ticket, they would have no more to do with
him; and after they had got me out of doors, they dragged me into
the big road, and they ravished me out there.[37]

Simril was raped by three of her white neighbors, Chester McCollum, Tom McCollum, and Jim Harper, who, in addition to assailing her physically and sexually, treated her to a barrage of insults that her examiners concluded was "of too obscene a nature to permit of publication" and proceeded to exclude from the official record.[38] Such selective omissions were unfortunately routine, suggesting that the speech act was for some more unsettling than the actuating violence.[39]

During the intervening years, klansmen conducted surreptitious raids throughout the former Confederate states, with freedwomen and girls their usual targets. Henry Willis testified in an illustrative case of a klan-style incursion upon the homes of freedpeople residing in Robertson County, Tennessee. After threatening Willis's mother with sexual assault, the culprits elected instead to rape his twelve-year-old sister, "one after the other."[40] The daughter of Edward Carter, a Mississippi freedman, was likewise molested by two local klansmen, John Cook and Diller Suddith, while performing her daily household chores. "She went to holler," her father explained, prompting one of her attackers to "put a leather girth on her neck, to prevent her hollering, and they carried her about a quarter or a half a mile from the house and they ravished her."[41] Georgia Governor Rufus Bullock cited the rape of three freedwomen in an anti-klan proclamation announcing rewards for the arrest and conviction of those responsible for a series of raids in that state. Among the episodes he enumerated was one that transpired in late 1870 on the plantation of Colonel Waltemire in which a band of approximately forty disguised men did "then and there, as is alleged, commit a rape upon the persons of three colored girls, named respectively Carrie Sanders, Delia Horton, and Kate Bogan."[42] In their depiction of klan gang rape, both as a crime that occurred with some regularity and generated data on prevalence and impact that are scant at best, these revelations are indicative of what is and is not knowable about much Reconstruction-era sexual violence.

Whipping and rape were by no means the only forms of sexual terror purveyed by the klans; genital torture and mutilation were also part of their repertoire.[43] Evidence suggests that men and women, most African American, were exposed to these abuses in roughly equal numbers, either as casualties of nightriding directed toward other ends or victims of savage premeditation.[44] In the same way that the antecedents of other sexualized punishments are readily discernible in the Old South, genital assaults were also perpetrated in slavery.[45] Outrages of this sort persisted throughout the Civil War, when they were carried out somewhat arbitrarily by soldiers from both camps,[46] and beyond, when they were administered with heightened ferocity and systematicity by the white supremacist klans.[47] Presaging events to follow, a Southern observer chronicled an atrocious act of wartime torture in which a group of Union soldiers stationed in Virginia seized two freedwomen, "turned them upon their heads, & put tobacco, chips, sticks, lighted cigars & sand into their behinds."[48] While this incident bears certain distinctive features that set it apart from others of its kind, it affords an unvarnished perspective on the intense sexualization of racial animosity that was rife throughout these years.

With the rise of the klans, malicious practices like these assumed even greater prominence. It was thus with little hyperbole that the protagonist in *A Fool's Errand*, Albion Tourgée's fictionalized memoir of the period, portrayed the Reconstruction experiment as marred by "the mutilation of men and women in methods too shocking and barbarous to be recounted," replete with tragic encounters that left freedmen "mutilated beyond description, tortured beyond conception," some "mangled," "despoiled of manhood!"[49] Indeed, the "Fool's" florid lament aptly evokes the myriad euphemisms then current to refer to klan castrations. Although it is impossible to calculate their frequency on the basis of extant sources, it appears that "cutting" was a favored weapon in the klansman's arsenal, one that was arguably as pernicious in the fear it induced as it was in execution. This dual stratagem is elucidated in a short passage from one of the many hate-filled rants published in the pages of Tuscaloosa's *Independent Monitor*. "The cutting and beating of the insolent fellow Balus . . . in [the] presence of crowds of his fellow niggers, has had a salutary influence over the whole of niggerdom hereabout. They now feel their inferiority, in every particular, to the white men."[50] Once more, the KKK exhibited its will to employ sexual violence to terrorize and diminish the freed black population. What is especially notable here is the assailant's literal aim at the sex organs of rival males whose genitals they had already mythologized. This preoccupation was recapitulated by white vigilantes of a slightly later era when they insisted that black men were inclined to sexually mutilate their (presumptively female) victims. Meanwhile, not only did klansmen far exceed any potential rivals in their deployment of these methods, but it was white men—reputable physicians and jurists eager to discipline real and imagined black offenders—who would later become the most avid proponents of punitive castration for sex criminals.[51] Some called for still harsher punishments, as when a South Carolina doctor declared, "let him wear the badge of Cain upon his brow, let the letter 'C' [castrated] be branded upon his forehead, and when recovery is complete let him depart free, a sexless warning to his race."[52] Wielding African Americans' historical experience of sexual terror against them, the editors of one respected medical journal went so far as to recommend that klansmen of the next generation assist in the operation.[53]

Numerous witnesses attested to the klans' peculiar fascination with the genitalia of freedmen.[54] John W. Long, a one-time klansman from North Carolina, rehearsed the notorious mutilation of an ex-slave, Nathan Trollinger, in multiple venues, admitting that a band of disguised men "gave [Trollinger] a thrashing and made him take out his privates and stick a knife through it . . . five or six times."[55] Henry Lowther, a freedman who endured similarly horrific abuse, related a klan attack upon another ex-slave, Bill Brigan. "The way they did him was, they tied him down on a log and took a buggy-trace to him, and whipped one of his seed out and the other very nearly out."[56] Furthermore, he maintained, a white man named Register "was castrated in an adjoining county."[57] As often happened, no coherent justification was provided for any of these offenses. However, such reticence was nowhere in view when the klan threatened George W. Hollowell: "'You have been fighting in the United States service; you are a Yankee, you black son of a bitch[,] and we are going to cut out your stones and skin you alive.'"[58] Nor was it present in a narrative depicting the torture of a Jackson County freedman accused of cohabiting with a white woman.

[T]he colored man was taken out into the woods, a hole dug in the ground and a block buried in it, and his *penis* taken out, and a nail driven through it into the block; that a large butcher or cheese knife, as they call it, very sharp, was laid down by him, and lightwood piled around him and set on fire; the knife was put there so that he could cut if off and get away, or stay there and burn up. Doctor Swinney said that he cut it off and jumped out.[59]

This passage illustrates one of several instances in which a former slave was confronted with the choice of death or castration, here, by his own hand.

Another klan mob wrought its vengeance through the genitalia of a North Carolina freedwoman. In the words of A. Webster Shaffer, a U.S. commissioner in Raleigh, it was the "most outrageous cutting" of a former slave that klansmen had yet to commit:

> They gave her the knife and made her cut the hair off, because she would not give them a pair of scissors. . . . Then they took her out of doors and cut her hair off for the second time; they had done it about four or five months before. They then whipped her and made her cut the hair off her private parts with a knife, and then they cut her with the knife two or three times—stabbed her with the knife in the same place. I could not ascertain any reason why they did it. She was not living with any white man. She was not doing anything, so far as I could ascertain by the testimony, that would justify it at all. It appeared to be mere fiendishness.[60]

Edwin Hull, a white railroad worker, alluded to an analogous incident where klansmen visited a group of contract laborers whose politics they reviled.[61] Among the injured was a young black woman, the daughter of one of the offending railroaders, who met with particularly sadistic treatment at the hands of disguised marauders.

> A: She stated—and I even saw the marks—that she had been whipped on her body and limbs. She also stated—which I did not see—that while she was prostrate on the floor, one of them lit a match and burned the hair off from her private parts.
>
> Q: Was she cut with a knife in any way?
>
> A: It appears to me she said she was, but I am not positive.[62]

Klansmen occasionally employed genital torture and mutilation to punish white women as well. A Georgia man recalled that nightriders had stripped, whipped, and mutilated a number of poor whites of both sexes. Evidently unmoved by these events, the witness allowed that the victims' status as "low characters" mitigated any putative harm.[63] During another klan raid, this one in North Carolina, a white girl on the premises of African Americans was stripped and cruelly lashed before her tormentors "lit a match and burned her hair off, and made her cut off herself the part that they did not burn off with the match."[64] More gruesome still is the testimony of a supposedly reformed klansman, Shaffer Bowens, regarding the brutalization of a white woman (identified only as "Skates") in which he had taken part:

> They was going to take that woman out; and they had a pot of tar and lime, and was going to pour her full of it. . . . Joe Harding said he was going to have it done; [he] went back and ordered her out; made her lie down and held up her clothes. . . . He then poured it into her, as much as he could; and took a paddle and rubbed it on her.[65]

Insofar as this substance was prepared and transported to the site of the assault, where at least one participant was seen instructing the others on its proper use, this diabolical punishment must have been contrived in advance.[66] Moreover, Bowen admitted that there was no special provocation for this attack;[67] it appears instead to have been but one of the innumerable acts of sexual terror committed out of "mere fiendishness."[68] Of course, not all of their explanations were so amorphous. Thus when klan members devised a hideous punishment for a white woman known to be cohabiting with a black man, the instigation was fairly unambiguous.[69] In response to her offense, "they took the woman, laid her down on the ground, then cut a slit on each side of her orifice, put a large padlock in it, locked it up, and threw away the key, and then turned her loose."[70] For two or three days she suffered, in excruciating pain and nearly immobilized, before finally sending for a local doctor who helped free her from the klan's torturous device.[71]

Klan lynching emerged under somewhat different circumstances than the sexual terrors examined to this point. Whereas antebellum lynch mobs had occasionally targeted slaves, both their status as property and the pretenses of noblesse oblige surrounding planter paternalism discouraged the use of lethal violence against them.[72] Although data were not systematically gathered until 1882,[73] historians cite factors such as these to explain white men's greater susceptibility to the crime in the years prior to emancipation. Extrapolating from this incomplete evidentiary base, it is generally conceded that lynchings, especially those involving black males, increased slightly during the Civil War and significantly thereafter, when freedpeople were at once divested of whatever modicum of security had inhered in their monetary worth and newly empowered to lay claim to the perquisites of white manhood so jealously guarded by their natural beneficieries.[74] Sir George Campbell, an English traveler, penned these reflections on lynching in the post-bellum South:

> One thing did astonish me during my tour, and that is, to find how much "Judge Lynch" survives, especially when the accused are blacks. I imagined he was a thing of the past, but I found that several lynching cases of atrocity occurred before I had been many weeks in the States; that is, hanging by popular movement without the intervention of judge and jury.[75]

Lynching was assuredly not "a thing of the past." As with other modes of sexualized violence, the Reconstruction klans were neither its originators nor its exclusive exponents. Rather, to borrow Allen Trelease's fitting locution, they "helped to institutionalize a practice which preceded and long outlived it."[76] In reifying the terror of the lynch mob, it is conservatively estimated that the KKK alone lynched upward of four hundred freedpeople between 1868 and 1871.[77] With its growing regional prominence and often grotesque finality, the specter of lynching would have doubtless loomed larger in the Southern black imaginary than it had in times past.

Some of the most overtly sexualized lynchings were those accompanied by castration. Consistent with what has been observed thus far, surviving descriptions of klan castration-lynchings are typically sparse, but telling. References to mutilation are ordinarily veiled, as in the murder of Jacob Lighter, said to have had "no superior in atrocity yet chronicled by any writer on crime."[78] In an 1869 proclamation, Governor Holden obliquely averred that "others, of both sexes, were subjected to indignities which were disgraceful not merely to civilization but to humanity itself."[79] A witness testifying in the lynching death of a former slave named Nelson Harris likewise affirmed that the victim had been castrated through casual reference to "the parts found."[80] Equally savage was the killing a black man whose tortured remains had been strewn by the roadside in the klan-ridden county of Maury, Tennessee. According to the freedman who happened upon this grisly scene, "he had been skinned. His skin was hanging over his neck, and his privates had been cut off and put in his mouth."[81] There is no perfect correlation between the type of violence inflicted and its asserted justification; yet the fact that Harris was accused, rightly or wrongly, of being "too intimate with some white woman" is key to understanding the violent sex that suffused his demise.[82]

Regardless of their substance, the stated motives for klan attacks must be broachied with caution. The importance of this caveat is baldly displayed in the lynching of Lewis Thompson, a South Carolina freedman whose only known offense was his service as a Methodist minister to the freed black community.[83] Once more, a witness was called to testify to the discovery of a murdered freedman. Thompson, he recounted, had been "stabbed—cut open . . . his privates were cut off, and his body was dragged along the road and stabbed—cut all about with stabs in the body."[84] There is a homoerotic cast to sadistic outrages like this one that would almost surely have been antipathetic to their perpetrators.[85] Even when genital mutilation did not accompany lynching, its prospect remained palpable. The conjunction of lynching and castration was therefore critical to the production of material and psychological reality within the implicated communities.[86] Just as the danger of sexual mutilation was "immanent in the entire procedure,"[87] so too was sex itself, for in their quest to possess, inscribe, and finally obliterate their victims, lynch mobs reified the toxic coalescence of sexual rage, desire, frustration, and obsession that impelled them to maim and kill.

This wave of sexual terror in all its varied manifestations exposes the nightriders' simultaneous attraction toward and repulsion from the body of a subordinated "other." On the one hand, they despised and denigrated their victims, and professed special contempt for imputatively African American traits; on the other, they were reflexively given to attacks that placed them in close, frequently intimate, physical proximity. Though most victims were black and male, countless others did not fit that description. The commonality among them was the challenge they posed—by their words, deeds, demeanor, their very being—to the maintenance of white supremacy. Discernible in each of the klans' terroristic methods are the disciplinary practices of slavery, a system that was ultimately sustained by the omnipresent threat of violence. Persisting throughout the Civil War, the techniques of sexual terror evidently became more prevalent and diverse after emancipation, an event that inflamed white anxieties about the social and political aspirations of their former slaves. That the ensuing onslaught was so thoroughly sexualized reflects the magnitude of these fears as well as their deeply personal nature. Klansmen were driven by multiple imperatives: to regenerate white manhood, severely depleted by the Civil War and its aftermath; to preserve racial hierarchy in the face of freedpeople's demands for access to the full benefits of citizenship; and, finally, to reassert their traditional right to sexual property in women of both races. With defeat on any of these fronts intolerable, klan members unleashed a quasi-military campaign that eventually engulfed the region.

These are some of the immediate conditions underlying the klans' heavy reliance on sexualized violence. There are others that predate them. In hindsight, it is apparent that all of the atrocities depicted here had clear antecedents in the slave South. Beyond affording a convenient model for emulation, racial slavery reinforced certain assumptions about the meanings of blackness and whiteness, masculinity and femininity, and legitimated white men's penchant for sexual abuse—a feature of the institution that roused vocal public opposition and in turn helped hasten its demise. Some of the most intransigent elements of Southern society simply donned new uniforms, reconstituting themselves in a more suitable guise: diffuse in organization and unconventional in tactics, klansmen sought to achieve through vigilantism what had eluded them on the battlefield. If blacks could not be lawfully enslaved, they could be wrested into a state of figurative bondage, much as sympathetic whites could be terrorized into retreat. Whereas the formal structure and relative discipline of the Confederate command served to limit the incidence of sexual violence, the klans did precisely the opposite. With most of their forays undertaken in disguise and under cover of darkness, adherents were emboldened by a sense of anonymity that was only amplified by their numbers.

It was no mere coincidence that klansmen so often preferred sexual violence to other alternatives. They did so for reasons both personal and pragmatic. Like others before and since, they found that violent sex was a satisfying and efficient means of accomplishing their ends. That the sexualized terror they purveyed was so ubiquitous, so idiosyncratic in its contours, yet so commonplace in its application lends further credence to this proposition; its extraordinary effectiveness in traumatizing, then subduing, vulnerable populations, thereby inflating the supremacists' perceived dominion, provides vital insight to answer the question why. Research has shown that systematic victimization of this kind engenders profound trauma that extends beyond those most directly affected to encompass those who may stand at a significant temporal, geographic, and imaginative remove. There is, of course, no identity of human experience across place and time; hence no viable interpretation of past events, however similar, can be founded on the wholesale imposition of knowledge derived from another era. But neither should a potentially illuminating strategy be categorically dismissed. Given an historical record replete with evidence of the traumatic effects of klan violence, much of it consistent with recent findings, modern empirical data may be judiciously extrapolated to help surmount the inevitable limitations of methods and sources.[88] In the case of sexualized terror, where documentation of subjective psychological perceptions is generally quite sparse, informed analogical reasoning can be invaluable in elcidating contemporaneous testimony. Imperfect as it is, this approach is infinitely superior to eliding the systematic assault on the minds and bodies of hundreds of thousands of men, women, and children, the overwhelming majority of whom were enforcedly illiterate and denied meaningful opportunity to bear witness for themselves. It is only by situating this traumatic history within the imbricating systems of race, gender, and sexual oppression that preceded and followed that its insidious legacy may be fully grasped and one day overcome.

NOTES

This essay is drawn in part from my prior work on the history of klan sexual violence. See Lisa Cardyn, "Sexualized Racism/Gendered Violence: Outraging the Body Politic in the Reconstruction South," *Michigan Law Review* 100 (2002): 675–867; and "Sexualized Racism/Gendered Violence: Trauma and the Body Politic in the Reconstruction South" (Ph.D. diss., Yale University, 2003).

1. Walter Laqueur, *A History of Terrorism* (1977; New Brunswick, N.J.: Transaction Publishers, 2001), vii.

2. See Jacky Hardy, "Everything Old Is New Again: The Use of Gender-Based Terrorism against Women," *Minerva* 19 (2000): 9.

3. I use the terms "Klan" and "KKK" to refer to the Ku Klux Klan itself and "klan," with a lower-case "k," to signify the broader category of post–Civil War white supremacist organizations of which the Ku Klux Klan was paradigmatic.

4. Frederick J. Hacker, *Crusaders, Criminals, Crazies: Terror and Terrorism in Our Time* (New York: W. W. Norton & Co., 1976), xi.

5. See especially Catherine Clinton, "Reconstructing Freedwomen" and Martha Hodes, "Wartime Dialogues on Illicit Sex: White Women and Black Men," in *Divided Houses: Gender and the Civil War,* edited by Catherine Clinton and Nina Silber (New York: Oxford University Press, 1992), and Hodes's subsequent contributions, "The Sexualization of Reconstruction Politics: White Women and Black Men in the South after the Civil War," *Journal of the History of Sexuality* 3 (1993): 402–417, and *White Women, Black Men:*

Illicit Sex in the Nineteenth-Century South (New Haven: Yale University Press, 1997).

6. Although there is no comprehensive history of slave sexual exploitation as of this writing, most scholars agree that it was widely endured by women and, to a lesser extent, men held in bondage. See, e.g., Catherine Clinton, "Caught in the Web of the Big House: Women and Slavery," in *The Web of Southern Social Relations: Women, Family, and Education*, edited by Walter J. Fraser, Jr., R. Frank Saunders, Jr., and Jon L. Wakelyn (Athens, Ga. : University of Georgia Press, 1985), 20, 23, 24, 25; Catherine Clinton, "'Southern Dishonor': Flesh, Blood, Race, and Bondage," in *In Joy and In Sorrow: Women, Family, and Marriage in the Victorian South, 1830–1900*, edited by Carol Bleser (New York: Oxford University Press, 1991), 57–58, 65–66, 67; Karen A. Getman, "Sexual Control in the Slaveholding South: The Implementation and Maintenance of a Racial Caste System," *Harvard Women's Law Journal* 7 (1994): 115, 142–143 (1994) ; Thelma Jennings, "'Us Colored Women Had to Go Through a Plenty': Sexual Exploitation of African American Slave Women," *Journal of Women's History* 1 (1990): 45–46, 60–66; Marie Jenkins Schwartz, *Born in Bondage: Growing Up Enslaved in the Antebellum South* (Cambridge, Mass.: Harvard University Press, 2000), 14, 44–46, 154, 161–162, 172–173, 174, 178, 197, 206–207; and Gloria Shepherd, "The Rape of Black Women in Slavery" (D.A. diss., State University of New York at Albany, 1988).

There are likewise few sustained historical discussions of Civil War sexual violence have yet been published; however, useful information on the topic may be found in a number of recent works. See, e.g., Stephen V. Ash, *When the Yankees Came: Conflict and Chaos in the Occupied South, 1861–1865* (Chapel Hill: University of North Carolina Press, 1995), 19–20, 158–159, 197–198, 200–201; Michael Fellman, *Inside War: The Guerrilla Conflict in Missouri during the American Civil War* (New York: Oxford University Press, 1989), 207–213; Thomas P. Lowry, *The Story the Soldiers Wouldn't Tell: Sex in the Civil War* (Mechanicsburg, Pa.: Stackpole Books, 1994), 31–32, 36, 39, 123–131, 136; Reid Mitchell, *The Vacant Chair: The Northern Soldier Leaves Home* (New York: Oxford University Press, 1993), 102–112; and Leslie A. Schwalm, *A Hard Fight for We: Women's Transition from Slavery to Freedom in South Carolina* (Urbana: University of Illinois Press, 1997), 102–103, 119–122, 247, 314–315 n. 23.

7. George C. Rable, *But There Was No Peace: The Role of Violence in the Politics of Reconstruction* (Athens, Ga.: University of Georgia Press, 1984), 95.

8. U.S. Circuit Court (4th Circuit), *Proceedings in the Ku Klux Klan Trials, at Columbia, S.C., in the United States Circuit Court, November Term, 1871* (Columbia, S.C.: Republican Printing Co., 1872) (hereafter *S.C. Klan Trials*), 582.

9. Ibid.

10. Ibid., 593–594.

11. In this, too, the klans could find ready inspiration in slavery's nefarious example. See Deborah Gray White, *Ar'n't I a Woman? Female Slaves in the Plantation South*, rev. ed. (New York: W. W. Norton & Co., 1999), 33; and Ervin L. Jordan, Jr., "Sleeping with the Enemy: Sex, Black Women, and the Civil War," *Western Journal of Black Studies* 18 (1994): 57.

12. Records of the Bureau of Refugees, Freedmen, and Abandoned Lands, (hereafter BRFAL), Record Group (hereafter RG) 105, vol. 30, Murders and Outrages, New Orleans, La., May 31, 1868, National Archives and Records Administration, Washington, D.C. (italics added). See also "The Ku-Klux," *New National Era* (Washington, D.C.), March 2, March 1871, p. 3.

13. Needless to say, there are other plausible explanations for the witness's choice of words. But the impression derived from thousands of accounts of klansmen descending on victims in their bedrooms and imposing what are often literally unspeakable acts of vengeance suggests that such language was purposefully obfuscating.

14. See U.S. Congress, Joint Select Committee on the Condition of Affairs in the Late Insurrectionary States, *Report of the Joint Select Committee to Inquire into the Condition of Affairs in the Late Insurrectionary States* (Washington, D.C.: Government Printing Office 1872) (hereafter *Klan Report*), 5: 1475. While klansmen may have enshrined the use of coerced terpsichorean exhibitions, their predecessor slave patrollers were known to command similar performances. See Gladys-Marie Fry, *Night Riders in Black Folk History* (1975; reprint, Chapel Hill: University of North Carolina Press, 2001), 146–147.

15. See George P. Rawick, ed., *The American Slave: A Composite Autobiography*, ser. 2 (Westport, Conn.: Greenwood Press, 1972) (hereafter Rawick, ed., *American Slave*, ser. 2], *The American Slave*, ser. 2], 10., 6 :, 350.

16. "The Ku-Klux," *New-York Tribune*, November 14, November 1871, p. 1.

17. U.S. Senate, Select Committee to Investigate Alleged Outrages in the Southern States, *Report on the Alleged Outrages in the Southern States, by the Select Committee of the Senate* (Washington, D.C.: Government Printing Office, 1871) (hereafter *Report on the Alleged Outrages in the Southern States*), 85. An elderly North Carolina freedman was likewise forced to simulate intercourse with another man's wife. See Records of the Adjutant General's Office RG 94, National Archives and Records Administration, Washington, D.C. (hereafter AGO), microfilm (hereafter M) 666, reel (hereafter R) 12, file (hereafter F) 1612, Letter from Edward Field to C. H. Morgan, October 3, 1871.

18. Slaves are also known to have suffered abuses of this kind. See, e.g., John Thompson, *The Life of John Thompson, A Fugitive Slave; Containing his*

History of 25 Years in Bondage, and His Providential Escape (Worcester, Mass.: John Thompson, 1856), 20.

19. See *Klan Report*, 4:613. During another encounter closely resembling this one, nightriders constrained a white South Carolinian to whip a former slave. See ibid., 3:366. Obversely, a mob of white men, this time undisguised, directed several freedmen to whip a white Republican in Alabama. See *Klan Report*, 9:695.

20. These cases pervade the literature on klan violence. Although the documentation proffered hereafter will be less thoroughgoing, the following catalog shows the scope and variety of evidence attesting to the sexualization of terror in the post-bellum South. See, e.g., AGO, RG 94, M 666, R 1, F 60, Outrages Committed by Persons in Disguise in the County of Alamance Since the 1st of December 1868, December 22, 1870; AGO, RG 94, M 666, R 12, F 1612, Letter from C. H. Morgan to Adjutant General, Department of the East, May 4, 1871, AGO, RG 94, M 666, R 67, F 2146, Affidavit of E. M. Mulligan, July 30, 1869, BRFAL, RG 105, M 999, R 34, Affidavit of Frank Dickerson, Nashville, Tenn., January 14, 1868; BRFAL, RG 105, B 91, Affidavit of Lewis Slegald, Tenn., July 8, 1868, BRFAL, RG 105, vol. 136, Assistant Adjutant General, Synopses of Reports, Washington, D.C., July 18, 1868; BRFAL, RG 105, vol. 136, Assistant Adjutant General, Synopses of Reports, Washington, D.C., October 29, 1868; Ku Klux Klan Papers, Rare Book, Manuscript, and Special Collections Library, Duke University (hereafter KKK Papers), Testimony of John W. Long [*State v. Tarpley*], 9; KKK Papers, Testimony of Sandy Sellers [*State v. Andrews*], 1; *Congressional Globe*, 42nd Cong., 1st sess., 1871, 155; U.S. House, *Sheafe vs. Tillman*, 41st Cong., 2nd sess., 1870, H. Misc. Doc. 53, 165, 299, 300; Alabama General Assembly, *Report of Joint Committee on Outrages* (Montgomery, Ala.: J. G. Stokes, 1868), 74–75; Austin Blair, *Enforcement of Fourteenth Amendment, Speech of Hon. Austin Blair, of Michigan, Delivered in the House of Representatives, March 30, 1871* (Washington, D.C.: F. and J. Rives and George A. Bailey, 1871), 4; North Carolina Senate, *Trial of William W. Holden, Governor of North Carolina, Before the Senate of North Carolina, on Impeachment by the House of Representatives for High Crimes and Misdemeanors* (Raleigh, N.C.: Sentinel, 1871) (hereafter *Holden Trial*), 2:1170, 1382, 1383, 1388, 1442, 1444, 1471, 1510, 1762; *Klan Report*, 2:167, 204–205; *Klan Report*, 3:36, 297, 350, 380, 403, 417, 436–437, 441, 521, 577, 580; *Klan Report*, 4: 697, 699, 701; *Klan Report*, 5: 1407; *Klan Report*, 6:18, 375–377, 386, 387, 389, 400, 401, 407, 463, 464, 465–466, 473, 479, 501–502, 566; *Klan Report*, 7:597–598, 642, 647, 669, 697, 732, 972, 1022, 1114; *Klan Report*, 10:1993–1994, 1997; *Klan Report*, 11:270, 326, 328, 485; *Klan Report*, 13:55, 59–60, 65, 73, 307; "The Ku-Klux," *New-York Tribune*, November 14, 1871, p. 1; "Ku-Kluxism! The Last Ku-Klux Outrage,

One Negro Murdered in Cold Blood, and Another Not Expected to Live,"
New National Era (Washington, D.C.), January 26, 1871, p. 1; Rawick, ed.,
American Slave, ser. 2, 14.2 : 15; *Report on the Alleged Outrages in the Southern
States*, lxvi, 85; "School Teacher Whipped in Bullock County," *Colored Tribune*
(Savannah, Ga.), June 3, 1876, p. 2; *S.C. Klan Trials*, 205, 283, 481, 482, 488,
490, 508, 511, 570; South Carolina General Assembly, *Report on the Evidence
Taken by the Committee of Investigation of the Third Congressional District under
Authority of the General Assembly of South Carolina. Made at Regular Session,
1869–70* (Columbia, S.C.: John W. Denny, 1870), 1063; Job E. Stevenson,
*Ku Klux Klan. Let Us Protect the People in the Enjoyment of Life, Liberty, and
Property, and Impartial Suffrage in Peace. Speech of Hon. Job E. Stevenson, of Ohio,
Delivered in the House of Representatives, April 4, 1871* (Washington, D.C.: F.
and J. Rives and George A. Bailey, 1871), 10, 11–12; "Still Another Ku-Klux
Outrage," *New National Era* (Washington, D.C.), February 23, 1871, p. 1; and
Tennessee General Assembly, Senate, Committee on Military Affairs, *Report
of Evidence Taken before the Military Committee in Relation to Outrages Committed by the Ku Klux Klan in Middle and West Tennessee* (Nashville: S.C. Mercer,
1868), 6, 20, 28, 46, 55.

21. See bell hooks, *Ain't I A Woman: Black Women and Feminism* (Boston: South End Press, 1981), 37–38. One of many firsthand accounts of the
stripping and whipping of slave women is reproduced in George P. Rawick,
ed., *The American Slave: A Composite Autobiography*, supp. ser. 1 (Westport,
Conn.: Greenwood Press, 1977) (hereafter Rawick, ed., *American Slave*, supp.
ser. 1), 4.2:464. Additional examples are set forth in Louis Hughes, *Thirty
Years a Slave: From Bondage to Freedom: The Institution of Slavery as Seen on
the Plantation in the Home of the Planter* (1897; reprint, Montgomery, Ala.:
New South Books, 2002), 41, 72; Charles L. Perdue, Jr., Thomas E. Barden,
and Robert K. Phillips, eds., *Weevils in the Wheat: Interviews with Virginia
Ex-Slaves* (Charlottesville: University Press of Virginia, 1976), 266, 267;
George P. Rawick, ed., *The American Slave: A Composite Autobiography*, ser. 1
(Westport, Conn.: Greenwood Press, 1972) (hereafter Rawick, ed., *American
Slave*, ser. 1), 4.1:180; Rawick, ed. *American Slave*, ser. 1, 5.3:244; Rawick,
ed., American Slave, supp. ser. 1, 4, 2, 466–467; and Thompson, *Life of John
Thompson*, 22, 25, 31, 32, 49.

22. *Klan Report*, 6:387.

23. Ibid., 6:377.

24. See Rawick, ed., *American Slave*, ser. 2, 16:100–101.

25. See, e.g., Wendell Phillips, *Speeches, Lectures, and Letters* (Boston: Lee
and Shepard, 1872), 108; [George Bourne], *Slavery Illustrated in Its Effects
upon Woman and Domestic Society* (Boston: Isaac Knapp, 1837), 27. On abolitionists' tactical manipulation of the imagery of sexual violation, see Dick-

son D. Bruce, Jr., *Violence and Culture in the Antebellum South* (Austin: University of Texas Press, 1979), 140; Karen Halttunen, "Humanitarianism and the Pornography of Pain in Anglo-American Culture," *American Historical Review* 100 (1995): 324–325; Karen Sánchez-Eppler, *Touching Liberty: Abolition, Feminism, and the Politics of the Body* (Berkeley: University of California Press, 1993), 14–49, 83–104; and Ronald G. Walters, "The Erotic South: Civilization and Sexuality in American Abolitionism," *American Quarterly* 25 (1973): 177–201.

26. See, e.g., J. D. Paxton, *Letters on Slavery; Addressed to the Cumberland Congregation, Virginia* (Lexington, Ky.: Abraham T. Skillman, 1833).

27. See, e.g., Thomas R. R. Cobb, *An Inquiry into the Law of Negro Slavery in the United States of America* (Philadelphia: T. and J. W. Johnson, 1858), 99; and William Goodell, *The American Slave Code in Theory and Practice* (New York: American and Foreign Anti-Slavery Society, 1853), 86. Minor exceptions to this rule emerged prior to the Civil War, when Georgia and Mississippi enacted legislation extending limited protection against rape to female slaves; but even here, race proved central to the law's practical application. Peter W. Bardaglio, *Reconstructing the Household: Families, Sex, and the Law in the Nineteenth-Century American South* (Chapel Hill: University of North Carolina Press, 1995), 68–69.

28. Most Civil War historians who have addressed the issue acknowledge that rapes were perpetrated by soldiers from both warring armies upon black and white women alike. That said, women who had been widely perceived as "unrapeable" in law and custom, because presumptively unchaste, would have been especially vulnerable in these years. See Victoria E. Bynum, *Unruly Women: The Politics of Social and Sexual Control in the Old South* (Chapel Hill: University of North Carolina Press, 1992), 118.

Trends in postwar assaults are discussed in Catherine Clinton, "Bloody Terrain: Freedwomen, Sexuality, and Violence during Reconstruction," *Georgia Historical Quarterly* 76 (1992):330–331; and Laura F. Edwards, *Gendered Strife and Confusion: The Political Culture of Reconstruction* (Urbana: University of Illinois Press, 1997), 199.

29. The persistent problem of white-male-on-black-female sexual violence in post-bellum Southern society has been noted by many historians, including Bardaglio, *Reconstructing the Household*, 195; Herbert G. Gutman, *The Black Family in Slavery and Freedom, 1750–1925* (New York: Random House, 1976), 393–399; Hodes, *White Women, Black Men*, 152, 160; Diane Miller Sommerville, *Rape and Race in the Nineteenth-Century South* (Chapel Hill: University of North Carolina Press, 2004), 148–149; and Allen W. Trelease, *White Terror: The Ku Klux Klan Conspiracy and Southern Reconstruction*

(1971; reprint, Baton Rouge: Louisiana State University Press, 1995), 232, 322, 341.

30. I have been able to locate only two cases documenting the rape of white women by klansmen during the Reconstruction period. See *Klan Report*, 8:549; and *Report on the Alleged Outrages in the Southern States*, 118. Where the rape of white women is referenced elsewhere, the perpetrators are not identified as belonging to any white supremacist order, though some may well have been so affiliated. See, e.g., *Klan Report*, 2:186; and *Report on the Alleged Outrages in the Southern States*, lxvi. It should not be inferred from this relative paucity of evidence that white women were spared the ravages of sexual terror; rather, it appears that nightriders preferred other modes of sexualized violence, such as stripping and whipping, when disciplining women of their own race.

31. *Klan Report*, 2:99–100 (italics added).

32. Indeed, these investigations prompted legislators to address the problem of klan rape in the halls of Congress. See, e.g., Daniel D. Pratt, *Extension of Ku Klux Act. Speech of Hon. Daniel D. Pratt, of Indiana, Delivered in the Senate of the United States, May 17, 1872* (Washington, D.C.: F. & J. Rives & George A. Bailey, 1872), 5, 13.

33. See, e.g., "Fiendish Cruelty, Hellish Barbarity!! Inhuman Treatment of a Freedwoman. A Relic of Barbarism—The Whipping-Post in Vogue," *Loyal Georgian* (Augusta, Ga.), October 13, October 1866, p. 3; "The Kentucky Kuklux," *New York Times*, November 8, November 1872, p. 3; "Kuklux in Kentucky," *New York Times*, August 26, August 1873, p. 1; "Outrages in the South," *New York Times*, October 13, October 1868, p. 4; "Palliation of the Ku-Klux by the Golden Age," *New National Era* (Washington, D.C.), October 3, October 1872, p. 2; and "The Southern States: The Ku Klux—Eleven Freedmen Almost Beaten to Death, Another Shot Dead, and a Mulatto Girl Whipped and Outraged, in One Night," *New-York Tribune*, March 17, 1869, p. 5.

34. An early assessment of the Reconstruction klans made lurid reference to their reliance on sex crimes. See J. A. Rogers, *The Ku Klux Spirit: A Brief Outline of the History of the Ku Klux Klan Past and Present* (New York: Messenger Publishing Co., 1923), 22–23. Yet the topic was studiously avoided in popular and professional histories for decades thereafter.

35. Clinton, "Bloody Terrain," 329.

36. "Horrible Outrage," *Loyal Georgian* (Augusta, Ga.), January 27, 1866, p. 2 (italics in original).

37. *S.C. Klan Trials*, 502.

38. Ibid.

39. Government officials habitually responded to such unwelcome information by effacing it. See, e.g., BRFAL, RG 105, M 821, R 32, Murders and Outrages, 27 July 1868 (stating that a murdered freedboy had been "mutilated in a manner of which decency forbids further description"); W. W. Holden, *Third Annual Message of W. W. Holden, Governor of North Carolina* (Raleigh: J. W. Holden, 1870), 156 (declaring that details of a freedman's genital mutilation were "not proper to publish"); *Holden Trial*, 2: 2008 (refusing to hear testimony concerning same-sex sexual violence); and *S.C. Klan Trials*, 789 (omitting descriptions of certain offenses, notably rapes, as "too indecent for public mention").

40. See BRFAL, RG 105, M 999, R 34, Affidavit of Henry Willis, Nashville, Tenn., October 23, 1866. See also BRFAL, RG 105, M 999, R 34, Affidavit of Amanda Willis, Nashville, Tenn., 23 October 1866.

41. *Klan Report*, 12:1084.

42. Ibid., 7:884.

43. See, e.g., ibid., 2:39; see also, Arthur F. Raper, *The Tragedy of Lynching* (Chapel Hill: University of North Carolina Press, 1933), 124.

44. Some of this evidence is merely suggestive, as when Brevet Major General J. J. Reynolds writes of freedmen who were "terribly mutilated" by outraging "desperadoes." See BRFAL, RG 105, Vol. 136, Assistant Adjutant General, Synopses of Reports, Washington, D.C., September 28, 1868. Analogous terms were used to describe some klan attacks. See, e.g., James Brewster, *Sketches of Southern Mystery, Treason and Murder. The Secret Political Societies of the South, their Methods and Manners. The Phagedenic Cancer on our National Life* (Milwaukee: Evening Wisconsin Co., 1903), 254–255; [William Woods Holden and Richmond Mumford Pearson], *Proclamations by the Governor of North Carolina: Together with the Opinion of Chief-Justice Pearson, and the Reply of the Governor* (Raleigh: Standard Steam Book & and Job Print., 1870), 10, 16, 31; Holden, *Third Annual Message*, 15, 16, app. 8, 14, 74; and *Holden Trial*, 1: 32.

45. See Rawick, ed., *American Slave*, ser. 1, 7:78; Dorothy Sterling, ed., *We Are Your Sisters: Black Women in the Nineteenth Century* (1984; reprint, New York: W. W. Norton & Co., 1997), 353; see also John W. Blassingame, *The Slave Community: Plantation Life in the Antebellum South*, rev. ed. (New York: Oxford University Press, 1979), 233, 263; Judith K. Schafer, "Sexual Cruelty to Slaves: The Unreported Case of *Humphreys v. Utz*," *Chicago-Kent Law Review* 68 (1993): 1313–1340 and Kenneth M. Stampp, *The Peculiar Institution: Slavery in the Ante-Bellum South* (1956; reprint, New York: Random House, 1989), 188.

46. There are numerous such cases in the files of federal courts-martial, including one in which a Union soldier attempted to rape a freedwoman

and, failing that, "pulled up her dress and threw a [flaming] torch between her legs." Records of the Judge Advocate General's Office (Army), Court Martial Case Files, M 2471, RG 153, NA, cited in Lowry, *Story the Soldiers Wouldn't Tell*, 123–124. In another, a Union soldier reportedly castrated a young boy "because he gloried in being a rebel." Charles W. Turner, ed., *Civil War Letters of Arabella Speairs and William Beverley Pettit of Fluvanna County, Virginia, March 1862–March 1865* (1988), 155, cited in Lowry, *Story the Soldiers Wouldn't Tell*, 130.

47. Contemporaries remarked on the nightriders' terroristic application of genital assault. See, e.g., "The Legislature," *Colored Tribune* (Savannah, Ga.), January 15, January 1878, p. 2; "The Effect of 'Improved Democratic Processes' at the South," *New York Times*, March 17, March 1871, p. 4; and Pratt, *Extension of Ku Klux Act*, 4, 5. This pattern has since been noted by several historians of the period. See, e.g., John Hope Franklin, *Reconstruction after the Civil War*, 2nd ed. (Chicago: University of Chicago Press, 1994), 155; Fry, *Night Riders in Black Folk History*, 159; Gutman, *The Black Family*, 394; Hodes, *White Women, Black Men*, 152, 154–156, 161; Leon F. Litwack, *Been in the Storm So Long: The Aftermath of Slavery* (New York: Alfred A. Knopf, 1979), 276–277; Trelease, *White Terror*, 202, 323–324; and Wyn Craig Wade, *The Fiery Cross: The Ku Klux Klan in America* (1987; reprint, New York: Oxford University Press, 1998), 78–79.

48. Henry J. H. Thompson Papers, Rare Book, Manuscript, and Special Collections Library, Duke University, Durham, N.C., Letter from Henry J. H. Thompson to his wife, June 20, June 1863, quoted in Bell Irvin Wiley, *The Life of Billy Yank: The Common Soldier of the Union* (1951; reprint, Baton Rouge: Louisiana State University Press, 1978), 114.

49. Albion W. Tourgée, *A Fool's Errand, by One of the Fools; The Famous Romance of American History*. Part II, *The Invisible Empire: A Concise Review of the Epoch on Which the Tale Is Based*, enl. ed. (New York: Fords, Howard, & and Hulbert, 1880), 241, 246.

50. "Niggers—Radicals—Ghosts," *Independent Monitor* (Tuscaloosa, Ala.), April 7, 1868, 2.

51. See S. C. Baker, "The Southern Negro—His Recent Erotic Tendencies—the Causes—Suggestions as to Prevention," *Carolina Medical Journal* 45 (1900): 89–94; Simeon E. Baldwin, "Whipping and Castration as Punishments for Crime," *Yale Law Journal* 8 (1899): 381–382; "Castration Instead of Lynching," *Atlanta Journal-Record of Medicine* 8 (1906): 457; F. E. Daniel, "The Cause and Prevention of Rape. —Sadism in the Negro," *Transactions of the State Medical Association of Texas* 36 (1904): 289–290; W. T. English, "The Negro Problem from the Physician's Point of View," *Atlanta Journal-Record of Medicine* 5 (1903): 470–471; and Hunter McGuire and G. Frank Lydston,

"Sexual Crimes among the Southern Negroes—Scientifically Considered," *Virginia Medical Monthly* 20 (1893): 122. For counterarguments, see J. A. de Armand, "Asexualization As a Punishment for Rape," *Medical Bulletin* 20 (1898): 55–57; and R. W. Shufeldt, *The Negro: A Menace to American Civilization* (Boston: Richard G. Badger, 1907), 144–146, 150.

52. Baker, "The Southern Negro—His Recent Erotic Tendencies," 94.

53. "An impressive trial by a ghost-like kuklux klan and a 'ghost' physician or surgeon to perform the operation would make of it an event the 'patient' would never forget, nor cease to talk about and enlarge upon. This would do away with the martyrdom effect of lynching as well as the demoralizing results of mob law. The badge of disgrace and emasculation might be branded upon the face or forehead, as a warning, in the form of an 'R,' emblematic of the crime for which this punishment was and will be inflicted." "Castration Instead of Lynching," 458.

54. See, e.g., *Klan Report*, 2:39. Although the site of bodily injury frequently remains unspoken, assertions respecting the widespread mutilation of freedmen's bodies strongly imply that these were commonly, if not uniformly, genital attacks.

55. *Holden Trial*, 2: 2007. Elsewhere, Long states, "They went and whipped Nathan Trollinger and made him draw out his 'tool' and peck it with his own knife." KKK Papers, Testimony of John W. Long [*State v. Tarpley*], 23. Trollinger's ordeal is also discussed in AGO, RG 94, M 666, R 1, F 60, Letter from W. W. Holden to General U. S. Grant, Enclosure, January 1, 1871, KKK Papers, Testimony of John W. Long [*State v. Andrews*], 2; and *Report on the Alleged Outrages in the Southern States*, xix, lxvi, 34, 36.

56. *Klan Report*, 6:359. Trelease refers to three cases, including those of Brigan and Lowther, in which freedmen in Wilkinson County, Georgia, were castrated by klansmen. See *White Terror*, 323–324. See also Hodes, *White Women, Black Men*, 156.

57. *Klan Report*, 6:360.

58. Ibid., 8:166. By contrast, a report presented by Governor Lindsay's recording secretary concludes that Hollowell, a visitor from the North, had provoked the Klan's enmity by committing several breaches of racial decorum—i.e., assuming "offensive airs" toward local whites, boasting of his marriage to "a wealthy white lady," and "asserting his equality with any white man." Ibid., 8:166.

59. *Klan Report*, 7:1120 (italics in original).

60. Ibid., 2:49.

61. Ibid., 65, 67–68.

62. Ibid., 2: 67.

63. Ibid., 7:1022.

64. Ibid., 2:37. See also Albion W. Tourgée Papers, Chautauqua County Historical Society, Westfield, N.Y. (hereafter Tourgée Papers), R 57, no. 11071, "KuKlux Outrages in Chatham County" (chronicling the chastisement of a woman during which raiders "cut the hair off her head & between her legs"). In addition to shearing and burning pubic hair, klansmen were known to cut and shave the heads of some male and female victims, a quasi-sexual form of humiliation that was of a piece with the klans' larger enterprise. See, e.g., BRFAL, RG 105, Records of the Assistant Commissioner for the State of Georgia, Statement of Johanna Gilbert, reprinted in *Standing upon the Mouth of a Volcano: New South Georgia*, edited by Mills Lane (Savannah, Ga.: Beehive Press, 1993), 94; Reports of Detectives of William W. Holden, General Assembly Session Records, Division of Archives and History, North Carolina Department of Cultural Resources, Raleigh, B 10, Report of Lieutenant McTaggart, March 4, 1870; Tourgée Papers, R 57, no. 11071, "KuKlux Outrages in Chatham County"; and *Klan Report*, 2:4. Similarly, a white teacher testified that klansmen "took me out of bed and cut off one side of my beard and one side of my hair." *Holden Trial*, 2: 1485. See also AGO, RG 94, M 666, R 1, F 60, Outrages Committed by Persons in Disguise in the County of Alamance Since the 1st of December 1868, December 22, 1870; *Holden Trial*, 2: 1708; and *Report on the Alleged Outrages in the Southern States*, lxvi, xci, 145. The descendant of a Union officer who participated in efforts to subdue the KKK in North Carolina emphasized the prevalence of hair-burning in the Klan Klan 's brutal panoply. See Elizabeth M. Howe, "A Ku Klux Uniform," *Publications of the Buffalo Historical Society* 25 (1921):30, 30 n. 16, 33. As with other sexualized violations, this one was not without precedent in Southern history. Years after her enslavement on a Mississippi plantation, an African American woman remembered that "[t]he female slaves often had their hair cut off, especially those who had long beautiful hair." Rawick, ed., *American Slave*, ser. 1, 17:168. Mildred Graves, an ex-slave from Virginia, endured much the same thing when she encountered a gang of marauding Union soldiers. "[B]out six o' 'em," she said, "stopped an' took a razor blade and cut off my hair. I had long black hair dat hung way down my back. I kicked an' fit as much as I could, but I couldn' stop 'em." Perdue, Barden, and Phillips, eds., *Weevils in the Wheat*, 121.

65. *S.C. Klan Trials*, 508. When asked to specify where the tar and lime had been placed, Bowens replied "I don't like to tell." Only when pressed did he admit, "He poured it in her privates,. " *S.C. Klan Trials*, 508. *Ibid.*

66. Ibid., 508–509.

67. Ibid., 509.

68. Ibid., 2:49.

69. Ibid., 7:1120.

70. Ibid., 7:1120.

71. See ibid.

72. See Eugene D. Genovese, *Roll, Jordan, Roll: The World the Slaves Made* (New York: Pantheon Books, 1974), 32–33.

73. The *Chicago Tribune* was the first to compile a comprehensive listing of all lynchings reported in the United States. See Stewart E. Tolnay and E. M. Beck, *A Festival of Violence: An Analysis of Southern Lynchings, 1882–1930* (Urbana: University of Illinois Press, 1995), 14–15 n. 4, 259. Corresponding tabulations were published in National Association for the Advancement of Colored People, *Thirty Years of Lynching in the United States, 1889–1918* (New York: National Association for the Advancement of Colored People, 1919); *Negro Year Book* (1914): 316; *Negro Year Book* (1952): 276–278; and Southern Commission on the Study of Lynching, *Lynchings and What They Mean: General Findings of the Southern Commission on the Study of Lynching* (Atlanta: Commission on Interracial Cooperation, 1931). Beyond these are untold others that remain uncounted.

74. See Rable, *But There Was No Peace*, 98. John Raymond Ross offers a somewhat different perspective, postulating that lynchings may have declined during the war years and surged dramatically thereafter. See "At the Bar of Judge Lynch: Lynching and Lynch Mobs in America" (Ph.D. diss., Texas Tech University, 1983), 102, 110, 112. His research indicates that "[i]n the Klan's peak year, 1868, the number of victims probably exceeded the 226 of 1892, the peak during the years for which there are reasonably reliable statistics." Ross, "At the Bar of Judge Lynch," 115.

75. Sir George Campbell, *White and Black: The Outcome of a Visit to the United States* (New York: R. Worthington, 1879), 171.

76. Trelease, *White Terror*, xxi.

77. See Richard Maxwell Brown, *Strain of Violence: Historical Studies of American Violence and Vigilantism* (New York: Oxford University Press, 1975), 214, 323. George C. Wright convincingly argues that, by restricting his study to fully documented cases, Brown has significantly underestimated the number of post-bellum lynchings. See *Racial Violence in Kentucky, 1865–1940: Lynchings, Mob Rule, and "'Legal Lynchings' Lynchings"* (Baton Rouge: Louisiana State University Press, 1990), 41.

78. "The Kentucky Kuklux," *New York Times*, November 8, November 1872, p. 3. See also Pratt, *Extension of Ku Klux Act*, 4.

79. *Holden Trial*, 1: 33.

80. See *Klan Report*, 8:2.

81. Tennessee General Assembly, *Report of Evidence Taken before the Military Committee*, 37. An Alabama freedman was threatened with an equally sinister punishment. See *Klan Report*, 8:166.

82. Ibid., 2:213.

83. See ibid., 4:1182–1183.

84. Ibid., 4:1184. See also ibid., 4:982, 994, 1031, 1182, 1183.

85. This line of inquiry is pursued in Trudier Harris, *Exorcising Blackness: Historical and Literary Lynching and Burning Rituals* (Bloomington: Indiana University Press, 1984), 22–24; and Robyn Wiegman, *American Anatomies: Theorizing Race and Gender* (Durham, N.C.: Duke University Press, 1995), 99.

86. See Wiegman, *American Anatomies*, 221 n. 3.

87. Joel Kovel, *White Racism: A Psychohistory* (1970; reprint, New York: Columbia University Press, 1984), 67.

88. See my prior work on klan sexual terror cited above above.

9

POLITICS AND PETTICOATS IN THE SAME POD

Florence Fay, Betsey Bittersweet, and the Reconstruction of Southern Womanhood, 1865–1868

Anne Sarah Rubin

"Dear Mister Editors of the Southern Home Journal," began a letter in that Baltimore newspaper's inaugural issue in November 1867. I got your per-lite letter last week a asking of me to write to you and tell the news down here in this "Deistrick," so called—and went right straight and jined a sewing society, besides making my old men take to going to lodge meetings again, that I might hear all as was a going; for I don't know which is the best place to pick up news—a sewing society where no gentlemen is admitted, or a mason's lodge where no ladies is allowed.

So opened the first of six "Letter[s] from Betsey Bittersweet" that graced the pages of the weekly *Southern Home Journal* in late 1867 and early 1868. This first paragraph—with its vernacular prose, political news, and satirical recognition of men and women's separate realms—introduced many of the themes that ran through these humorous columns. Supposedly the correspondence of a North Carolina woman, Betsey's letters mixed discussions of Reconstruction politics with domestic complaints about shifting racial and social relations within postemancipation households.[1] This mixture of humorous political and domestic complaints, written in the voice of a middle-class white Southern woman, could also be found in "Florence Fay Arrows," a column that appeared for several months in another regional weekly, the *Field and Fireside*.[2] Like Betsey Bittersweet,

Florence Fay relied on exaggerated humor and convoluted phrasings to express her social and political critiques, although she rarely used dialect. Compared to Betsey Bittersweet, Florence Fay's messages tended to mock Northerners less and criticize white Southerners more. Her writings stressed the plight of the common Southerner, and she frequently sent her arrows flying in the direction of the intellectually and socially pretentious "small fry" or "mushroom aristocracy."[3]

Both the *Southern Home Journal* and the *Field and Fireside* claimed a broadly regional readership. The *Southern Home Journal* was published in Baltimore between November 1867 and mid-1869. Its masthead proclaimed it was "Devoted to Choice Literature, Biography, History, Poetry and the News," and its eight pages were filled with a mixture of serialized fiction, poetry, humorous pieces, reminiscences of the war, and general essays. Despite the claims that "THE Publishers of the SOUTHERN HOME JOURNAL design making this paper strictly a literary publication of the South, not in the spirit of 'contention, but rather emulation,' avoiding everything of a political nature," the paper gradually became more politicized, particularly in 1868, when it ran editorials expressing opposition to the impeachment of Andrew Johnson and opposing the presidential candidacy of Ulysses S. Grant.[4] The *Field and Fireside*, a continuation of the wartime *Southern Field and Fireside*, was published in Raleigh, North Carolina, and it too focused on fiction and poetry as opposed to overtly political writings.

Both Betsey Bittersweet and Florence Fay criticized the Union government and Union soldiers, complaining about white Southerners' political subjugation. As such, they provided an outlet for white Southern bitterness and resentment toward the Republican party, the Freedmen's Bureau, and the freedpeople themselves. The ladies' sharp tongues were not, however, limited to outsiders. To varying degrees, both Betsey and Florence turned their wit on themselves, addressing the behavior of white Southern women as well. They rebuked Northern women (and implicitly their Southern sisters) for demanding the vote; they warned against the dangers of overt flirtatiousness; and they condemned women who were more interested in matters outside the home than the comfort of those within.

In so doing, writers like Betsey Bittersweet and Florence Fay sought a resolution to the "crisis in gender" that had arisen out of the Civil War. Just as the war and its aftermath forced a redefinition of Confederate into Southern or American identity, so too did it challenge Southern notions of appropriate gender roles. During the war, women had expanded their sphere of sanctioned activity from the privacy of the household to the public world of nursing, charity, and work. Women took part in political discussions, urged men to enlist and fight, and resisted the Yankee invaders, all the while publicly maintaining a posture of ladylike femininity. Men were encouraged to fight through appeals to both their masculine honor and fortitude and their duty to protect white Southern womanhood. Losing the war implicitly challenged gendered notions of male masculinity. As men tried to resolve this blow to their honor and self-esteem, they sought to reassert control over women, both at home and in public.[5]

This struggle played out both within the household and in the pages of newspapers and magazines, memoirs, novels, and travel accounts. Women were not so quick to relinquish the power of speaking their minds on a variety of political and social topics. Much has been written in recent years about the roles of Southern white women in creating and sustaining Confederate nationalism during the Civil War, but we know comparatively little about the parts they played in reshaping Southern identity after the war. As Reconstruction began, Southerners engaged in public and private debates about how to maintain their identity in the face of the loss of their Confederate nation. Throughout the first years of Reconstruction, Southerners engaged in a region-wide conversation about how to preserve their Confederate past in the Reconstruction present. White Southern men who had supported the Confederacy were devastated by its defeat, and returned home to shattered political and personal landscapes. Southern men and women struggled to reaccustom themselves to one another after years of being apart. Despite their being forced back into the private sphere of home and family, women continued to publicly express their distaste for Yankees.

It became almost a cliché for postwar visitors to the South to comment on the unreconstructed nature of its white women.[6] "The men are rather more inclined to reconstruction than the women," observed one visitor to Charleston after the war, a comment that was repeated in almost every travel account. "The men of North Carolina may be 'subjugated,'" Northern journalist Whitelaw Reid observed: "But who shall subjugate the women?" A visiting Englishman found the bitterest hostility to the North "among the women, who have nothing to do but to stay at home and nurse their wrath."[7] This image of the unrepentant Southern woman, shunning Yankee soldiers as she persisted in her Confederate rebelliousness, was a holdover from the war years, when women under occupation resisted the invaders by using particularly feminine strategies. Southern men remarked on their women's uncowed spirit with a mixture of admiration and condescension: admiration for the women's lasting dedication to the cause, condescension for their stereotypically emotional responses.[8]

White Southern men relied on these stories of female intransigence to perform a sort of political ventriloquism. The manhood of conciliation demanded that white Southern men censor their public disapproval of the Union for reasons of political expedience. But men also recognized that, for the most part, gender insulated women from Yankee reprisals, freeing them to say and act as most white Southerners felt. Thus, by publicizing stories of women snubbing Northerners, men were able to express their bitterness toward the conquering Yankees while at the same time offering assurances that their loyalty to the Union could no longer be called into question—the better to regain their confiscated property and political rights. This more public role to which women had become accustomed during the war, however, threatened men's social dominance at home. Such vehemence could be seen as unladylike, almost masculine, and ought to be tempered.

Praise for unreconstructed women could be a double-edged sword— useful when directed at Yankees, problematic when directed at Southern men. Even as women were being implicitly praised for their unreconstructed ways, they were also being cautioned against overstepping the bounds of propriety. Attacking the Yankees was fine, but when a woman like Fanny Downing could write a poem berating Southern men for being unwilling to labor, a poem that included the following stanza, it was time to do something.

> Let Southern woman's red lips curl,
> And barbed shafts of satire hurl
> At men, who should, except for shame
> To womanhood, bear woman's name!
> We love not cowards, let it be
> Danger, or duty, which they flee![9]

For each approvingly related tale, there was another with an attitude of superiority on the editor's part, often in the same magazine, if not the same issue.

Thus, when a "Virginia lady" wrote to the *Land We Love* asking "at what time [did] our 'late enemies' become late," editor D. H. Hill responded in feigned amazement "What a question to propound to a loyal Editor in

District No. 2!" Hill reminded the woman that Southern whites needed to take the moral high ground. Similarly, he counseled another female subscriber who was concerned about how to treat "our late enemies" that "it is a safe rule to recognize the gentleman and man of honor wherever found, of whatever creed, sect, or nation."[10] Women needed to understand that war was like a business negotiation or a game: you fought your hardest while it was going on, but then you needed to be gracious in defeat (or victory) and put the battles behind you.

Women were both subtly patronized and overtly put back in their places at home, out of the realm of political discourse. By publishing an editorial mocking Lucy Stone and other Northern women who petitioned Congress for suffrage, the editors of the *Field and Fireside* sent a clear message to their female readers. The editorial scoffed at the suffragists' rationale that women should be given the franchise—that since African Americans were being given the vote, so, too, should it be granted to white women, declaring that "these 'women' surely *are* men, for no woman would ever have designed to aspire to negro equality."[11] Femininity required retreat from politics.

While the stories of defiant Southern women snubbing federal officers or crossing the street to avoid walking under an American flag are standard elements of Reconstruction narratives, they represent just two ways that women expressed their displeasure toward the Union. Former Confederate women also used the culture and medium of print—specifically postwar Southern newspapers and magazines—to insert themselves into this discussion of Southern identity. As Southern women rebuilt their own and their families' lives, they sought to preserve some of the public sphere for themselves, and many continued to use the explicitly public forums of poetry, fiction, and newspaper columns or essays. There seemed to be a utility in writing in a female voice, a perception among Southerners that women were more free to complain about the Union occupation. Often they wrote in a stereotypically feminine style, using sentimental verse to praise Southern soldiers, memorialize "the heroic dead," and call for charitable support of widows and orphans. They might also write to defend themselves against charges of disloyalty, as did a Mississippi lady who justified Southern women's decisions to marry Northern men on the basis of their fears of spinsterhood.[12] At other times, however, women used their platforms to criticize fellow Southerners, particularly men, whom they saw as forgetting the sacrifices of the past and being unwilling to work to return the South to prosperity.

These tensions over women's place become quite clear in the Betsey Bittersweet and Florence Fay columns. Indeed, the idea of political ventriloquism takes on particular salience in these two instances, because their form represented a departure from typical female types of writing. Neither Betsey Bittersweet nor Florence Fay fits neatly into the paradigm of domestic fiction or sentimental poetry in which the vast majority of women—either the well-known Northerners Harriet Beecher Stowe or Louisa May Alcott or the lesser known Southerners Margaret Junkin Preston, Fanny Fielding, or Fanny Downing—tended to write. One scholar of this literature has explained that "women's voices were to parallel the attributes of the cult of domesticity itself: to be passive, submissive, domestic, and self-denying." Betsey and Florence, as we shall see, were none of these.[13]

The Betsey Bittersweet and Florence Fay columns were unlike any other female newspaper writings. Their use of vernacular, even coarse, humor, as well as their anger and bitterness, made them unlike the sentimental fiction penned by other female contributors to the *Southern Home Journal* and the *Field and Fireside*. In many ways, they seem more typical of men's writings. There were a few mid-nineteenth-century female humorists, although they were all Northerners. Those Southern women who used humor tended to be local colorists, and tended also to write after the war.[14] Not surprisingly, humor written by men and women also tended to differ in their treatment of women in general, and of the emerging women's rights movement in particular. Women tended to be more sympathetic toward both their sex and their aspirations. In general, when a male humorist wrote about women's rights, he did so by presenting a figure of a coarse- or ridiculous-looking woman. More often, men's writings about women featured parodies of women's rights speeches, or direct disapproval of attempts by women to challenge social stereotypes.

The author of the Florence Fay letters is unknown, and therefore may have been either a man or a woman. The Betsey Bittersweet column, for all her masculine characteristics, was actually written by Mary Bayard Clarke, a prolific author best known for her poetry and essays. The Bittersweet letters represent somewhat of a departure for her, in terms of both their angry tone and satirical style. Her criticisms of the Radicals are especially interesting in light of her husband's joining the Republican party in late 1868. Certainly, Clarke felt the need to use a pseudonym to mask her unladylike expressions.[15]

Although there were enough similarities between the two columns to make analyzing them together both logical and useful, they were quite different in both tone and format. Betsey Bittersweet's letters were more explicitly concerned with politics, perhaps a function of the tumultuous months in which they were written. Every letter addressed political and racial tensions, and several dealt with North Carolina's second Reconstruction constitutional convention. Betsey also freely mocked African Americans for wanting to vote, and women for moving outside of their traditional place within the home and family. The letters were all written in dialect, with frequent misspellings and malapropisms, locating them squarely in the tradition of the antebellum Southwestern humorists, Northern characters like Artemus Ward, and Betsey's extraordinarily popular regional counterpart, Bill Arp.[16] Florence Fay's columns were less predictable. About half of them had to do with more social topics, whether in the form of diatribes against snuff-dipping or saloon-keeping or mocking attacks on social pretensions. Those that dealt with politics criticized both Yankees and ex-Confederates. When Florence Fay turned to political matters, she was more likely to complain about their effects on ordinary people in the form of economic hardships than to condemn black voting or white disfranchisement.

Betsey Bittersweet began her correspondence with the editors of the *Southern Home Journal* by expressing her sympathies for "the ex-queen of the United States," Mary Todd Lincoln. Betsey reported on a rumor that the "Radikills" (referred to in other letters as the "Redy-to-kills") were skimping on their financial support for Mrs. Lincoln, forcing her to sell off her old clothes. Betsey was shocked to discover that the widow's pension totaled seventeen hundred dollars a year, remarking that "republic's is ongrateful and that's a fact. Why that aint more'n twice as much as some private widows lives on, and to expect a public one to be satisfied with it is jest like them Radikills." This sarcasm was typical of her writings. Betsey went on to tell her husband that if she were in a similar position, rather than resort to selling her old clothes, she would pen an exposé of the situation, and "get it worked up into sich a book as the Democratick papers would pay me well for." She spun a series of potential titles for her serialized work:

One week I'd come out with a story called "The four S's, or the Secret Story of the Sable Set—Seward, Sumner, Stanton, and Stevens;" and the next I'd give the sequel to it, and call it "One Queen of Diamonds versus Four Knaves of Spades." And if that did'n't do the business, next week I'd come out with "The Loyal League, or Lace and Loot," and follow that with "The Black Cashmere, or the Blanket Contract," or the "Long Red Shawl, or Last Radikill Shift," or "The True History of the Public Pocket Handkerchief, and the Pocket it came out of, told by the Pocket it went into." And then I'd collect 'em all in a book, and call it "Rampant Radikill Revelations," or "The Public Washing of the Loyal Lincoln League Linen," and my fortune would be made.

Betsey uses her femininity to express her criticisms of the Radicals in two ways. First, rather than address their political policies directly, she attacks obliquely, through the figure of Mary Todd Lincoln, though it would be a mistake to think that Betsey had any great sympathy for the martyred president's wife. Then she couches her criticism of the radicals in a female form, that of titles for sentimental romances, the very sort that graced the pages of the *Southern Home Journal* itself.[17]

Just as Betsey looked back at the Civil War to make her political points, so too did Florence Fay. For example, when she addressed the question of "Patriotism" in January 1866, she charged that, despite "the vast amount of Patriotism there is at the present day between the two oceans . . . you can't always tell the genuine from the spurious article from the cut of the cloth." You can't tell a patriot from a pocketbook, she reflected ruefully:

until you find the latter convenience suddenly wrenched from your hand, on the principal thoroughfare, leaving a piece of the chain around your victimised finger, by something in blue breeches and army cap; and you look after the said breeches and cap as they widen the distance between you and them, with astonishing rapidity, and think what a surprising quantity of *Patriotism* must have got under those breeches and cap to give the fingers of that flying something the itch, and butter its heels.

In effect, patriotism was nothing more than an excuse to steal from the common people.[18]

Florence Fay devoted most of her essay to a mocking assessment of "Patriotism"—by which she meant Unionism, a recognition of North Carolina's divided population, perhaps—under both the Confederacy and Reconstruction. She described Patriotism calling at your house during the war, asking if you have a husband in the "rebel" army. You feed it, and it goes off without paying, and you look at Patriotism's back as it goes over the sill, and hope that it may always keep its toes in the present direction. Then you turn the bolts in the locks of your doors, and open your upper windows and when Patriotism makes you another call, there's nobody home but your poodle, whose little but loud mouth tells the news to patriotism through the keyhole.

Implicit in this picture was a real resentment of the ways Southern civilians had been treated at the hands of both their enemy invaders and their own Confederate government, a resentment that continued unabated into peace time. As she explained:

Patriotism had wide-awake eyes and cautious feet. It crept about between two days and very carefully and commendably choked old hens and young porkers, lest they should lay "secesh" eggs in the morning and utter a "rebel" squeak at day break, and so commit treason against the flag.

Patriotism claimed orchards and gardens as its own, by right of conquest—it made "dumplins and things" of the fruit, and very properly cut down the trees to cook 'em with.

Everything was *patriotic*; from the little nigger with both hands full of stolen candy, whistling "I wish I was in Dixie, hoo-ray!" *down* to the larger and lighter complexioned animal in blue and brass, singing musically, "We'll be gay and happy, too-hie!"

Patriotism, in the form of loyalty to the Union, had only given Southerners hardship and deprivation. Patriotism was money-grubbing and selfish. "Patriotism looked handsome and well until it put its industrious hands into its Uncle's pocket, in its anxiety to protect its purse, and got its fingers so pinched it disfigured its face. May the Lord bless Patriotism to the full extent of its merits, and keep its dear hands out of Uncle Sam's and his daughters pockets, and its precious feet away from poultry yards and pig pens."[19] Florence Fay's oblique yet humorous indictment of patriotism reflected white Southerners' disconnection from the rhetoric of postwar American nationalism. But because the anger came in the voice of a woman, it was softened and made less threatening. Florence Fay also took aim at the Yankees themselves, specifically the "Blue Devil or politely speaking, bonnie *Blue Beëlzebub!*"—the Northern officers who persisted in flirting with Southern women. She painted the Federals as leering lechers, unwilling to take no for an answer. "If you say to Blue Beëlzebub, 'get thee behind me satan,'" Florence Fay warned her female readers, "and succeed in pushing him from before your eyes, he'll bend over your shoulder and whisper in your ear; such and so pertinacious is a Blue Devil!" Florence Fay, protected by her lightly mocking tone, seized the opportunity to not only impugn the occupiers' present motives (that of seducing Southern women) but their past performance:

> Blue Devils are brave dogs, and "die in the last ditch" with the Prince of Orange, when battling with an inferiour force; but pusillanimous puppies in combat with equal numbers, and wheel suddenly and run rapidly from a bold and well-panoplied adversary, with delicately dropped oars and slender narrative modestly dangling between their posterior propellers.

In short, a fair fight would send the "Blue Devils" running away with their tails between their legs. While a male newspaper editor or author might have feared such an outright insult to the occupiers, the masks of humor and gender protected Florence Fay.[20]

Florence Fay directed her ire against white Southerners and Union soldiers, with African Americans almost entirely absent from her columns. The same could not be said for the more critical, more acerbic Betsey Bittersweet, who reported several nasty practical jokes at the freedmen's expense. In one instance, she described a new "Yankee invention" that had supposedly been keeping the freedmen from "stealing the corn and cotton from out'n the fields." What was this miraculous invention? Nothing less than fertilizer made from the bones of Union soldiers found on Southern battlefields, according to Betsey's Cousin Jane. It worked, according to Betsey, by playing on black fears of being "hanted," while also getting in a not-so-subtle dig at purported Yankee barbarity.[21] In a different letter, Betsey's husband tricked a group of African American men on their way to vote by convincing them that if they deposited their Radical tickets in the ballot box they would no longer have proof of their registration, and have "nothing to show for your mule and forty acres." Better they should drop Conservative tickets in the box, and hold onto their Radical ones. By using this image of the foolish freedmen, a staple of postwar white Southern (and nationally Democratic) rhetoric, Betsey signaled her essential conservatism. While the medium of a woman taking on a public political stance though newspaper commentary might be new, the message of racial, gender, and political hierarchies was not.

In the same letter, Betsey went on to complain about something even more ridiculous in her eyes: the spectacle of her female cook asking for time off

> "to forge all the notes in the county." "To register all the votes, you mean, don't you?" ses I. "Well," ses she, "and there aint much difference between the two." "No," ses I, "there aint, but what's the need of your going? You cant vote, 'cause you are a woman, and you might as well stay and git dinner." But she 'lowed she was'nt going to do no sich thing. "I'm as black as eny body," ses she, "and I knows my rights and am a gwine to the court-house after 'em."

The cook then comes to Betsey to ask for a basket in which to bring her franchise home. When asked if she knew what she was going after, what the franchise was, the woman replied:

> Well not 'zactly Miss Betsey, but that there Northern gentlemen as spoke 'tother day, sed as how God A'mighty had give us niggers the 'lective franchise, same as he gave the children of Israel manna in the dessert; he sed we was brought out of the land of bondage by Marse Moses-Lincoln, and now we was to taste the good things in store for us; and in course he's gwine to give us something good to eat better'n them rations of hard tack and salt beef they's been putting us off with till things get settled.

In Betsey's eyes, black women were foolish to overstep their bounds and expect something denied to white women. This anecdote highlighted the belief that African Americans had no idea what the franchise was, that they were simply sheep being led about by Northerners. Betsey's final complaint was that while her cook was off getting the franchise, she had to do her work and get her own dinner, which highlighted the persistent Southern complaint that emancipation had resulted in an erosion of ladylike prerogatives.[22]

Three of the six "Letters from Betsey Bittersweet" dealt with the most pressing political question of the winter of 1867–1868: North Carolina's Republican constitutional convention. She first traveled to the capital to hear William Holden and Zebulon Vance speak. Betsey was quite partial to the latter, whom she described as having "nothing provisional 'bout him." Indeed, Betsey claimed that his speech warning the freedmen that they would never rule the South was so inspiring that it moved a group of Union soldiers watching the proceedings to jump out of their seats and yell out: "'Give it to 'em Guv'nor, give it to 'em; this is the white man's country, and while bagonetts and bullets is to be got, niggers shan't rule it.'" Thus, this section of her letter does double duty: it endorses Zeb Vance's defiance while turning the Union occupiers into buffoons, no better than the freedmen who feared fertilizer.[23]

In her next letter, Betsey turned her attention to a letter written by Union General Ewing in which he likened the Southern states to "magazines, full of powder and percushon caps." According to Betsey:

> Southern wimen is like percushion caps, not much harm in 'em by themselves, tho ther's a good deal of noise ef you set 'em off. But jest attach 'em to a gun that's loaded and primed, and they'll do some mischief when they explode, I kin tell you. Let the sweet, harmless critters alone, Mr. Home Journal, for making their men folk shoot true, when they do go off, and vote to suit them.

She then takes issue with Ewing, who believed that the only way to keep the magazines from exploding was to guard them:

> I kin tell him, and you too, that packed in these magazines along of the powder and the percushion caps, is ever so many brimstone matches, and squirming around among all this here ammunition is a passel of political rats that quit the Confederate ship when she was about to sink, and being disappointed in gitting of a nibble at the big Union cheese, theys now a doing of ther best to light the matches, explode the powder, and blow things up in spite of the bagonets [bayonets].

She advises both Adams and Ewing to "invent a Yankee rat-trap, something like a Sherman's Wringer, you know" and catch all of the "rats" who are encouraging the blacks to listen to speeches rather than work in the fields. After that, "we may make a crop, which will allow the Yankees to make money out'n the South once more; and that will do more toards quieting of them and reconstructing things ginerally, than any gospel that kin be preached or pistel that kin be fired."[24] Betsey's letter carries a serious political message: a demand for home rule, a warning that politicians North and South were jeopardizing the fragile stability of the Reconstruction South, and a bitter recognition that all most people cared about was profits. But related in a humorous way, and by a woman, the words seemed less ominous, less threatening.

Betsey then wrote from the so-called North Carolina Constitutional Convention in Raleigh, mocking all of the delegates, but especially the newly enfranchised African Americans and the Radical Republicans. "And I can tell you, Mister Home Journal," she explained, "that the fight lays between the Conservatives and the niggers, for the white Radicals in this convention aint got sense enough even to be the puppets of the X.P.G., Mr. W. Holden, and the niggers have, and is accordingly elevated to that dignified position." Much of her letter was devoted to her desire to witness and report on the convention herself, "and not be dependent on no 'irresponsible stripling'" for her information. But it seems that to sit in the observers' gallery would have been improper, and so Betsey's solution was to disguise herself "in a short-tailed dress, with a red wig on, and the hair all skewered in the top of my head, with a little hat the size of a saucer stuck on in front and a pair of green specks stuck on." By adding a false nose and a blue veil, she had transformed herself into

> a nigger marm on her travels, anxious to hear the debates in a convention of the wisdom, learning, and ability of North Car'liner. The Southerners will be glad if I am satisfied with listening and don't want to take a part; and as for the Radikils, they will think, no matter what I do, its all for the glory of God and to make money.

In this instance of political ventriloquism, it was precisely Betsey's femininity that allowed her to cross boundaries, though always in the service of the conservative white South.[25]

The "Letter from Betsey Bittersweet" and "Florence Fay Arrows" also allowed men to resolve some issues of what has been called the more personal or domestic "crisis in gender" that engulfed the South after the Civil War. Several historians have suggested convincingly that, as the war drew to its bitter conclusion, the defeated Southern soldiers, bred in a patriarchal, honor-bound society, felt emasculated by their loss.[26] Their manhood and valor had been tested and had fallen short on the battlefield. Consequently, it would need to be reasserted at home. One of the many reconstructions Southern whites faced after the war involved that of male-female relations, and one of the media in which it played out was in the press. By presenting themselves as practical and conciliatory and women as intemperate and hysterical, men sought to reconstruct the divisions between the public and the domestic, the rational and the emotional.

This use of a woman's voice and figure could have other meanings, for not only did Betsey take aim at Reconstruction politics but (along with Florence Fay) she addressed social relations and appropriate female behavior. Clearly Betsey thought it inappropriate, if not completely ridiculous, for her cook to seek the franchise. But what of *her* political interests, *her* trips to the capital and convention? Betsey justified her actions carefully, and in so doing delineated the boundaries of acceptable female behavior. Betsey freely admitted that she usually went to visit her cousin Jane in Raleigh when "there's anything a stirring at the Capital," even though she thought "as a general rule politics and petticoats is too p's as oughten to be in the same pod." What made her behavior acceptable was that it wasn't her fault. Rather, the blame lay with the Union and the Radicals: "sense they've turned our men into wimen—or tried to do it by disfranchising of 'em—we wimen, who was always counted politically with the niggers, you know, is got demoralized, and has gone into politics like Senator Pool did into the Confederate service, 'jest to embarrass things.'" With this throwaway line at the beginning of a letter, Betsey neatly encapsulated the fears and resentments of ex-Confederate men. Their world had been turned upside down with black voting, imposed from the outside, and the next threat to stability could only come from one place: from women exercising the franchise. This was not an entirely irrational fear on the part of North Carolina's men, for the very convention that Betsey supposedly attended, along with others throughout the South, put in place new property rights for married women, and others saw proposals (voted down) for white female suffrage.[27]

Betsey was careful, however, not to go too far, and she pointedly condemned Northern women for wanting to vote. As Betsey saw it, "what does a woman want to vote for, when at the very least she can always, if she understands her rights, make at least one man vote as she pleases?" Women had plenty of rights already:

> a right to our own way, when we can git it without a row in the family; and a smart woman kin always do that, if she goes the right way to work. And we've a right to pat and pet and coax our men folks, now a pulling of the right rein, then a twitch of the left, and then holding both of 'em sorter easy but firm; like you do sperited horses, till you can turn 'em any way you want to,

and make 'em think all the time they're agoing of ther own way instead of yours.

By expressing concern over women taking too public and political a role, Betsey argued for a return to antebellum gender conventions. At the same time, though, she realized that for many women such a retrenchment would be impossible: "But I ain't of opinion that she has a right to be a man, or even pretend she's one; and ef she is obliged to wear the britches for the good of the family, her skirts ought to be long enuf to hide 'em." If a woman had to take charge for the sake of her family, and many women did, she needed to do so in a way that preserved her man's virile image.[28] In doing this, Betsey also reflected what would become a longstanding trend in Southern history—that of the antisuffrage woman, best exemplified a generation later by Rebecca Lattimer Felton.

Like Florence Fay complaining about the high costs of patriotism and its tendency to result in extra work for white women, Betsey Bittersweet also expressed her dismay with the shape of postwar Southern social relations. In the same letter in which she mocked her cook for seeking the franchise (and leaving her to get the family's dinner), Betsey complained that the Freedmen's Bureau had been invented "jest to make Southern ladies have to do their own work, like Northern ones does, so as they would by their cute contrivances." These contrivances to which Betsey referred included "Union Washing Mashins" and "Sherman's Wringers." In a letter dated January 1, 1868, she lamented how much work Christmas was for the mistress of the house without slaves to assist in the preparations, noting that "it was a very good thing in the old time when we had servants and money and could keep it like ladies and gentlemen, but it don't suit these times." She proposed a radical solution:

And, while we are a reconstructing, I vote to reconstruct Christmas, and appint that hereafter it shall fall on the twenty-ninth day of February instead of on the twenty-fifth day of December. Thanksgiving belongs to the Yankees, fourth of July to the niggers, and Christmas ought to belong to the white folks.

By adopting the persona of the overworked Southern lady, Betsey was able to voice Southern complaints about the changes in public ritual (specifically the celebration of the Fourth of July by freedpeople) that had accompanied Reconstruction.[29]

Florence Fay was less concerned with explicitly resolving the crisis in gender by removing women from the public and political sphere, and more interested in defining appropriate and ladylike behavior for her female readers. She spoke out against snuff-dipping by women—and by men; she mocked flirtatious "wee women," who attend church for the sole purpose of catching men's attention. The wee woman at home was no better:

> She enters the parlor with the self conscious dignity of a queen, sets the heel of her right foot into the instep of her left, forms a semi-circle with the right, then the "left wheel"—crawfishing; dips, squats, shows her teeth, slides, and then swims off to the farthest sofa; half drops, crosses her small jeweled hands systematically upon her belt buckle, and sits like a wax doll in a show window— afraid to be natural, lest she should not appear womanly. . . . She sings like a swan: and you'd think she was in the last agonies of a dying one, but for the evident soundness of the lungs under those catch-me-quick eyes rolled so far towards her brain pan that nothing is visible but the whites.

By puncturing pretensions, Florence Fay told women to retrench. The overt flirtatiousness of the war years was inappropriate for peacetime; women were no longer to take the lead, in either public or private.[30]

While she frowned at flirtations, Florence Fay was not opposed to marriage. Indeed, in one column she provided advice (to both men and women) on choosing a mate, in the process painting a picture of desirable postwar Southern gender behavior. Women were cautioned against "a masculine" who drinks with his friends, who attends church either too frequently or not often enough, who "squirts great sluices of tobacco juice," or who is prone to jealousy. "Take it for granted," Florence Fay advised, "if your lover is an imp, your husband will be the d—! [devil]" Men were given even more specific advice in choosing a proper lady. The ideal bride should not be overly interested in fashion, and men were warned to

> *Prenez garde* of her who sports every color of the rainbow about her pinched-up form, and any quantity of gay ribbons streaming from her waterfall. Marry her, and she'll soon push you into defrauding the Government of two hundred thousand dollars, and you'll

very speedily "bring up" at the penitentiary, with your ladie fayre flirting around to theaters, operas, etc., with popinjays and *patriots* during your imprisonment.

Nor should men choose a woman who constantly scolded the servants, for a bad mistress would never make a good wife. "You may learn a woman's worth from a domestic's tongue more certainly than you can get the truth from Robert Tomes' 'History of the great American Rebellion' or General Big Failure Butler's 'reports,'" references to popular histories of the war. Finally, men were warned against choosing a woman who clamors

loudly for equality with man, and thinks said equality consists in the right of poking bits of paper into the ballot box on election days—tricked out in trowsers, a short frock and shingled hair. Marry her and she'll make you feel as cheap as the famous tower at Bermuda Hundred was sold, if you are a Southern man. Marry her and if you are a "foreigner" she'll help you vote southern plantations into small farms for contrabands and "furrin squatters."

In this last advice, Florence Fay closes the circle, neatly linking the personal and political. Even marriage for whites in the postwar South had public consequences. A good wife was one who stayed home, and a good wife was one who endorsed a return to the political status quo of the antebellum years. A politicized wife, one who sought the franchise, was no better than a Yankee.

Although the "Letters from Betsey Bittersweet" and "Florence Fay Arrows" shared much in terms of both tone and content, they appear to have been aimed at different audiences. Betsey's letters—with their more overtly political content, use of feminine disguises, and more vernacular language, in the tradition of the (male) Southwestern humorists—seem to have been written for men. Women, including, at times, Betsey herself, are clear objects of ridicule. The letters are not really concerned with delineating the boundaries of appropriate female behavior, or at least not for white women. Class, too, is important in these letters. Betsey is presented as somewhere between lower and middle class, not so well-bred as to speak properly or have several servants, but not so badly off as to be entirely without domestic help or other resources. While one could imagine elite men chuckling over her malapropisms, it's difficult to imagine what lessons upper-class women might take from her adventures. Florence Fay, however, occupies a more indeterminate class position. She is much more concerned with limiting roles and opportunities for women, reminding them to stay away from men, cautioning them against appearing too forward or flirtatious. At the same time, some of her writings, as in the Blue Devil column, were every bit as coarse and earthy as Betsey's.

What might readers have taken away from these columns? Did they take the advice to heart, or were these writings simply amusing diversions? Politically, Betsey was clearly preaching to the choir in the disgust she felt toward both the Radicals and the freedmen. Women could do little with Betsey's suggestions and examples. Florence's advice might have been taken more to heart, though plenty of women continued to flirt with Union soldiers and white Southern men alike. These columns broke no new ground in their content. Their significance lies in their form and tone. Betsey and Florence, for all the humor inherent in their writings, were strong women taking a public stance on issues that mattered to them. By ranging broadly over issues of both private and public significance they signaled an expansion, however slight, of women's purview during the tumult of Reconstruction.

NOTES

1. These letters are written in dialect; I have transcribed them as is, without using "[sic]." Unless otherwise indicated, spellings and punctuation are original.

2. Unless otherwise qualified, when I use the words "Southern woman" or "Southerner" in this article, they refer to whites who supported the Confederacy and objected to Reconstruction.

3. "Florence Fay Arrows: Small Fry," *Field and Fireside*, December 23, 1865; "Florence Fay Arrows: Mushroom Aristocracy," *Field and Fireside*, December 30, 1865. These columns appeared in late 1865 and early 1866, about two years before Betsey's letters in the *Southern Home Journal*. The *Field and Fireside* was a continuation of the wartime *Southern Field and Fireside*, a weekly paper published first in Augusta, Georgia, and then in Raleigh, North Carolina. It, too, consisted of a mixture of serial fiction, poetry, and political writings.

4. "Prospectus of the Southern Home Journal," *Southern Home Journal*, December 28, 1867.

5. For a provocative study of the intersection of race, class, gender, and Reconstruction in Granville County, North Carolina, see Laura F. Edwards, *Gendered Strife and Confusion: The Political Culture of Reconstruction* (Urbana:

University of Illinois Press, 1997). See also Drew Gilpin Faust, *Mothers of Invention: Women of the Slaveholding South in the American Civil War* (Chapel Hill: The University of North Carolina Press, 1996), 248–254; LeeAnn Whites, *The Civil War as a Crisis in Gender: Augusta, Georgia, 1860–1890* (Athens: University of Georgia Press, 1995), 132–159; Catherine Clinton, *Tara Revisited: Women, War, and the Southern Plantation Legend* (New York: Abbeville Press, 1995), 160–174.

6. Nina Silber, *The Romance of Reunion: Northerners and the South, 1865–1900* (Chapel Hill: University of North Carolina Press, 1993), 26–28. I am only looking at these stories as they appeared in Southern publications and through Southern eyes, since other historians, Nina Silber in particular, have examined the Northern writings. Silber argues that Northerners used these stories as further evidence of the degraded state of Southern gender roles and relations. Southern men, already emasculated by their losses on the battlefield, were seen as all the more weak because of their inability to control their womenfolk.

7. Gail Hamilton, *Wool-Gathering* (Boston: Ticknor & Fields, 1867), 301–302; Whitelaw Reid, *After the War: A Tour of the Southern States, 1865–1866*, edited by C. Vann Woodward (New York: Harper & Row, 1965), 46; Robert Ferguson, *America during and after the War* (London: Longmans, Green, Reader, and Dyer, 1866), 208.

8. Silber, *Romance of Reunion*, 26–28; Gaines M. Foster, *Ghosts of the Confederacy: Defeat, The Lost Cause and the Emergence of the New South, 1865–1913* (New York: Oxford University Press, 1987), 29–31.

9. Fanny Downing [Mary J. Upshur], "To Proud to Work," *Land We Love* 2 (April 1867): 444.

10. *Land We Love* 3 (July 1867): 269; *The Land We Love* 1 (August 1866): 304.

11. *Field and Fireside*, January 20, 1866, 20.

12. "Sic Transit," *Crescent Monthly* 1 (October 1866): 323. The same poem also appeared in *Land We Love* 2 (November 1866): 16.

13. Martha J. Cutter, *Unruly Tongue: Identity and Voice in American Women's Writing, 1850–1930* (Jackson: University Press of Mississippi, 1999), xv.

14. The female vernacular humorists included Frances Berry Whitcher, who used both dialect and the figure of the Widow Bedott to depict her neighbors in western New York state during the 1840s; Marietta Holley, and her folksy but well-traveled Samantha Smith Allen; and Ann Stephens, who constructed a male persona, Jonathan Slick, for her critiques of New York City's upper class. In her study of women's vernacular humor, Linda Morris argues that women's writings differed from those of men in significant ways.

First, female humorists tended to write for a female audience, and chose as their subject the place of women in so-called genteel society. Women like Whitcher, Holley, and Stephens were social critics, dedicated to skewering social pretensions. Male humor, and in particular the work of the antebellum and wartime Southwestern humorists like Augustus Baldwin Longstreet and George Washington Harris, tended to be more masculine, with an emphasis on fighting, hunting, and politics. Indeed, vernacular humor became popular throughout America in the 1830s and 1840s, the same years that saw the emergence and rise of the doctrine of separate spheres; styles in humor reflected trends in society as a whole. Linda A. Morris, *Women Vernacular Humorists in Nineteenth-Century America* (New York: Garland, 1988), 2, 14–21.

15. See Terrell Armistead Crow and Mary Moulton Barden, *Live Your Own Life: The Family Papers of Mary Bayard Clarke, 1854–1886* (Columbia: University of South Carolina Press, 2003), xlv, 250–253. I thank Jane Turner Censer for alerting me to this.

16. Interestingly, the first Arp letters written during the war by Charles Henry Smith were written in dialect, but his postwar humor columns were not. See David B. Parker, *Alias Bill Arp: Charles Henry Smith and the South's "Goodly Heritage"* (Athens: University of Georgia Press, 1991).

17. "Letter from Betsey Bittersweet," *Southern Home Journal*, November 23, 1867, p. 7.

18. "Florence Fay Arrows: Patriotism," *Field and Fireside*, January 1, 1866.

19. Ibid.

20. "Florence Fay Arrows: Blue Devils," *Field and Fireside*, March 24, 1866.

21. "Letter from Betsey Bittersweet," *Southern Home Journal*, December 21, 1867, p. 8.

22. Ibid., December 7, 1867, p. 8.

23. Ibid., December 21, 1867, p. 8.

24. Ibid., January 4, 1868, p. 8.

25. Ibid., March 21, 1868, p. 5. Betsey's letter is dated February 21.

26. See Whites, *Civil War as a Crisis in Gender*, 132–150; Foster, *Ghosts of the Confederacy*, 26–29.

27. "Letter from Betsey Bittersweet," *Southern Home Journal*, December 21, 1867, p. 8. Suzanne D. Lebsock, "Radical Reconstruction and the Property Rights of Southern Women," in *Half Sisters of History: Southern Women and the American Past*, edited by Catherine Clinton (Durham, N.C.: Duke University Press, 1994), 110–135.

28. "Letter from Betsey Bittersweet," *Southern Home Journal*, January 4, January 1868, p. 8.

29. Ibid., December 7, 1867, p. 8, and February 2, 1868, p. 8.

30. "Florence Fay Arrows: Wee Women," *Field and Fireside*, January 20, 1866. Florence Fay also sent arrows flying in the direction of grumblers and saloon-keepers. See "Florence Fay Arrows: Grumblers," *Field and Fireside*, January 27, 1866, and "Florence Fay Arrows: Stray Arrows," *Field and Fireside*, February 3, 1866.

10

THE CONFEDERATE RETREAT TO MARS AND VENUS

Thomas J. Brown

They are a study in the art of contrast. The marble statue to the fallen Confederate soldiers of South Carolina stands in front of the principal entrance to the state capitol (fig. 1). Leaning on his rifle as he looks directly down Main Street from a height of forty feet, he commands the precise point at which the channels of government and business power meet in Columbia. The bronze statue to the Confederate women of South Carolina sits diametrically across from the State House, about an equal distance from the building, in a chair on a low pedestal (fig. 2). With her back to the street, surrounded on three sides by shrubbery atop a restraining wall, she looks up from the Bible resting on her lap. The carefully coordinated inscriptions on the two monuments underscore that the models of virtue shared an abiding commitment to the Lost Cause. The men were "TRUE TO THE INSTINCTS OF THEIR BIRTH, / FAITHFUL TO THE TEACHINGS OF THEIR FATHERS, / CONSTANT IN THEIR LOVE FOR THE STATE," and the women were "UNCHANGED IN THEIR DEVOTION, / UNSHAKEN IN THEIR PATRIOTISM, / UNWEARIED IN MINISTRATIONS, / UNCOMPLAINING IN SACRIFICES." The inscriptions also emphasize that this common loyalty provided a basis for mutual respect and affection. The soldiers monument declares that it has been "ERECTED BY THE WOMEN OF SOUTH CAROLINA"; the monument to women answers that it was "REARED BY THE MEN OF THE STATE." Together, the monuments to the exemplary Confederate man and the exemplary Confederate woman naturalize the South Carolina State House—their house—and situate the

Figure 1. Muldoon, Walton & Company, South
Carolina Soldiers Monument (1879). Photograph
by Thomas J. Brown.

public realm in a timeless order of sexual differentiation and harmony
epitomized by the gendering force of war.

Historians have learned to be skeptical of the notion that the Civil War
so simply perpetuated an ancient martial reinforcement of distinctions
ordained by biology. To the contrary, the scholarship of the past fifteen
years has shown that the sectional conflict reflected and sparked vigorous
contests over gender ideals and that remembrance of the war provided a
vehicle for advancing a variety of views of manhood and womanhood.

Figure 2. Frederick W. Ruckstuhl, Monument to
South Carolina Women of the Confederacy (1912).
Photograph by Thomas J. Brown.

The monument to fallen Confederate soldiers unveiled at the South Carolina State House by women in 1879 and the monument to Confederate women juxtaposed with it by men in 1912, both the first memorials
of their type to be placed in a former Confederate capital, offer useful
points for charting the trajectory of ideas about gender and relations
among male and female organizations in the public culture of the Lost
Cause. A look at the funding, design, inscriptions, and dedications of the
paired landmarks suggests the extent to which a wartime consensus over

gender roles fragmented over three decades and the ways the culture of commemoration strained as well as strengthened relations among white Southern men and women.

The stresses of the war years and their immediate aftermath shaped the decade-long work of the South Carolina Monument Association (SCMA). The founding of the SCMA was part of the process of defining women's role in the mobilization of white South Carolinian opposition to Reconstruction. Columbia women arranged for the organizational meeting to take place during the November 1869 state fair, the first such gathering since the war and an important forum for strategists making plans to reverse the political upheaval that had recently placed Republicans in control of the state legislature. Sponsored by the State Agricultural and Mechanical Society under the direction of future Democratic governor General Hagood Johnson, the 1869 fair coincided with the formation of several other statewide networks, including the Confederate Survivors' Association, headed by Democratic leader General Wade Hampton; the Young Men's Christian Association, directed by future Democratic party chair Colonel Alexander Haskell; and the South Carolina Club, promoting social interaction among young gentlemen, guided by future Democratic paramilitary commander General Martin Gary. Though no transcript survives of Hampton's address to the first meeting of the SCMA at Washington Street Chapel on November 4, he most likely suggested to them, as he did to a similar Virginia group four years later, that their project reflected "no keen sense of private bereavement" but was "more sacred in its aims and more patriotic in its object." The SCMA chose a president who combined both motives, Louisa McCord, the mother of a fallen soldier as well as an accomplished Southern polemicist and a leading figure in wartime nursing and soldiers' aid societies. McCord demonstrated that she certainly understood the SCMA to be a political organization: six months after she took the position she resigned in protest against the short-lived Union Reform strategy of Democratic alliance with conservative Republicans, declaring that "to our beloved dead, principles are a nobler monument than marble."[1]

Before she resigned, McCord composed a public appeal addressed to the women of South Carolina that eloquently summarized the political premises of the SCMA. Her statement envisioned the SCMA as a group defined by emotional and tangible sacrifice, established to parallel as well as honor the soldiers' "great sacrifice of pure purpose." McCord announced that membership dues had been set "at the lowest point practicable" in order to broaden opportunities for participation to those "who, having little to give, have still the right, through tears and suffering, to join us in the fulfillment of this most sacred duty," and she exhorted other South Carolinians to "give to us freely according to your means, give generously; give gratefully to the memory of those who gave their lives for us." Consistent with this principle, the group raised money almost exclusively through donations, disdaining bazaars, raffles, and benefit entertainments. McCord expressly invited men as well as women to contribute, but the project figured women as the leaders of the community undertaking and as self-sacrificing counterparts to fallen soldiers at the metonymic monument.[2]

This vision of women as representatives of South Carolina took on a special concreteness amid the effort to resist Reconstruction by establishing institutions that would rival the Republican government. From the outset, the women sought to place their monument in a conspicuous public location. When soil instability frustrated the initial plan to set it atop a hill in Sydney Park with a commanding view of the city, they reluctantly accepted the gift of a site outside the front gate of Elmwood Cemetery while they continued to raise funds for the statue. After the Democratic recapture of political control in 1877, the legislature granted the SCMA's petition for a site at the capitol and paid for the relocation of the base from Elmwood Cemetery, ratifying the women's claim to act on behalf of the state.

If the SCMA departed from antebellum patriarchy by asserting political leadership and placing women alongside fallen soldiers on a plane of citizenship defined by sacrifice, the image of manhood that was advanced by the organization contrasted equally sharply with the ideal of mastery that slaveholding had fostered. The most obvious expression of this alternative image was the statue that the SCMA ordered from Muldoon, Walton & Company, for ten thousand dollars, in July 1873. Identified by SCMA secretary Isabella Martin in the official organization history as "a picket 'in for' a night's duty," the soldier wearing a cloak on his shoulders to ward off the midnight chill and holding his rifle upright with bayonet fixed was an example of the figure that with slight variations would eventually be found in more than a thousand communities across the country. At the time the SCMA placed its order, about forty single-figure sentinels had been dedicated, all but one in the North. The SCMA, which reported proudly that all members of the Muldoon firm and all workmen on the Columbia job were Confederate veterans, was decidedly not attempting to emulate its Northern counterparts. Instead, its design selection evoked an intersectional wartime culture of sentimentality that historian Alice Fahs has recently traced in popular literature. As Fahs notes, the picket was a key icon in this representation of the Civil War because he embodied the soldier as an individual, not as a part merged into a mass, and offered an opportunity to imagine his thoughts during long, lonely vigils. Popular songs emphasized that in those hours the sentinel mostly dwelt on the sweetness of home. For example, in "All Quiet on the Potomac," widely circulated on both sides of the line, the night guard envisioned his children ("the two on the low trundle-bed / Far away in the cot on the mountain") and then turned to his wife:

> The moon seems to shine as brightly as then,—
> *That night* when the love yet unspoken
> Leaped up to his lips, and when low-murmured vows
> Were pledged to be ever unbroken.
> Then drawing his sleeve roughly over his eyes,
> He dashes off tears that are welling,
> And gathers his gun close up to its place,
> As if to keep down the heart-swelling.[3]

Moreover, the extreme vulnerability of the isolated picket encapsulated all soldiers' limited control over their fate in the staggeringly deadly war. To be sure, Martin reported that "the most striking characteristic of the statue" was the "full manly strength" of the determined expression on the soldier's face, "which seems to say 'the cause I defend is a just one, and my soul is enlisted in it.'" But that mid-Victorian ideal of "full manly strength" was defined by endurance of privation rather than the aggressive exertion of force.[4]

The SCMA added a South Carolina twist to these widely shared principles by asking the sculptor to model the face of the statue from a photograph of Beaufort native Stephen Elliott. The choice was in some respects peculiar, for the monument explicitly honored men who died in the performance of duty, and Elliott lived until 1866, though he never fully recovered from wounds sustained late in the war. Moreover, the well-born Elliott had entered the Confederate army as an officer and risen to the rank of general, which conflicted with the focus of the statue on the ordinary private as an emblematic figure. But as the commander at Fort Sumter for the first nine months after the fall of Fort Wagner in September 1863, Elliott's stoic perseverance through constant bombardment had come to personify a heroic manhood defined by steady fortitude rather than dashing battlefield charges. A poignant eulogy delivered to the state legislature by historian and politician William Henry Trescot capped this reputation by describing Elliott as a typical South Carolina soldier who "simply did his duty where his country put him." Though fame eventually found him, Elliott had "indulged in no fretful longing for promotion, no impatient anxiety for a sphere of larger ambition," during months of "arduous but comparatively obscure service" before his assignment to Fort Sumter. Another eulogist stressed that Elliott brought to Fort Sumter the strength he had gained in his wartime religious conversion, an experience that the sentimental image of soldiers often highlighted and that— like unglamorous, self-effacing toil—was central to prescribed ideals of womanhood. Even a quarter-century after the dedication of the Columbia monument, remembrance of Elliott would prompt the reflection that "the bravest are the tenderest often and that man is at his best when some womanly thought ennobles him, just as womanhood is soundest with a touch of manliness to make it strong."[5]

The SCMA invited Trescot to expand on his portrait of the representative South Carolina soldier by commissioning him to write the inscription for its monument. The result was a masterpiece of its genre, reprinted in literary anthologies and magazine articles and reproduced on at least ten other Confederate monuments around the South; more than a century later, V. S. Naipaul reported that it deservedly remained known in South Carolina as a poetic expression "of the South's idea of itself."[6] Noting that the text "ought to be true and simple and yet there is an element of ornateness that a monument inscription requires," Trescot built his composition around an insistent parallel structure that highlighted the qualities of deliberateness and equipoise in the Confederate soldier. In arguing that the dead "HAVE GLORIFIED A FALLEN CAUSE / BY THE SIMPLE MANHOOD OF THEIR LIVES," he located that simple manhood in "THE PATIENT ENDURANCE OF SUFFERING,/AND THE HEROISM OF DEATH." The inscription on the front of the monument echoed the popular songs of the Civil War by emphasizing the close connections between loved ones at home and soldiers who

IN THE DARK HOURS OF IMPRISONMENT,
IN THE HOPELESSNESS OF THE HOSPITAL,
IN THE SHORT, SHARP AGONY OF THE FIELD,
FOUND SUPPORT AND CONSOLATION
IN THE BELIEF
THAT AT HOME THEY WOULD NOT BE FORGOTTEN.

The inscription on the reverse side of the monument further elaborated a vision of masculinity consistent with the sentimental ideal. Trescot stressed that moral purity, and particularly a strong sense of self-restraint, had guided the soldiers through life and into the afterlife. He enjoined future strangers looking at the monument to

RECOGNIZE THAT THESE WERE MEN
WHOM POWER COULD NOT CORRUPT,
WHOM DEATH COULD NOT TERRIFY,
WHOM DEFEAT COULD NOT DISHONOR.[7]

The dedication ceremony on May 13, 1879, not only praised the power of self-restraint exhibited by the dead but tested its presence among the living. Long remembered by whites as "one of the greatest days, it may be the greatest, that ever [Columbia] has known," the spectacle marked the first time after Reconstruction that former Confederate supporters in South Carolina "with a feeling of sureness that they were a free people let themselves loose in a mighty jubilation."[8] Excursion trains from around the state brought a crowd estimated at up to fifteen thousand people. The *Charleston News and Courier* relayed breathlessly that the streets were alive "with military either marching in glittering bodies or strolling upon the pavements and commingling with the civilians." The SCMA and its supporters took pride, however, that the excitement did not overwhelm the self-possession of participants. The *Columbia Register* reported that of the more than a thousand former soldiers in arms, "not a man was intoxicated." The SCMA official history declared it "one of the largest, most enthusiastic, and at the same time most orderly, harmonious and satisfactory demonstrations that Columbia has ever seen."[9] When emotions did overflow, it was not in the direction of boisterousness; rather, newspapers reported that old soldiers were moved to tears by the pathos of the day, which reached its climax in the unveiling of the monument by four young women orphaned by the war, who were escorted by four young veterans who had each lost an arm for the Confederacy.

The SCMA's choice of General John Preston as the orator of the day further clarified the ideas about gender associated with the monument. The transformation Preston identified in contrasting "the wild enthusiasm with which [the soldiers] began the fight, and the stern religious courage with which they met all its terrible trials" aptly expressed the masculine ideal of the SCMA. As former head of the Conscription Bureau, moreover, Preston personified military service as an acceptance of duty rather than an exercise of voluntarism, and he emphasized that Confederate soldiers had no equals in "calm endurance and fortitude, in meek submission to and humble reliance on the God of all Truth."[10] Preston's administrative position also made him a representative of the rights of noncombatants, such as the women of the SCMA, to address the meaning of the war. This point produced some controversy when his bombastic defense of secession and resistance to Reconstruction drew objections that "denunciation and vituperation . . . come with ill grace from one who saw no active field service." Preston's defenders grounded his right to speak for the community in terms often applied to women: he had served the Confederacy faithfully in a capacity appropriate for his physical condition, and he had lost a son to the cause.[11]

Preston's remarks on women in his oration more directly recognized them as entitled by their sacrifices to represent the public. Suggesting that the Wayside Hospital in the Gervais Street railroad depot, where female volunteers had rendered assistance to seventy-five thousand soldiers passing through Columbia, "would have been as grand a monument to these women as that granite and marble is to the dead soldier," Preston stressed not that the hospital initiative had demonstrated feminine solicitude and tenderness but that the "earnest, active, efficient, working sacrifice" had left "fair, delicate women, wasted, haggard, tottering beneath burdens which might have crushed the stoutest of us." He further pursued the motif of a monument to women's sacrifices by pointing out that the soldier statue looked toward the neighborhood most devastated in the February 1865 burning of Columbia. Observing that it was "placed on the spot where these women stood shelterless, in the black winter night, with their old men and half-naked children gazing thitherward at their crumbling houses . . . burned to the ground by those who had slain the men whose effigy overtops the column," Preston asked: "Is not this monument meant, in part, to commemorate that scene?" He rhetorically urged the SCMA to "go, ladies, and call your sculptor here, and bid him complete his half-told tale and carve there, in deep relief, your own images, crouching and shuddering, and huddling around the base."[12] A jarring reminder of Confederate military impotence amid white South Carolinians' celebration of their victory over Reconstruction, Preston's vivid picture of an implied component to the monument presented the collective ordeal of soldiers and female and quasi-female civilians as the epitome of the broader system of gender equivalencies and transferences embedded in the work of the SCMA. The marble memorial promised to stand as a permanent declaration that white Southern men and women shared a common experience, a unified public authority, and overlapping sets of moral virtues.

Despite the reinforcement it received from the SCMA, the early postwar commemorative construction of white Southern manhood and womanhood faced substantial challenges by the late 1870s. The tension was first evident in Columbia in the observance of Memorial Day, where an 1876 squabble that Democratic strategist Alexander Haskell called a "war of men against women" dramatized the emergence of veterans as rivals to women's leadership of Confederate commemoration. The chief institutional fruition of this trend was the United Confederate Veterans (UCV), which did not share the SCMA's idealization of the sentimental Confederate soldier. The UCV's model man was distinguished by his martial prowess rather than his lonely vulnerability, and while he grandly appreciated the support he received from women at home, he was also sustained by his political principles and his comrades. This vision of gender roles sought to limit women to honoring men without the opportunities for independent public expression that the Columbia soldiers monument had provided, an arrangement most vividly exemplified by the distinctive Southern practice of selecting attractive young unmarried women to play prominent roles in veterans' reunions as "sponsors" of delegations. As historian Gaines Foster has noted, this "ritual presentation of virgins to veterans" affirmed the aging ex-soldiers' manhood.[13]

Women did not meekly accept a subordinate position in Confederate commemorative culture. In Columbia, the primary vehicle for reassertion of their centrality was the Wade Hampton Chapter of the United Daughters of the Confederacy (UDC), formed in 1895, which launched two major projects articulating ideas about gender, the establishment of the Confederate Record and Relic Room and the publication of *South Carolina Women in the Confederacy* (2 vols., 1903–1907). But the women, too, departed from the model of the Columbia soldiers monument. The Relic Room, placed by the legislature in 1901 in a room at the State House that looked out on the statue, devoted relatively little attention to the ties between soldiers and their families and focused not on nameless privates but on the Confederate leaders whose success and power within the disciplined military hierarchy offered a template for civilian class stratification. And rather than emphasizing women's sacrifice as a metonymic link to soldiers, the museum and book stressed the resourceful productivity of Confederate women. The contemporary implications of this zealous commemoration of women's contributions became increasingly sensitive during the 1890s, as women began to enroll in the University of South Carolina and the woman suffrage movement reached the state.

Apart from its affinities with civil and political tendencies that brought women into controversial terrain, Confederate commemoration itself proved to be a site of recurrent conflict between men and women. In 1906, for example, the UDC "most enthusiastically adopted" a resolution urging the UCV to "dispense with the offices of Sponsor and Maids of Honor" at its upcoming meeting and ensure "that the entertainments for that occasion be such as are adapted to aged Confederate Veterans."[14] The resolution hinted not only that the veterans should reclaim their dignity but also that they should show more appreciation for the female virtues documented in the Relic Room and in *South Carolina Women in the Confederacy*. A proposal by veterans to organize a public tribute to Confederate women offered an opportunity to act on this hint.

Like the similar state memorials that followed it throughout the South, the South Carolina monument to Confederate women exposed friction between men and women even as it honored their partnership. White Southern women began to criticize the regional campaign for a monument to their beloved wartime women heroines almost as soon as the annual UCV meeting endorsed the idea in 1896.[15] Their resistance was partly a continuation of a struggle for control of the Confederate commemorative agenda, which intensified in 1899 when the UCV passed along to the UDC responsibility for the slow-moving effort to place an expensive monument to Jefferson Davis in Richmond; the UDC firmly opposed undertakings that would distract veterans from fund raising for the Davis monument, and after its dedication in May 1907, women continued to claim authority to weigh the intended tribute to Confederate women against other priorities, like the establishment of residential facilities for indigent veterans. Moreover, women showed little enthusiasm for a public monument as an instrument for recognizing and perpetuating their model of womanhood. Their preference for a home for Confederate widows pointed up a complaint that deepened when General C. Irvine Walker of Charleston took charge of the UCV monument committee and pressed for adoption of a single monument design that would be replicated at the capitols of all of the former Confederate states. Walker argued that this plan would avoid geographic rivalries while containing costs and would also testify to the unanimity with which Southerners revered Confederate women. But the striking departure from the highly decentralized process that was placing soldiers monuments in communities throughout the South underscored a difference in the ways the projects balanced two goals. Memorials like the soldiers monument at the South Carolina State House invited remembrance of each man who had died in the war. In contrast, the proposed tribute to women sought more to sanction an abstract ideal than to recognize the specific historic achievements of particular individuals. And insofar as that ideal sought to guide future generations, many women expressed less confidence in the influence of a monument to be commissioned by the UCV than in the establishment of a college for women, or if fund raising could not hope to achieve so much, the endowment of college scholarships.[16]

Women's dissatisfaction with the proposal, widely shared in South Carolina, made it plain that men's inflexible commitment to a monument as a form of commemoration constituted a defiance of women as much as a tribute to them. A supporter in Chesterfield sounded the keynote of the initiative when he declared that "it is always safe to follow the women, but the boys of the '60s will not follow them in this."[17]

The leadership of South Carolina in the regional commemorative movement resulted from distrust of the UCV's process and eagerness to turn the venture to political and economic advantage. With the veterans' effort at a standstill, rising young legislator John G. Richards, Jr., moved to bring the effort to fruition in South Carolina. After consultation with editor William Elliott Gonzales of *The State* newspaper of Columbia, he introduced a bill in January 1909 that provided for an appropriation of seventy-five hundred dollars toward a monument, to become available upon the contribution of an equal amount by "the male inhabitants of South Carolina." Upon passage of the measure two months later, *The State* immediately launched a front-page campaign to raise the matching funds that remained a prominent feature of the newspaper for the next six months. The daily exhortations appealed not only to readers' admiration for Confederate women but also to the pride and rivalries of contributing localities, to the point that a supporter felt obliged to clarify that receipts forwarded from Rock Hill reflected "a sincere sympathy with the effort to do honor to the noble women of the Confederacy and not an effort to outdo some other town or county." Sharply different from the community of sacrifice envisioned by the South Carolina Monument Association, this strategy placed *The State* at the forefront of South Carolina boosterism, and readers did not fail to notice that "the monument to the women is likewise a monument to the loyalty and influence of your paper."[18]

The selection of an artist for the monument reflected similar opportunism. Three weeks after passage of the legislation, Gonzales wrote to invite a design proposal from sculptor Frederick W. Ruckstuhl, whose equestrian statue of Wade Hampton had been unveiled at the State House in 1906 and who was presently working on a statue of John C. Calhoun for the state to place in Statuary Hall in the United States Capitol. One week later, Ruckstuhl received the commission for the monument from the supervisory committee created by the legislation, which consisted of Walker as chair, Gonzales as secretary and treasurer, and Richards and two other members. Gonzales and Ruckstuhl may have hoped that the separate action of the South Carolina committee, with Walker as a figurehead, would prompt Walker's UCV committee to adopt Ruckstuhl's design for the multistate project.[19] At the least, the quick commitment to Ruckstuhl protected South Carolina from the danger that the state would be pressured toward acceptance of an aesthetically or ideologically objectionable design endorsed by the veterans' committee. South Carolina leaders' experience with Ruckstuhl had familiarized them with his academic style, which reflected an outspoken hostility to the cultural forces of modernism, and his appreciation for the business rationale for investment in public art. Beautification of the State House grounds, he told South Carolinians, was "a mere commercial proposition and investment, with heavy profits."[20]

The possibility that the UCV committee might adopt an unacceptable design was not simply a hypothetical danger by the time the promoters of the South Carolina monument offered the commission to Ruckstuhl in April 1909. As several scholars have recounted, a chorus of criticism greeted the committee's approval of Louis Amateis's proposal for a statue of a woman brandishing an unsheathed sword and a Confederate flag with an exhortation to "UPHOLD OUR STATE RIGHTS." Historians' emphasis on the clear antisuffrage overtones in veterans' distaste for "this brawny Southern Amazon. . . . declaiming like a candidate for the Legislature" makes it somewhat puzzling that such a politicized model of womanhood ever won the endorsement of Walker's group, a success best explained by the energy with which Amateis's design stressed that white Southern men had fought, and continued to fight, to assert their rights.[21] Upon the overwhelming rejection of Amateis's proposal at the annual UCV meeting in June, the committee sent another mixed signal by turning to the design of twenty-three-year-old Belle Kinney, the daughter of a Confederate veteran (fig. 3). Commendation of the only woman sculptor to enter the UCV competition implied a recognition of the creative powers and commemorative authority of women, but if Walker sought to curry favor with the UDC, he again miscalculated, for commemora-

Figure 3. Belle Kinney, model of proposed monument to Confederate women. Reprinted from *Confederate Veteran* 18 (March 1910): 97. Courtesy of South Caroliniana Library, University of South Carolina.

tive activists concluded that patronage of the Nashville ingenue, like Walker's wholehearted enthusiasm for reunion sponsors, merely demonstrated that veterans were "so susceptible to a winning smile and pleasant manner!"[22] Though the UCV scrambled to salvage the plans for a unified Southern tribute and eventually placed Kinney's monument at the capitols of Mississippi and Tennessee, Ruckstuhl's design (fig. 4) more thoroughly revealed Confederate veterans' ideas of gender.

In some fundamental respects, the conceptions were quite similar. Both artists envisioned the Confederate woman at the end of the war,

Figure 4. Frederick W. Ruckstuhl, model of monument to South Carolina women of the Confederacy. Reprinted from *Confederate Veteran* 20 (May 1912): 245. Courtesy of South Caroliniana Library, University of South Carolina.

marked for Kinney by the fallen soldier to whom the woman extends a palm and for Ruckstuhl by the "very simple dress, to the wearing of which most of the Confederate women had been reduced by the misfortunes of war." Homespun dress notwithstanding, Ruckstuhl, no less than Kinney, eschewed emphasis on the wartime work that the UDC had celebrated in the Confederate Relic Room and in *South Carolina Women in the Confederacy*. In Ruckstuhl's case, that decision partly reflected a determination that public art should adopt a more socially stratified frame of visual reference than the popular culture that had shaped the SCMA's soldier statue.

He reported that "a good Southern friend of mine" had suggested that the monument might "strike the popular chord better than a symbolic one" by depicting the Confederate woman "engaged in some characteristic work for the soldiers, such as sewing, knitting, nursing, or making hospital supplies," for she had earned this honor "not merely in her quiet endurance of hardships and suffering, but also and primarily in the works which she did." Ruckstuhl rejected the suggestion as a simplistic illustration that "lowered my point of view to the mental grasp of the mass of men who are too harassed by labor ever to get the time to study the secrets of successful monumental art." A more symbolic composition, he argued, would enable "the great and wise" to elevate the intellectual and spiritual level of the masses and would represent a truth that transcended the Civil War. He chose to present his ideal Confederate woman "in the simple act of holding listlessly in her lap the Bible. . . . She has lifted her eyes from the book, source of her inspiration, and is lost in a far-away meditation over the past and future of her people." "No higher activity than this, nor a more characteristic one, could be imagined," he added.[23]

In addition to their shared focus on the end of the war rather than women's wartime work, both artists showed the Confederate woman receiving a crown of laurel—in Kinney's design from Fame, and, in Ruckstuhl's design from a figure he called the Genius of the State. Most important, both compositions rendered the woman humbly unaware of this honor. Placed on an ornate chair of state, crowned by an allegorical being who has landed so suddenly that her wings flare up to halt her momentum, and approached by two cherubs, Ruckstuhl's subject "does not hear, nor know of the noise and hubbub," in part because that tribute takes place in an otherworldly realm but also in part because her ruminations leave her oblivious to everything about her. The artist aimed for a "sphinx-like seriousness" and "serene repose" in her face, though its blank look struck another sculptor as "without expression or feeling."[24]

This portrait of extreme detachment illustrated the way in which Ruckstuhl's work not only presented an ideal of devout, passionless, and modest womanhood but also helped to redefine the ideal of manhood it was designed to balance at the South Carolina state house. Juxtaposed with a woman lost in meditation while listlessly holding a Bible, the soldier statue embodied the alertness essential to effective action more clearly than it had when understood as a sentimental stereotype of midnight reverie. The lonely fortitude honored in the monument to women helped to erase the notion that solitary reflection had been an important dimension of the male experience of the war at the same time that it elided the impetus to organizational activism that had been one of the most memorable aspects of the female experience in the Confederacy. Contrary to John Preston's praise for the volunteers at Wayside Hospital, supporters of the later monument project noted that white Southern women had benefited from "none of the inspiration which a united host creates" and had struggled to carry on "not to the inspiring music of the military band or in that excitement of the battlefield which leads to self-forgetfulness, but on the deserted plantation."[25]

Several differences between the works of Kinney and Ruckstuhl highlighted the deepening of gender distinctions at Columbia. Kinney's image of a woman placing a palm of martyrdom on a slumped soldier holding a broken flagstaff stirred protests that "the design has singled out one feature, Appomattox alone," from the Confederate epic. In Ruckstuhl's monument, the throne on which the Confederate woman regally sat and the heavenly Genius of the State, resembling the classical alighting of Winged Victory, provided assurances that the South had ultimately prevailed. Consistent with the New South boosterism of his fund-raising campaign for the monument, William Elliott Gonzales's inscriptions repeatedly drove this theme home. With remarkable readiness to leave the war behind, he observed that

THE TRAGEDY OF THE CONFEDERACY MAY BE FORGOTTEN
BUT THE FRUITS OF THE NOBLE SERVICE
OF THE DAUGHTERS OF THE SOUTH
ARE OUR PERPETUAL HERITAGE.

The greater drama, he suggested, came during the postwar period. Ruckstuhl singled out the conclusion to the main inscription as the passage that best expressed the mood of the monument:

IN THE REBUILDING AFTER THE DESOLATION
THEIR VIRTUES STOOD
AS THE SUPREME CITADEL
WITH STRONG TOWERS OF FAITH AND HOPE
AROUND WHICH CIVILIZATION RALLIED
AND TRIUMPHED.

This formulation not only passed over recognition of the innovative wartime work of Confederate women in favor of remembrance of their static "UNCONQUERED SPIRIT" but also assigned them a purely transitional role. Forced by the war into reduced circumstances, like the heroine of the monument, the South had proudly returned to power and prosperity with the aid of women. That extraordinary aid was no longer necessary. Unlike the soldiers monument, or Belle Kinney's model, Ruckstuhl's monument did not identify commemoration as a venue for women's continued participation in public life. To the contrary, the sculptor underscored the exclusion of women in an inscription of his own. One of the cherubs carried a commission from the General Assembly, affixed with the state seal, "to show that the men ordered the monument by passing a law for its erection."[26] The device imagined the legislature not as the representatives of the men and women of South Carolina but as a gathering of its men.

Controversy over Kinney's images of the female body similarly illuminated boundaries that Ruckstuhl drew between the sexes. Critics assailed Kinney's modernistic modeling of Fame as "Amazonian" for flouting rules of taste and refinement in its "large, bold features and massive form," "brawny neck," "slovenly arrangement of attire," and undraped knee protruding into the center of the composition. Ruckstuhl, who regarded modernism as tantamount to Bolshevism, followed academic conventions of feminine beauty. One observer wrote that to compare the allegorical figures in the two works "would be to compare the rugged oak to the graceful and delicate jasmine."[27] Another set of complaints focused on Kinney's sexually charged portrait of the Confederate woman. *The State* huffed: "We do not consider appropriate, the representation of the Southern woman of the Confederacy as a beautiful girl of 20 or 22, appearing in a costume with low neck and short sleeves, and we can not determine whether the 'expression of exquisite sadness' is on account of the soldier or the fact that the only covering for her unquestionably beautifully shapely legs is a misty, gauzy something that would give Comstock the horrors. She is magnificent, but she is not a woman of the war." In contrast, Ruckstuhl intended his demurely dressed model of womanhood to be between forty and forty-five years old. Though "still handsome" in the eyes of the sculptor, she did not challenge any double standards of morality as a sexually active, independent young woman. If Kinney's young woman bid farewell to male protection, Ruckstuhl's middle-aged woman looked forward to rehabilitating male leadership.[28]

Ruckstuhl's rejection of youth as an attribute of the Confederate woman marked a significant change between wartime images of womanhood, which had often focused on soldiers' mates, and Lost Cause gender ideals, which much more frequently centered on soldiers' mothers.

Monuments to Confederate women dedicated in Macon, Georgia (1911), Little Rock, Arkansas (1913), Raleigh, North Carolina (1914), and Jacksonville, Florida (1915), depicted Confederate women with young children, highlighting the centrality of mothers to the generational transmission of white Southern values. The trend fit into a broader social and cultural pattern of increased emphasis on motherhood that drew upon antifeminism and white Protestant anxieties about the pace of family formation amid the tide of southern and eastern European immigration into American cities. Not coincidentally, Mother's Day was established in the United States during the years South Carolina was planning its tribute to Confederate women. One of the contributors to the Columbia project described it as "a monument to the women of Confederacy—rather, the mothers of the Confederacy, truly to 'Mother.'"[29]

Ruckstuhl's symbolic program connected his specific vision of Confederate womanhood to an overarching maternal ideal, for the image of a woman pausing from the reading of scripture for the visit of a glorifying angel evoked traditional iconography of the Annunciation as the first stage in the transformation of the Word to flesh (fig. 5). To be sure, the exemplary Confederate woman differed from Mary not only in her lack of interaction with the angel but in that she was already a mother. But Ruckstuhl was less concerned with the births of the actual men who fought in the Southern armies than with the conception of the ideal Confederate soldier in the wake of defeat. As he well knew, the remembrance of martyrs who "fell in a cause, though lost, still just, / And died for me and you" drew relentlessly on a Christian framework.[30] Acknowledgment of women's contributions to the unfolding of this legend attached the highest significance to their Lost Cause commemorative work, but Ruckstuhl did not undercut the sacred ideal by suggesting that it was a manufactured product. Like the Virgin, the Confederate woman had come as close as possible to divinity by accepting the postwar role assigned to her for her purity and by providing an inspirational example of gentle strength amid sorrow.

At the dedication of the South Carolina monument to Confederate women on April 11, 1912, principal orator Joseph Barnwell, who had fought in the war as a Citadel cadet, reserved the conclusion of his address for a summary of the significance of the project. Noting that "field after field has been opened for your energies and few occupations or employments are now closed to you which you care to enter," Barnwell urged his female listeners to learn from Confederate women that an expansion of social usefulness did not require surrender of feminine grace and beauty

Figure 5. Paolo Veronese, *The Annunciation*, c. 1580.
Samuel H. Kress Collection, National Gallery of Art.
Image © 2005 Board of Trustees, National Gallery of Art,
Washington, D.C.

or replacements for female influence. "The deeds I have attempted to describe, the devotion I have tried to picture, did not come from unsexed and denatured women," he declared. While leaving unspoken the continued inequality he obviously envisioned in the workplace and political arena, he warned that the felicity of private life also depended on recognition that "you are not, and cannot be, men," for "love and admiration are as well worth winning as an acknowledgment of superiority or cold respect."[31] Barnwell's remarks provided an apt gloss on the order of the universe imagined by Ruckstuhl's design, which was encapsulated by the two cherubs accompanying the Genius of the State. The male cherub carried an armful of roses that, "boy-like, he did not even bother to tie into a bouquet," instead rushing forward "full of enthusiasm" to present them; the female cherub meanwhile advanced "timidly" with the legislative scroll, "as if half afraid to approach the great lady."[32] The perfect realm of the angels, like the Confederate saga it absorbed, was divided permanently on natural lines of sexual difference.

Far from a complement to the soldier statue in front of the main entrance of the capitol, the monument to Confederate women installed a diametrically opposite understanding of gender roles. Appreciation for permeable, interpenetrating gender traits had given way to constructions that defined masculinity as either a gregarious, impulsive assertion of widely shared rights or a privileged command of power and that described femininity in terms of either graceful purity or hard-earned achievement of resourceful competence. Both sets of alternatives withdrew from the cross-class availability of wartime ideals and fused gender, in divergent ways, to class hierarchies. Through the debates over these formulations, the cultural crucible of the Civil War had come to represent not a blurring but a sharpening of distinctions between men and women. The effect of this transformation on the personal relationships of white Southerners inspired by the Lost Cause is difficult to document, but the increasing clashes between male and female commemorative organizations from the dedication of 1879 to that of 1912 suggest that the domestic bliss implied by the symmetry of the tributes was tempered by the distance between the monuments at the northern and southern edges of the South Carolina State House.

NOTES

1. *Columbia Daily Phoenix*, November 5, 7, 9, 16, 18, 20, 1869; "Memorial Address of General Wade Hampton," *Southern Magazine* 13 (August 1873): 225; Louisa S. McCord to the Board of Managers of the South Carolina Monument Association, June 17, 1870, in *Louisa S. McCord: Poems, Drama, Biography, Letters,* edited by Richard C. Lounsbury (Charlottesville: University Press of Virginia, 1996), 386–387. On the prominent presence of women in South Carolina resistance to Reconstruction, see W. Scott Poole, *Never Sur-*

render: Confederate Memory and Conservatism in the South Carolina Upcountry (Athens: University of Georgia Press, 2004), 67–73, 128–131.

2. *Columbia Daily Phoenix*, November 26, 1869 (quotation); *Columbia Reporter*, May 14, 1879; *The South Carolina Monument Association: Origin, History and Work, with an Account of the Proceedings at the Unveiling of the Monument to the Confederate Dead, and the Oration of Gen. John S. Preston, at Columbia, S.C., May 13, 1879* (Charleston, S.C.: News and Courier Book Presses, 1879), 69–70. Daniel J. Sherman, *The Construction of Memory in Interwar France* (Chicago: University of Chicago Press, 1999), chap. 3, describes a similar conception of sacrifice in fund raising for war memorials.

3. Richard B. Harwell, *Confederate Music* (Chapel Hill: University of North Carolina Press, 1950), 82–83.

4. *South Carolina Monument Association*, 13, 48; Alice Fahs, *The Imagined Civil War: Popular Literature of the North and South, 1861–1865* (Chapel Hill: University of North Carolina Press, 2001), 118–119. Compare with LeeAnn Whites, *The Civil War as a Crisis in Gender: Augusta, Georgia, 1860–1890* (Athens: University of Georgia Press, 1995), chaps. 6–7, attributing the ascendancy of a self-sacrificing male ideal in the postwar South to Confederate defeat, and Poole, *Never Surrender*, 156–157, reading the Columbia monument of 1879 as a symbol of more aggressive antebellum Southern masculine values that continued, despite Appomattox, to flourish until the 1880s.

5. *In Memoriam. Gen. Stephen Elliott* (Columbia, S.C.: Julian A. Selby, 1866), 7–8, 14, 21; "Gen. Stephen Elliott, C.S.A.," (Columbia, S.C.) *State*, May 7, 1903; John M. Bryan, *Creating the South Carolina State House* (Columbia: University of South Carolina Press, 1999), 91. Comparison of photographs of Elliott and the original statue (destroyed by lightning in 1882) indicates that the Italian sculptor with whom Muldoon contracted may not have acted on the suggestion. A newspaper commentator reported that "we recognize not the remotest resemblance," though the article shows that the SCMA's intention was widely known. *Columbia Register*, May 11, 1879.

6. See "Confederate Monument at Columbia, S.C.," *Confederate Veteran* 15 (March 1907): 127; George Armstrong Wauchope, *The Writers of South Carolina* (Columbia, S.C.: State, 1910), 398–400; J. C. Hungerpiller, ed., *South Carolina Literature* (Columbia: R. L. Bryan, 1931), 222; V. S. Naipaul, *A Turn in the South* (New York: Knopf, 1989), 99 (quotation), 107. Confederate monuments that borrow from Trescot's inscription include works in Newnan, Georgia (1885); Staunton, Virginia (1888); Fayetteville, Arkansas (1897); Elberton, Georgia (1898); Eufaula, Alabama (1904); Gadsden, Alabama (1907); Cartersville, Georgia (1908); Cross Hill, South Carolina (1908); Millen, Georgia (1909); and Burgaw, North Carolina (1914).

7. W. H. Trescot to Isabella D. Martin, February 14, 1879, Martin MSS, South Caroliniana Library (hereafter SCL), University of South Carolina. For the full inscription, see Thomas J. Brown, ed., *The Public Art of Civil War Commemoration: A Brief History with Documents* (Boston: Bedford, 2004), 40–41.

8. W. W. Ball, "Columbia in Reminiscence," undated newspaper column, Ball Papers, SCL.

9. *Charleston News and Courier*, May 14, 1879; *Columbia Register*, May 15, 1879; *South Carolina Monument Association*, 46.

10. Ibid., 42–43.

11. *Chester Reporter*, May 15, 1879 (quotation); *Columbia Register*, May 20, 1879; *Charleston News and Courier*, May 22, 27, 1879.

12. *South Carolina Monument Association*, 40, 44.

13. Gaines M. Foster, *Ghosts of the Confederacy: Defeat, the Lost Cause, and the Emergence of the New South* (New York: Oxford University Press, 1987), 137.

14. *Minutes of the Thirteenth Annual Convention of the United Daughters of the Confederacy, Held in Gulfport, Mississippi, November 14–17, 1906* (Opelika, Ala.: Post Publishing Company, 1907), 27.

15. The monument to Confederate women unveiled in Fort Mill, South Carolina, in 1895 was the first of several community monuments on the theme. For overviews of the UCV initiative, see Foster, *Ghosts of the Confederacy*, 175–178; Cynthia Mills, "Gratitude and Gender Wars: Monuments to the Women of the Sixties," in *Monuments to the Lost Cause: Women, Art, and the Landscapes of Southern Memory*, edited by Cynthia Mills and Pamela H. Simpson (Knoxville: University of Tennessee Press, 2003), 183–200; Elise L. Smith, "Belle Kinney and the Confederate Women's Monument," *Southern Quarterly* 32 (summer 1994): 7–31.

16. In addition to the works cited in note15, which trace this controversy through the pages of *Confederate Veteran* magazine and the minutes of UDC conventions, see the untitled editorial in *Lost Cause* 3 (May 1900): 184; "Judge Keiley Contributes," *Lost Cause* 4 (August 1900): 10; Florence Ballard, "The Woman's Monument," *Lost Cause* 4 (February 1901): 104; "An Appeal for the Memorial to the Women of the Confederacy," *Lost Cause* 6 (March 1902): 122–123; "Address by Dr. G. H. Tichenor, Chairman Southern Women's Monument Committee," *Lost Cause* 7 (December 1902): 66–67; "Plea for Confederate Home," *State*, February 22, 1909, p. 3; "Men Will Pay Tribute to Confederate Women," *State*, March 24, 1909, p. 1; "A Daughter Commends the Plan," *State*, March 27, 1909, p. 1; "F. W. Ruckstuhl Was Selected," *State*, April 2, 1909, p. 1; "A Misunderstanding," *State*, April 6, 1909, p. 4.

17. "Increased Interest in Women's Monument," *State*, March 18, 1909, p. 1.

18. "How the Fund Grew in The State's Care," *State*, April 11, 1912, pt. 2, p. 1 (first quotation); "York County Active in Monument Fund," *State*, May 15, 1909, p. 1 (second quotation). "Monument Fund Had Lovely Day," *State*, August 22, 1909, p. 3 (third quotation).

19. "F. W. Ruckstuhl Was Selected"; "Concerning Southern Woman's Monument," *Confederate Veteran* 17 (August 1909): 372; "Sculptor Interprets the Memorial," *State*, April 12, 1912, p. 4.

20. "Ruckstuhl Says We Are Growing," *State*, May 15, 1909, p. 2. On Ruckstuhl's social thought, see Albert Boime, *The Unveiling of the National Icons: A Plea for Patriotic Iconoclasm in a Nationalist Era* (New York: Cambridge University Press, 1998), 279–282, 343–363.

21. Smith, "Belle Kinney and the Confederate Women's Monument," 13.

22. Margaret Drane Tichenor to Margaret L. Watson, March 1910, Tichenor Scrapbook, Eleanor S. Brockenbrough Library, Museum of the Confederacy, Richmond, Virginia.

23. "Sculptor Interprets the Memorial."

24. Ibid.; Pompeo Coppini to Margaret Drane Tichenor, January 24, 1912, Tichenor Scrapbook, op. cit.

25. "A Northern Tribute," *State*, February 3, 1909, p. 4.

26. "Sculptor Interprets the Memorial."

27. Margaret Drane Tichenor, "Open Court," undated typescript ("Amazonian," "brawny neck," "slovenly"); Florence Murphy Cooley, "Monument to Confederate Women" (Jacksonville, Florida) *Sunday Times-Union,* undated clipping ("amazonian," "bold features," "rugged oak"), both in Tichenor Scrapbook, op. cit.

28. "Concerning Southern Woman's Monument"; "Miss Kinney's Design," *State*, August 17, 1909, p. 4 ("consider appropriate"); "Sculptor Interprets the Memorial" ("still handsome"). Anthony Comstock had been synonymous with the regulation of sexual order since the 1873 passage of the federal antiobscenity legislation known as the Comstock Law.

29. Smith, "Belle Kinney and the Confederate Women's Monument," 24–26; Kathleen W. Jones, "Mother's Day: The Creation, Promotion and Meaning of a New Holiday in the Progressive Era," *Texas Studies in Literature and Language* 22 (summer 1980): 175–196; "Monument Fund Is Increasing," *State*, April 16, 1909, p. 1 (quotation). Fahs, *Imagined Civil War*, 121–128, emphasizes that maternal figures were important during the war, but her book also provides abundant evidence that soldiers' wives and sweethearts enjoyed a significance that would later decline.

30. See Charles Reagan Wilson, *Baptized in Blood: The Religion of the Lost Cause, 1865–1920* (Athens: University of Georgia Press, 1980). Quotation from Abram J. Ryan, "The March of the Deathless Dead," in *Poems: Patriotic, Religious, Miscellaneous,* 25th ed. (New York: P. J. Kennedy and Sons, 1880), 76.

31. "Addresses at Monument Unveiling Yesterday," *State*, April 12, 1912, p. 13.

32. "Sculptor Interprets the Memorial."